A Child, A Family, A School, A Community

Susan L. Gabel and Scot Danforth
General Editors

Vol. 4

The Inclusion and Teacher Education series is part of the Peter Lang Education list.
Every volume is peer reviewed and meets
the highest quality standards for content and production.

PETER LANG
New York • Bern • Frankfurt • Berlin
Brussels • Vienna • Oxford • Warsaw

Diane Linder Berman and David J. Connor

A Child, A Family, A School, A Community

A Tale of Inclusive Education

PETER LANG
New York • Bern • Frankfurt • Berlin
Brussels • Vienna • Oxford • Warsaw

Library of Congress Cataloging-in-Publication Data

Names: Berman, Diane Linder, author. | Connor, David J., author.
Title: A child, a family, a school, a community: a tale of inclusive education /
Diane Linder Berman and David J. Connor.
Description: New York: Peter Lang, 2017.
Series: Inclusion and teacher education; vol. 4
ISSN 2373-695X (print) | 2373-6968 (online)
Includes bibliographical references and index.
Identifiers: LCCN 2017014415 (print) | LCCN 2017000772 (ebook)
ISBN 978-1-4331-3323-7 (hardcover: alk. paper)
ISBN 978-1-4331-3322-0 (paperback: alk. paper) | ISBN 978-1-4331-4018-1 (ebook pdf)
ISBN 978-1-4331-4019-8 (epub) | ISBN 978-1-4331-4020-4 (mobi)
Subjects: LCSH: Inclusive education.
Classification: LCC LC1200 (print) | LCC LC1200 .B47 2017 (ebook)
DDC 371.9/046—dc23
LC record available at https://lccn.loc.gov/2017014415
DOI 10.3726/b11257

Bibliographic information published by **Die Deutsche Nationalbibliothek**.
Die Deutsche Nationalbibliothek lists this publication in the "Deutsche
Nationalbibliografie"; detailed bibliographic data are available
on the Internet at http://dnb.d-nb.de/.

To
My husband David, and my two wonderful sons
Forever making me smile

–Diane

To
My cousins Jacqueline & Paul Johnstone
and all members of their ever-growing family

–David

CONTENTS

Foreword by Jan W. Valle   xiii
Introduction   xvii
Prelude: Summer 1972   xxv

Chapter 1.   Leaving a Restrictive Environment Behind   1
Chapter 2.   Climate   13
Chapter 3.   A Free and Appropriate Education (FAPE):
              How Appropriate is Misery?   25
Chapter 4.   First Impressions: Instantaneous Behavior Shaping   41
Chapter 5.   Behavior: Addressing Impulsivity   53
Chapter 6.   Creating Classroom Community:
              Embracing Difference   71
Chapter 7.   Friendship: Reversing the Status Quo   87
Chapter 8.   Communication: Balancing High Expectations
              with Acceptance   103
Chapter 9.   Setting Goals: Letting the Child be the Guide   119
Chapter 10.   Extraordinary Extra Curriculars   133
Chapter 11.   The Informal Bending of Boundaries   151
Chapter 12.   Grade 5 in the Penthouse   167

Chapter 13.   Teaching in My City   183
Chapter 14.   Brothers   201
Chapter 15.   Graduating Boulder   215

               Ongoing Questions: Dialogue   231
               Epilogue   241
               Index   249

LIST OF ILLUSTRATIONS

1.	Leaving a Restrictive Environment Behind	2
2.	Climate	14
3.	A Free and Appropriate Education (FAPE): How Appropriate is Misery?	26
4.	First Impressions: Instantaneous Behavior Shaping	42
5.	Behavior: Addressing Impulsivity	54
6.	Creating Classroom Community: Embracing Difference	72
7.	Friendship: Reversing the Status Quo	
8.	Communication: Balancing High Expectations with Acceptance	88
9.	Setting Goals: Letting the Child be the Guide	120
10.	Extraordinary Extra Curriculars	134
11.	The Informal Bending of Boundaries	152
12.	Grade 5 in the Penthouse	168
13.	Teaching in My City	184
14.	Brothers	202
15.	Leaving Boulder	216

ACKNOWLEDGEMENTS

Joint acknowledgements: We would like to thank series editors Susan Gabel and Scot Danforth for approving this project. In addition, we thank all the staff at Peter Lang who helped guide us through this process to production. We are deeply indebted to the principal and staff at Boulder Elementary School who allowed us into their world so we could do our best to capture what they do.

Diane's acknowledgements: I would like to thank Don Behrman, cousin and friend who has been a wonderful supporter and sponsor of my writing as well as my interest in Disability Studies. I wish to thank Brigitte Bentele for reading the draft version and giving me detailed feedback. I am grateful always to my mother for all of her support as well.

David's acknowledgements: As always, I thank my family members in the U.K. who support me in whatever I choose to do. In addition, I thank Dr. Jennifer Samson of Hunter College who relieved me of my duties, and served as Interim Acting Chairperson of the Special Education Department when I was on sabbatical in spring 2016. Finally, I am grateful to my friends for making me feel at home in Buenos Aires where I spent my sabbatical writing this book—*muchas gracias* to Martha Berman, Mickey Vail, Max Dasso, & Gustavo Gordillo de Quilmes.

FOREWORD

This significant contribution to the Disability Studies in Education (DSE) series takes the reader inside a model inclusive elementary school that embodies DSE tenets within its everyday practices. It is also, perhaps more importantly, the story of a school community that changes the life of a family and a school community changed by a family. Told in a "double-voiced" format by Diane, the mother of a child with a disability (who is also a classroom teacher and teacher educator) and David, a DSE scholar/teacher educator, the authors clearly and skillfully render how the *personal is political* through the integration of storytelling and DSE theory. In each chapter, Diane shares a narrative that reveals a particular point along her family's journey, followed by David's analysis of the narrative using DSE theory. For readers unfamiliar with the tenets of DSE, the volume is an excellent introduction to the application of DSE to a real-life school and family context.

This is the story of a family; however, it is not without significance that it is a story told by a mother. Although the father appears within the narrative, it is without question a mother's story. As a fellow DSE scholar who writes about mothers of children with disabilities, I have argued elsewhere that the experience of motherhood necessarily intersects with the social influences of the culture within which a woman carries out her role as mother—and

American culture persists in holding mothers responsible for the outcome of their children to a greater degree than fathers. In the case of disability, mothers are held to even greater responsibility for motherhood gone "off-script". Mother and child become inextricably bound by perceived imperfection. Pressures intensify as children with disabilities become increasingly defined in terms of their relationship to an established norm of social and academic performance. As illustrated within Diane's story (and supported within the literature), mothers are more likely than fathers or couples to engage with school personnel and with far greater frequency and intensity.

I have long contended that we need only to look to mothers of children with disabilities for the most reliable assessment of special education practices. Mothers *intimately* experience how public schools respond to disability. In sharing her story, Diane contributes a powerful and cogent account of outcomes resulting from the segregation of her son in one district and his full inclusion in another. She takes the reader into the interior of her family where outcomes matter in the daily business of living—rendering visible the significant impact of each school context (and its accompanying responses and choices in regard to disability) upon not only the child with a disability but also the entire family. Accompanying Diane's narratives are David's analyses that serve to "connect the dots" by moving the reader from the micro-context of a single family to the macro-context of society and culture where conceptualizations of disability originate and influence schooling.

Unlike more traditional special education research that seeks generalization, this narrative study is meaningful for its *specificity* of detail about one child with a disability and the school professionals who serve him. At the heart of Diane's story lies the significance of *context*— a departure from the historical emphasis that special education has placed upon objectivity. The reader learns what works for a particular child with a particular disability in a particular school context—and the take-away is to consider how to apply what works here in another equally particular context. Diane acknowledges that her positionality as English-speaking, White, middle-class and married influenced her access in securing a more appropriate context for her son and writes about her concern for the children who remain in settings her son was able to leave. Yet, it is also worth noting that there is much to glean about what works in this particular inclusive environment that can be applied to other contexts. As Diane's story reveals, what works has more to do with the *embodiment* of a school-wide philosophy of inclusion than any kind of funding distribution.

This volume should appeal to an audience of teacher educators, researchers, administrators, pre-service and in-service teachers, advocates, parents, policymakers, and the general public with and without disabilities. It speaks to the critical need to develop philosophical practices in regard to inclusion (in contrast to mere strategy implementation), to recognize and attend to sites of ableism within our ways of seeing and acting in the world, and to acknowledge and learn alongside a multiplicity of voices whose life experiences intersect with disability. Inclusion, the authors remind us, is not an educational method to learn and implement but rather a decidedly human way of being in the world that requires ongoing negotiation of a particular context in which we give ourselves permission to listen, think, risk, consider, ask, see, collaborate, challenge, love, reflect...and dream!

--Jan W. Valle

INTRODUCTION

This book grows out of Diane's desire to paint a portrait of a school in New York State that successfully included her son, Benny, who had previously "failed to function" in two exclusionary/highly restrictive special education classrooms in New York City. In contrast to the city schools, The Boulder School welcomed Benny and supported him and his family in finding ways to ensure his inclusion within all aspects of schooling (Note: pseudonyms are used throughout for children, school, and faculty). In turn, Benny's presence and participation within the school grew over the years and significantly influenced its general culture in a myriad of positive ways. At the same time, the school also provided an oasis for Diane's younger son, Adam, who excels academically and socially. In contemplating the same school and the same teachers who met the needs of her two children with such dramatically different learning profiles, Diane felt compelled to chronicle how, and explore why, this school was successful whereas so many others in her experience had not been.

David's interest in creating this text lies in the fact that Diane had shared this school's story with him. He became drawn to the challenge of "capturing" and analyzing a school that has attempted to develop an authentic inclusive educational experience for students—a process that is ongoing, admittedly imperfect, yet earnest. Despite major policy changes in regard to inclusive education over the past three decades, there have been very few clear examples of successful inclusive schools in scholarly works (Danforth, 2014; Hehir & Katzman, 2012) and documentary media (Habib, 2007; 2011) that can be shared in teacher preparation classes. In conversations with Diane, David could see how what was being done at the school to ensure authentic inclusion was, in fact, unsurprisingly, very much in tune with a Disability Studies in Education (DSE) framework. For this reason, he believed it would be worthwhile to document—and discuss—an example of where a "real life" example of inclusive education evolved with what he believes is a DSE-disposition that helps educators, parents, students, and community members best understand and approach how to "do" inclusion.

We both work as inclusive educators in the same teacher education program at Hunter College, part of the City University of New York. David developed the required inclusion course for all general and special educators to have a DSE-framework through which to understand inclusion as everyone's responsibility and a student's civil right (Valle & Connor, 2010). For the past three years Diane has integrated her personal story into the course and has brought Boulder staff to speak to her students. Each semester, 5 to 8 Boulder staff members, including the principal, speak to her classes. When Diane spoke extensively with the Boulder staff, they often defer to "instinct" when explaining how they create their school culture. This response, and graduate students' questions about positive examples of inclusive settings became a primary motivation for her to write this book. While Boulder faculty present with a refreshing absence of technical jargon, we recognize that their general attitude and effective programs are in line with many elements that form the basis of DSE. We also recognize that in order to accurately document Boulder's approach to inclusive education, a deeper analysis is needed. In an effort to capture what is possible, it is our hope that by analyzing and reflecting upon a school that embodies a DSE-simpatico approach, other teachers and administrators can become familiar with these ideas and see how they can apply within any educational or community setting.

Interactive Format

The format of this collaborative book reflects our mutual interest in inclusive education as citizens and teachers, and our disparate yet arguably connected roles as parent and researcher who are motivated by our belief in the civil rights of providing disabled children access to a quality educational experience. After exploring multiple options of how to structure the book, we decided to craft the text in what can loosely be seen as a conversation between us as authors. There are fifteen chapters written by Diane in which she chronicles her journey and that of her family over the last decade. She begins by describing her disillusion with, and disbelief of, the limited placements offered within New York City's District 75, a separate structure for children and youth with moderate, severe, and multiple disabilities (Berman, 2009). Exasperated, she searched elsewhere in New York State to find a school that she believed would be a potentially "good fit" for Benny. What follows may be considered the core of the book, a series of largely sequential chapters that each foregrounds a key element of inclusive education by illustrating how that particular element looked in the context of educating Benny, partnering with her family, building relationships with teachers, and the pinnacles and pitfalls of consciously creating an inclusive community. The style and tone is descriptive prose in the genre of memoir, making the story purposely accessible and of interest to a wide variety of people, including parents, administrators, policy makers, pre-service and in-service teachers, and academics. Because it is a memoir, all quotations and conversational exchanges are Diane's recollections.

After each of Diane's chapters, David takes the opportunity of further exploring the content through deepening an analysis of the many issues raised in the contextualized history of Benny and his family, Benny's classroom experiences, and the evolution of the Boulder School. Conceptualizing Diane's narrative as describing an authentic example of successful inclusive education rather than "a case study" (with its problematic shades of medicalized language), David analyzes how a family and a school strive to "get things right" without any blueprint, rather than excluding Benny from an education alongside his sibling and peers. The story provides a rich, layered picture of what can be done, often by an informed sense of trial and error, when parents, principal, teachers, and community share a common ideal. It also provides an opportunity to actively link DSE to practice, as much of what occurs in this story is—without the participants consciously knowing it—intimately connected to a DSE framework (Connor, Gabel, Gallagher, & Morton, 2008). By utilizing the tenets of DSE and culling from a wide range of DSE research, David seeks to show ways in which practice is related to theory, and theory to practice, while encouraging the growth of DSE work to be *practical* and explicitly tied to students, families, classrooms, schools, education systems, and policies.

Analysis of Chapters

To ensure a degree of consistency, every chapter was analyzed with three broad yet interconnected areas in mind:

(1) *What are some important everyday issues about inclusive education raised within the narrative?* How did these examples highlight areas such as personal and professional responses to human differences? What were some successful activities used in the inclusive classroom? What were some examples of problem-solving approaches? What were some examples of strength-based perceptions of students?
The purpose of this approach is to recognize and specifically name examples of context-based inclusive practices.

(2) *How do elements of the narrative relate to aspects of Disability Studies in Education?* What are some connections between DSE to the organization of the school, principal, faculty members, children, and parents? How do these connections resonate with existing literature within DSE?
The purpose of this approach is to illustrate examples of Boulder's conscious inclusive practices being subconsciously simpatico with the tenets of DSE.

(3) *What are some personal connections made with the narrative?* In what ways do the issues described touch upon my own observations of almost three decades within education? How do the issues relate to my thoughts about as a citizen, a former teacher, a district professional development specialist who advocated for inclusive practices, and professor of inclusive education?
The purpose of this approach is to both personalize the response and broaden the discussion to many issues related to inclusive education and teacher education.

After each chapter, all three strands are woven together in a short response designed to share observations, create more connections between the issues, and raise further questions about how we create successful inclusive classrooms and schools.

A Brief Description of Chapters

Chapter 1, *Leaving a Restrictive Environment Behind,* serves to map out the journey. Diane begins at the end of a successful inclusionary elementary school experience for Benny and looks back on the thoughts and fears her family had when leaving a restrictive setting years before. She examines the reasons why some parents cling to the "safety" of a segregated school experience for their children who have disabilities. Providing a panoramic view of the story, Diane sets the scene for details to be shared in the following chapters. David's commentary focuses on the broad issues and questions raised by DSE with respect to inclusive and segregated education.

Chapter 2, *Climate*, provides a close up of Boulder as Benny prepares to graduate. The visionary and passionate principal, Clark, is introduced. David reflects on the importance of a creating an atmosphere of true equity and contrasts this with the often prevailing view that inclusion must be "earned," and can only be done so as the child approaches "normalcy."

Chapter 3, *A Free and Appropriate Education (FAPE): How Appropriate is Misery?* takes us back to the dismal conditions in the second of two self-contained class placements in NYC. Readers visit the chaotic classroom hidden far away from everything and witness the abuse these children had to endure daily. Diane questions how "appropriate" this placement is for any child, and David critiques the use of a "continuum of placements," part of the provisions made within IDEA which can support *and* undermine efforts toward inclusion.

Chapter 4, *First Impressions: Instantaneous Behavior Shaping*, describes Benny's family move to the suburbs. Immediately, Benny's joy indicates that he is much more aware and insightful than anyone could have predicted, with the cloud that had loomed large over him for months receding immediately. David discusses the way family perspective is critical but often overlooked. He speaks to the immediate manifestations of the social model in a suburban school and discusses the way many successful communities embody the social perspective without even being aware of the terminology.

Chapter 5, *Behavior: Addressing Impulsivity*, narrates how although Benny loved his new school from the start, his behavior still proved challenging. Diane charts how positive interventions that Boulder put in place to help support Benny in his classroom worked. David begins to address the specific elements of the program and philosophy at Boulder that enable the flexible approach to inclusion to take root, while contrasting some of these elements with observations of other less successful programs.

Chapter 6, *Creating Classroom Community: Embracing Difference* reveals some of the creative use of natural supports at Boulder. In many instances, Boulder developed community based activities, specifically designed to support Benny. These drew upon the talents and interests of all of the students.

David connects these initiatives to Universal Design for Learning and differentiated learning. DSE also comes into play as it addresses the naturalistic growth that occurred when Benny was given opportunities to form friendships and converse in ways that were accessible to him at the time

Chapter 7, *Friendship: Reversing the Status Quo*, chronicles how in encouraging conversation and relationships between Benny and his peers, these friendships began to move out of the classroom. Boulder staff embraced Benny's interests, instead of trying to extinguish them, developing them into areas of expertise and shared experiences with peers. David addresses the isolation felt initially by Diane and her family, linking it to the sociology of other oppressed and stigmatized groups.

Chapter 8, *Communication: Balancing High Expectations with Acceptance*, recognizes how difficult it can be to know what to expect from a child who learns in his or her own way. In this chapter we meet a teacher who was determined to have Benny grow academically in her class. The crucial role of communication is explored. David contrasts the experiences of parent and teacher and reflects on the importance of flexibility and keeping expectation high with solid yet malleable supports ready to be implemented.

Chapter 9, *Setting Goals: Letting the Child be the Guide*, focuses on how school personal look to the IEP for guidance, yet we argue the value of viewing the IEP interpreted as a minimalistic guide. Despite meeting his goals in grade 3, Benny wanted to push himself more. Creative problem solving led his parents and teachers to design more opportunities for him to become a vocal member of the school, despite his language disabilities. David couches this within the framework of a strength based perspective as well as theories of "presumed competence," both necessary for this type of growth to occur.

Chapter 10, *Extraordinary Extracurriculars*, documents the huge array of activities offered by Boulder. Diane shares how these events are spread through the year, marking the seasons, creating a culture unique to Boulder by offering multiple invitations to participation within school life. David considers the goals of contemporary education—academic, social, and emotional—and the importance how these influence families and communities in many ways.

Chapter 11, *The Informal Bending of Boundaries*, explores the absence of traditional limitations. Clark's unconventional leadership style breaks many established rules that have come to be commonplace in educational institutions. David discusses the way that this style contributes to the success of the inclusion program, questioning the purpose of "boundaries" and whose interests they serve. By considering the bending, even absence, of traditional boundaries, David advocates moving "out of the (traditional) box" educators often trapped within.

Chapter 12, *Grade 5 in the Penthouse*, showcases how this grade holds a special place in the development of skills needed for success in middle school. Diane shares aspects of Benny's and Adam's experiences in grade 5, each educated within an inclusive classroom. David comments on the atmosphere created in this grade via the goals of the teacher that are simple yet somewhat novel in providing an academically rigorous year.

Chapter 13, *Teaching in My City*, chronicles how David invites Diane to teach within the Special Education master's degree program at Hunter College. As she shapes the course on inclusion to education majors at the college, she has the opportunity to see how intertwined her personal and professional lives have become. The staff of Boulder visits Diane's classes at Hunter every semester, holding a roundtable discussion with her students. David, who attends, speaks to some of the issues raised by these present and future teachers, many of which inform this book.

Chapter 14, *Brothers*, features Diane sharing her thoughts as the parent of two children with very different learning profiles. She discusses the initial conflict she and her husband had in trying to respond to the different developmental patterns between their two boys. The opportunity to educate the brothers in the same type of classroom was pivotal in the positive family dynamics that have ensued. David discusses the ways in which families have to wrestle with difficult choices and at times create their own path in unchartered territory. He places Diane and her family's journey in the context of their growth towards a social model of understanding disability.

Chapter 15, *Leaving Boulder*, describes the end-of-year rituals at Boulder and how they impact Benny and Adam. Diane reflects on a lifetime of educational rituals she has been through, and what they symbolize. With a cautious sense of optimism, David uses examples from Boulder, along with other schools, to advocate for the continued growth of inclusive practices.

In the penultimate section called *Conversation*, we thought it would be interesting to wind down the book with an actual conversation, symbolic of how we have tried to structure this interactive work from the beginning. We share what writing the book has meant to us, including what we have learned, what we still need to know, and lingering questions that we still have.

Finally, in *Epilogue*, Diane takes the opportunity to share some recent discussions with Benny and Adam. They talk about their impressions of middle school, their future, and their voice in the ongoing mission to create a world where everyone is welcome and all people are given opportunities to contribute fully.

In closing, most of all, we hope you enjoy reading this book—and our telling of a successful inclusion story. Furthermore it is our deep desire that this story might change the world, make it more accessible for some who, like Benny, might otherwise be excluded. We know that it is those folks who come into the world wired a little differently who have the power to take us all to new and glorious places, so long as we open our classrooms and our hearts.

References

Berman, D. L. (2009). *Beyond words: Reflections on our journey to inclusion*. Harrisburg, PA: White Hat Press.

Connor, D. J., Gabel, S. L., Gallagher, D. & Morton, M. (2008). Disability studies and inclusive education--Implication for theory, research, and practice: Guest editor's introduction. *International Journal of Inclusive Education, 12*(5–6), 441–457.

Danforth, S. (Ed.) (2014). *Becoming a great inclusive educator*. New York: Peter Lang.

Habib, D. (Producer and Director). (2007). *Including Samuel*. [DVD]. Available from http://www.includingsamuel.com/home.aspx

Habib, D. (Producer and Director). (2011). *Who cares about Kelsey?* [DVD]. Available from http://www.whocaresaboutkelsey.com/

Hehir, T. & Katzman, L. I. (2012). *Effective inclusive schools: Designing successful school-wide programs*. San Francisco, CA: Jossey Bass.

Valle, J. W., & Connor, D. J. (2010). *Rethinking disability: A disability studies guide to inclusive practices*. New York: McGraw-Hill.

PRELUDE: SUMMER 1972

My family rents a summer home on Fire Island. There are no cars. We walk barefoot and I learn to ride my bike without training wheels. The water seems to be everywhere and the air smells a little like pickles and sprinkles my face with salty droplets. I do not even miss my home; I could live here forever. I count the days. At first thirty seem like forever, but then they begin to slide away and I do not want to leave. It feels like a fairy tale come to life. We go to the bay and then the beach and carry groceries home in a tiny wagon. My mom lets me play outside alone and walk by myself all over. I make a lot of new friends.

I meet Jill while trying to learn to fish. She comforts me when I cry because of the worm and then the fish which twist on the hook until we can pull them off and throw them back, now damaged and it seems like a really mean thing to do to them. She is older than I am by a whole four years, almost ten. But she likes me and it feels good to have an older girl, with beautiful hair, want to play with me. She has puffy reddish cheeks as if she is wearing makeup but I know she is not. She seems to know so much, I guess, because she is ten. She has a freely flowing kindness that washes over me like the foamy waves at the beach. We play together every day and every evening until the sky becomes darker than the ocean and the waves seem to light up as they come crashing into the shore. I go to bed late on Fire Island. I play until I can barely hold up my head and my mom and dad carry me to my bed. Some days I do not even remember to brush my teeth.

One day I get a splinter from all the wood around and it is very deep. My mom tries to get it out with tweezers but she cannot. Jill stays with me, right by my side, even though my finger is bloody and I am shrieking at the top of my lungs. Nothing seems to scare her and she holds my hand just the right way while my mother sterilizes a sewing needle and fishes for the splinter while I try to wriggle away. I can feel her kindness throughout my body; it calms me, it makes me happy even though I am in pain. I wonder if I could ever do the same for anyone. Maybe when I am 10, like she is, I tell myself, but I am not so sure I could ever be that strong.

Later that night, after my finger is bandaged and Jill has gone home, my mother tells me that Jill has something called Down syndrome. She tries to explain to me what this means but I scream and block out her words. I do not want to hear. It makes no sense; the words she is using and her tone that is calm and all-knowing is making me mad. She is trying to explain my friend to me, but only I know my friend. I feel like I am breaking, splitting, and I cry and yell. She tells me Jill might seem a little slow and that people with Down syndrome are very nice to everyone. I tell her that Jill is not slow and she is not kind because of some word. A deep sadness grows inside that spreads quickly all over my body. It begins to burn me and I hurt more from that than I did minutes ago from the splinter. My mother keeps talking in that soothing tone and inside, for the first time, I feel like I can't trust her and this makes me scared and mad. I want to run away, back a few minutes to a time when Jill was just Jill standing beside me with her soft pink hands around my throbbing finger.

All night long I toss and turn, sweating though a cool breeze blows. When the light of dawn comes into my room, I begin to calm down but those words have already begun to change me into a person I do not ever want to be.

LEAVING A RESTRICTIVE ENVIRONMENT BEHIND

There is rarely a day or even an hour in which I do not think about where we might have been had we not been able to turn our lives upside down to move our son, Benny, into an inclusive classroom just shy of eight years ago. Sometimes the feeling is sharp and painful, piercing me to my toes. Other times it comes in with softness and warms me in ways that I have come to know as simply delightful. I live with these waves of emotion as constant and steady as the shifts in light from day to night. And for Benny this chance has meant life itself. This opportunity has brought him into the world in new ways, enabled him to find talents and strengths he never knew he possessed, and given him friendships which nourish him in vital ways. Benny is by no means "cured" of his developmental delays or the eight diagnoses he amassed by the time he was three years old including, but not limited to, Pervasive Developmental Disorder—Not Otherwise Specified (PDD-NOS), and severe receptive and expressive language disorders. Yet inclusion has given him opportunities that no restrictive environment would have been able to provide. Inclusion has given him a chance to take part in all that interests him, interacting with his peers in ways that enable the entire community to grow.

Adam, my younger child, a boy filled with a sophistication and sensitivity, reaps the rewards of this move. Boulder has given him the gift of time

spent in a truly nurturing extension of family. Better yet, he has been able to attend school alongside his brother, and they serve as mutual role models each inspiring the other to move out into the world with greater confidence, in a dance which would not be nearly as elegant or elaborate had they been sent to different schools.

Often, I wonder where we would have been individually, and collectively as a family, had we accepted the recommendations of our first school district and moved Benny to a class for the multiply disabled, in the special education district, commonly known in New York City as District 75. Originally Benny was placed in what's known as a "12-1-1 class" (12 children, 1 teacher, 1 parapro-fessional) in our local elementary school. Typically students in this class have a wide range of disabilities, including learning and language disabilities, Attention Deficit Hyperactivity Disorder (ADHD), and/or mild sensory issues. Each class at the elementary level spans three grade levels, K-2, or 3–5. This was already a more restrictive placement than we were comfortable with, but the district thought he needed an even more restrictive setting. The class that they (the principal, school psychologist and teachers at two schools) unanimously agreed he needed was housed in a school far from home. Benny would have had to ride a bus for many hours a day to attend this sort of class. The class was an "8-1-1 class" (8 children, 1 teacher, 1 paraprofessional). They felt he would benefit most by being with other non-verbal children, who had similar needs. As an educator, this scenario did not make sense to me. I wanted Benny to be in a class with chil-dren from whom he could learn and who could learn from him. I wanted Benny exposed to, and engage with, the general education curriculum.

Rarely does a day go by that an image of a child, like Benny, who was rec-ommended to District 75 rather than placed in a fully inclusive general edu-cation class, comes to my mind. These images are fleeting, often they follow him, ghost-like, from the car as I drop him at drama club or the performance choir. Sometimes the image settles like a soft cloud beside us as we sit together on the couch to prepare for an algebra test. I reach out and touch Benny's still soft pink cheek and kiss him while he looks right at me and asks again why I cry so often with "happy tears." One day I will explain to him that I cry for the children who were left to languish in tiny classrooms without a chance to grow, without parents who do not have the knowledge or skills to advocate ferociously for their child. Today I just tell him I am so proud of him and all he has accomplished. He tells me he loves me too and we go on with our busy days and nights, following a schedule as fast-paced as any teenager in the New York City area often does.

I am conscious also of the fact that my husband and I sought options from a position of privilege and power. As white, middle class educators with fluent use of the English language, we had access to many resources that other parents do not. We could easily ask for recommendations. We could research and then articulate what we desired. We were confident in the abilities that we saw in our child while top doctors told us repeatedly that he had very limited potential. Despite this position of power and advantage, we recognized that we needed more; that alone, even coupled with the best of intentions and our belief in our son was not enough to ensure academic and social growth. We desperately needed a partnership with Benny's school and we needed a school that would work with his strengths.

We did not consider the districts that had specialized programs for children with autism spectrum disorders. In fact, we purposefully steered clear of those districts. I was tired of hearing from the specialists in autism. They seemed to miss the essence of Benny when they looked at him through their medicalized lens and decided ahead what his program of therapy should be. Instead we went for simplicity, choosing a neighborhood school with a principal who made an immediate connection to Benny and promised us to make it work. We selected a school which, at that time, had never had a child like Benny, where most of his teachers confessed to me they were initially scared to teach him but quickly found it incredibly rewarding. It was not science, but rather instinct, that led us to choose this school, which did more for Benny and Adam than David and I could have ever imagined possible.

Seemingly suddenly, in having chosen this school, I have been transported from those early years of anguish and fear to a new place, one with wide open spaces and majestic views, a place from which anything and everything seem possible for Benny. This personal transformation was not one limited to mother and son. The entire family has felt the immediate ripples of Benny's growth as they radiate out in ever expanding circles of celebration. Even in the best of communities, finding the right balance of support and opportunity can be daunting. Over the years we, his parents and teachers, have learned to look toward Benny for direction as he best understands his needs for support and independence. Together in close communication, we work to create a program that offers both challenge and support. Benny has taught us all the importance of learning new ways to *listen*. In his quiet yet determined manner he has found ways to be in control of his education.

From the beginning, upon initiation of evaluations and therapies at the age of two, his disabilities felt constraining, a fact of life that imposed more and more constrictions upon our lives. I had to be home for hours of therapies each day. A return to full time work was not feasible given the amount of time and attention I needed to spend on coordination of his services, and on the new navigation necessary to thrive as a parent in the world of the special needs child (more on that term soon). I was afraid to entrust his care to anyone else. The extra responsibilities needed to help Benny interact with others and to tame his frequent meltdowns were daunting, even for me, a mom who loved him more than life itself. While my instinct told me that Benny was full of potential and promise, the kinder therapists and doctors cautioned me about my optimism, while those with less sensitivity reprimanded me brutally, for being a mother in denial.

With the perspective of time and experience, I have come to understand Benny's differences as a liberation of sorts, an expansion of the narrow confines of normal. This understanding has opened up parts of me that have lain dormant for most of my life. They touch on so much: my ability to parent, to teach, and to interact fully as a human being. It is only of late that I have begun to see Benny's disabilities as something other than fixed, etched in stone, but rather as a constellation of attributes that make him unique, that give him areas of intense struggle right alongside talents which flow from him with the greatest of ease. The placement of our younger son Adam in this very same inclusive school has, I think, enabled Adam to develop into a wonderfully imaginative, compassionate, and quirky young boy. His academic growth was enhanced, not curtailed by this placement. These experiences have shown me what an injustice we do by deciding for all children what their potential might be, and by limiting their experiences through creating classrooms that have so little stimulation and so few opportunities to learn.

On my long journey to this place where Benny stands proud, I have met many families who were not as fortunate. It is too easy to fall into traps set by an educational system that can be hostile to human differences, with teachers and administrators who prefer to send children off to extremely restrictive settings rather than to take the time to find what the child needs in order to function and develop. Parents do not realize that the curricular gap will only widen over time between lower level and grade level classrooms. The very words we must use shape our conception of disability, prepare us for lower expectations, and disappointment. As soon as a child is "diagnosed" the family becomes steeped in a new language of sorts. Personally, I find it difficult to speak of Benny's differences as most of the language available places such immediate and profound limitations on him. I especially dislike the term "special needs," a word that tries to sound helpful, soft and gentle, but more often strains to justify a separate educational experience. I cannot stand "disabled" as the obvious implication is that the person so described lacks some sort of ability or, worse yet, is devoid of ability at all. It is a paradox that we must choose from these words that impose such limitations while at the same time, guarantee services needed to grow.

I know that without the chance to learn amongst his peers, Benny would not have been able to develop the wide array of talents he enjoys today. I know that without typical peers who spoke to him with such earnestness, he might not be conversational. I know that without the chance to share in so many events Adam and Benny would not be the best of friends as they are. Adam would not be able to reap the benefits that come naturally from having an older brother.

I write to shine a spotlight on Boulder School, a place that balances support and growth. Administrators and teachers rarely, if ever, referred to Benny by any diagnostic labels, yet were all able to provide him with valuable accommodations and supports. Since we entered the school on a cold February day in 2008, they have been by my side letting me know with great excitement about all of the talents they have been able to nurture in my son. They embraced us as a family from the start and never for a moment allowed me to question our right to be a part of this community. They have taught me how to step back as a parent and how to expect nothing short of miracles in my son.

***

The term "Least Restrictive Environment" (or LRE for those fluent in the many acronyms within educationalese) is one of those phrases that most people take for granted, and few question. It had always left me with a sense of unease, but it wasn't until reading Lipsky and Gardner's classic book Inclusion and *School Reform: Transforming America's Schools* (1997) that I became aware that it is predicated upon the degree of containment imposed upon people, a concept based upon jailing criminals. It has a subconscious ring of, 'Prisoners with good behavior receive more privileges.' It is also one of the foundations of special education law, enshrined in Pubic Law 94–142, originally in the form of The Education of All Handicapped Children Act (1975) and now reauthorized as the Individuals with Disabilities Education Improvement Act (2004). Like much of special education, it is well intended, but also had far-reaching, unforeseen consequences, including its use to keep children out of general education classes (Brantlinger, 2004).

Benny's story begins with his placement in an exclusive NYC district, reserved only for students deemed as having moderate, severe, and/or multiple disabilities. District 75 is an unusual place that I have described at length before, illustrating its tradition of largely resisting inclusive education as it flies in the face of some parental desires, professional job placements (administrators, teachers, paraprofessionals), and the Department of Education's (DoE) policy to have a centralized system of more restrictive environments (Connor, 2010). I have friends who are teachers that work within District 75, and live with the ambivalence of wanting their students to be more included in general education classes, but are fearful that general education teachers (and school personnel in general, including safety officers, sometimes referred to as "Security") would not understand behaviors, tics, quirks, and moods of many children identified as disabled. For example, if a safety officer tells a student identified as behavior disordered to take off his hat, and the student says, "Fuck, no," in a zero-tolerance environment, the student will be suspended, despite the legal provision of having a Behavior Intervention Plan (BIP). As one District 75 teacher I know has said, "If we don't exist, then our kids would be kicked out of the regular schools"(Clark, 2016, personal communication).

We understand that these issues are complicated. At the same time, because District 75 does exist, it is often seen as the automatic default placement for many students, such as Benny, who do not fit the expected mold of what a student should be or be able to do. It may be easier in terms of allocating systems to support administration, budget, and professional personnel, but most of District 75 does not provide meaningful options to children like Benny. On a related note, there has been a growth of a small network of schools involved in the ASD Nest Program that cultivates sites to support children with autism in general education placements (Bleiweiss, Hough, & Cohen, 2013; Cohen & Hough, 2013). However, this system has relied upon the relentless advocacy of an experienced mother who fought for the option of inclusive classes for children with autism. In the case of Diane's family, these options were beginning to become available, but then had not been sufficiently established. As she acknowledges, the cultural capital of middle-class, white parents, often dissipates in the face of placement options, a phenomenon verified in research (Hale, 2011). In other words, while they have some clout based on socio economic status and race, and—crudely put—would therefore likely have more options not provided to working class, poor, and immigrant parents, of color, the "capital" they have is not enough to get them what they need.

One of the most haunting parts of this chapter is Diane's realization that so many other children have not had the same chance as her son. She is acutely aware of now living in a parallel universe where education fits Benny instead of Benny not fitting into the educational settings as they are currently constructed. This co-existence of the "possibility" and "impossibility" of inclusion, she knows, creates vastly different lives of children who strive to meet their unimposed potential compared to children whose potential has been imposed upon them—through unstimulating, restrictive environments that stunt their emotional, social, and academic growth. What kind of child would we see if Benny had never left District 75? It is painful to think that most of the peers he left behind are still there and, I strongly suspect, have never been able to approximate their potential.

Because District 75 is considered a more restrictive environment, it is problematic on many levels. The ratio of students with disabilities within racial categories are not reflected equally, with the majority of students being students of color, and many being placed there when given the category of Emotional Disturbance or Behavior Disorders (ED/BD) (Connor, 2010). Sometimes, the least experienced teachers are placed in the most restrictive environment by the Department of Education (DoE). At the request of the DoE, my college created a program for new teachers who are hired and then placed in District 75. Some classrooms are "6:1:4" (six students, four paraprofessionals, one teacher) and prove to be extremely challenging for a novice teacher. Parents of children with autism who have placed their children in such settings have reported seeing them regress in terms of communication and behaviors (Ginsberg, 2003). This is unsurprising when a class full of students with the same label have only each other to learn from in terms of behavior. As a former teacher of students labeled with Behavior Disorders who all were placed in the same class, I saw first hand how the students reflected each others' undesirable behaviors, cultivating a skewed sense of class norms, not having access to general education and diverse peers as natural role models.

In shifting the focus, I want to also call attention to the powerful effect of inclusive education when it is done well on parents and children. Many parents fear including their children with disabilities in general education classes as they see it as taking a risk of subjecting their child to a hostile environment created by teachers who do not feel adequately prepared to teach their children (Priestly & Parvaneh, 2002), with an increased likelihood of bullying by nondisabled peers if teachers do not provide supportive social environments

(Humphrey & Symes, 2010). Others feel it is akin to African-American children having been on the front lines of racial integration of schools—and the unfairness of schools being the "pilot" for forging integration at large throughout all aspects of society. These fears are understandable, and yet, when inclusion is done well—that is, responsibly—with the input of parents, such as in the case of Boulder, it works far better than exclusion. What is of interest in Boulder is a level of honesty and openness about trying to find the best way to include children. Diane writes, "…most of his teachers confessed to me they were initially scared to teach him but quickly found him incredibly rewarding." I have always been fascinated by teaching the most "difficult" student in a class, and think this way of framing the situation actually helps teachers. First, unpacking why a student is considered difficult to teach helps us constantly grow as educators. Second, not seeing the child as a problem, but rather a challenge to reach, shifts a teacher's position from being reactive to proactive. In other words, instead of responding to a pre-assigned label that implies the child and his/her needs are already "known," finding out about the child oneself as an educator—a puzzle to put together, a mystery to be solved, as someone with a history, an individual with likes and abilities that a teacher must personally come to know, then guides how to best respond to his/her needs. Third, once teachers come to personally know their students, they have "reached" them. Once reached, students are far easier to teach, as they have a genuine connection with their teacher, a certain degree of trust. The teacher then provides support—academic, social, and emotional—that nourishes the intrinsic satisfaction of being a teacher.

As mentioned in our introduction, one purpose of this book is to illuminate ways in which the philosophy of DSE is already in action, although it may not be explicitly recognized and formally identified as such. This chapter, like others in the book, serves as a "slice of life" that relates to those who are grounded within a DSE approach to education. The tenets of DSE states that we "assume competence and reject deficit models of disability," (Connor et. al, 2008, p. 448) something that Diane and her husband did, but personnel in the initial schools did not. In addition, DSE serves to "promote social justice, equitable and inclusive educational opportunities, and full and meaningful access to all aspects of society for people labeled with disability/disabled people" (p. 448), something Boulder school has done as part of who they are. And while a third tenet reads DSE "privileges the interests, agendas, and voices of people labeled with disability/disabled people" (p. 448), I also suggest that this can be, and is often, done with family members whose advocacy shapes the opportunities of and possibilities for their disabled child or sibling, as can be seen in many memoirs and testimonials (Cutler, 2004; Ginsberg, 2003; Harry, 2008; Jacobson, 1995; Lavani, 2011, 2014; Mukho-padhyay, 2003; Park, 2001; Sauer, 2007; Simon, 2002; Valle & Aponte, 2002; Valle, 2009; Ware, 2006).

Considering this chapter in terms of DSE theory, Diane recognizes "the oppressive nature of essentialized/categorical/medicalized naming of disability in schools, policy, institutions, and the law." Many of us have, and continue to struggle with the notion of labeling. On one hand, it makes things "under-standable," allows for government funding, school budgeting, services and allocated resources, power to the individual under the law, and so on. On the other hand, it oversimplifies the complexities of being human to reductive descriptors (into which some people are forced), inscribes identities, stigma-tizes, provokes discrimination despite such illegality, and reduces options and possibilities for accessing all realms of life enjoyed by nondisabled people. In once talking about labels to a major self-advocate and motivation speaker for ADHD, he shrugged, "You're damned if you have them, and you're damned if you don't," revealing deep and unresolved ambivalences that we all have about labels. After all, they open doors for some things, and close them for others; they work to enable some people, and actively disable others.

In terms of expanding our understanding of disability, so it is not con-fined to medical, scientific, and psychological fields, it can also be argued that Diane's family focused upon "political, social, cultural, historical, and indi-vidual understandings of disability" (Connor, et. al., 2008, p. 448). They saw Benny's uniqueness within all of these realms, along with the implications of each specific realm for him, whereas the massive school system saw Benny as a unit to be placed within the order of existing things, and that placement was District 75. In contrast, and in line with DSE, Diane's family supported "the education of students labeled with disabilities in non-segregated settings from a civil rights stance" (p. 448). They saw no compelling reasons for what was essentially a form of local government's containment of their son, a story that sounds all too familiar to other parents in their advocacy for their child to have a "full inclusion" education (Lipton, 1994). Given the rhetoric of federal policy in the form of No Child Left Behind (2001), there is great irony in that Diane and her family had to leave a more restrictive environment behind in NYC, so Benny would not be left behind in terms of his growth in academic, social, and emotional domains.

References

Bleiweiss, J., Hough, L., & Cohen, S. (2013). *Everyday classroom strategies and practices for supporting children with autism spectrum disorders*. Lenexa, KS: AAPC Publishers.

Brantlinger, E. (1997). Using ideologies: Cases of non-recognition of the politics of research and practice in special education. *Review of Educational Research, 67*(4), 425–459.

Clarke, E. (2016). Personal communication.

Cohen, S., & Hough, L. (Eds.) (2013). *The ASDC nest model: A framework for inclusive education for higher functioning children with autism spectrum disorders*. Lenexa, KS: AAPC Publishers.

Connor, D. J. (2010). Adding urban complexities into the mix: Continued resistance to the inclusion of students with cognitive impairments. In P. Smith (Ed.). *Whatever happened to inclusion?* (pp. 157–187). New York: Peter Lang.

Connor, D. J., Gabel, S. L., Gallagher, D. & Morton, M. (2008). Disability studies and inclusive education--Implication for theory, research, and practice: Guest editor's introduction. *International Journal of Inclusive Education, 12*(5–6), 441–457.

Cutler, E. (2004). *A thorn in my pocket: Temple Grandin's mother tells the family story*. Arlington, TX: Future Horizons.

Education for All Handicapped Children Act of 1975, PL 94–142, 20 U.S.C. 1400 *et seq.*

Ginsberg, D. (2003). *Raising Blaze: Bringing up an extraordinary son in an ordinary world*. New York: Harper Collins.

Hale, C. (2011). *From exclusivity to exclusion: The LD experience of privileged parents*. Rotterdam: Sense.

Harry, B. (2008). *Melanie, bird with a broken wing: A mother's story*. New York: Paul H. Brookes.

Humphrey, N. & Symes, W. (2010). Perceptions of social support and experience of bullying among pupils with autistic spectrum disorders in mainstream secondary schools. *European Journal of Special Needs Education, 25*(1), 77–91.

Individuals with Disabilities Education Improvement Act (2004), U.S.C. 1400 *et seq.*

Jacobson, D.S. (1999). *The question of David: A disabled mother's journey through adoption, family, and life*. Berkeley, CA: Creative Arts Book Company.

Lalvani, P. (2011). Constructing the (m)other: Dominant and contested narratives on mothering a child with Down syndrome. *Narrative Inquiry, 21*(2), 276–293.

Lalvani, P. (2014). The enforcement of normalcy in schools and the disablement of families: unpacking master narratives on parental denial. *Disability & Society, 29*(8), 1221–1233.

Lipsky, D. K., & Gartner, A. (1997). Historical background of inclusive education. In D. K. Lipsky & A. Gartner (Eds.) *Inclusion and school reform: Transforming America's classrooms* (pp. 73–83). Baltimore, MD: Paul H. Brookes.

Mukhopadhyay, T. R. (2005). *The mind tree: A miraculous child breaks the silence of autism*. New York: Arcade.

Park, C. C. (2001). *Exiting nirvana: A daughter's life with autism*. New York: Little, Brown, & Company.

Priestly, M., & Parvanah, R. (2002). Hopes and fears: Stakeholder views on the transfer of special school resources toward inclusion. *International Journal of Inclusive Education*, 6(4), 371–390.

Sauer, J. S., (2007). No surprises, please: A mother's story of betrayal and the fragility of inclusion. *Journal of Intellectual and Developmental Disabilities*, 45(4), 273–277.

Simon, R. (2002). *Riding the bus with my sister*. New York: Plume.

Valle, J. W. (2009). *What mothers say about special education: From the 1960s to the present*. London: Palgrave McMillan.

Valle, J. W., & Aponte, E. (2002). IDEA and collaboration: A Bakhtinian perspective on parent and professional discourse. *Journal of Learning Disabilities*, 35, 469–479.

Ware, L. (2006). Diego's life without her. *Equity & Excellence in Education*, 39(2), 124–126.

· 2 ·

CLIMATE

September 2012 brought in the last parent evening I would attend for Benny at The Boulder School. Even though I still would have Adam there for two years after Benny graduated, in June 2013, I had already sensed that the intensity of the experience had begun to weaken, stretched thin by the forces which moved me to look ahead to the next few years and begin to imagine him in middle school, switching classrooms, and choosing electives. I enjoyed the evening, especially hearing Clark, principal extraordinaire speak. I remembered, early on in my experience at the school, sitting in the audience trying to make sense of his words but feeling confused. Finally, once Benny had grown so, I could listen with pure pleasure, finally understanding the goals of the school, ultimately feeling like we belonged, that we were not outsiders trying to impose a child with disabilities upon a classroom of typical peers. He spoke to both to us, the parents he knew so very well, and the novices to Boulder, new to an educational approach that is different than any they have experienced to date. I knew that to some of the new folks, his words seemed far away, perhaps not even real. Standing up in front of the parent body, Clark told us that he wants his students to enjoy their days in elementary school, he wants them to develop *all* sides of themselves, not merely the academic. "Any school can teach reading, writing and mathematics," he would say each year in a slightly different way, continuing,

"I want my children to learn about themselves, to develop confidence, to discover talents and interests, and to become courageous and proud." He talked about the relationships developed here, the friendships among faculty and between parents and staff, and his hope that Boulder would continue to be family for all who have ever been connected to it. He then briefly described some of the unique programs and events designed to bring the community together--a menu of delectable options, many of which are currently being cut from elementary school budgets.

His voice, while full of passion, can be squeaky, bursting with the capriciousness of youth. The first few times I heard him speak like this, I did not really take him seriously. His words fell so far from all I have experienced in education over the past 40 years, both as student and teacher, that I dismissed his promises as idealistic gestures that could not be realized.

In the spirit of confession I also felt these words fell far from my son, who entered his school despite the advice of many educational experts and developmental pediatricians. Benny was lucky to be making it through the day at first, and the thought that he would progress to a place where he could develop a passion for learning and awareness of his skills and strengths seemed a fantasy in which I had little right to indulge. So for the first few years I let Clark's words sprinkle around me, bursting above and landing always somewhere else, just out of reach, but never out of sight. Quizzically, I would look over and study these promises; I would try to understand what he meant, hoping to take some of it back to my own teaching, still unclear how these words might apply to Benny. Suddenly as dawn comes after the darkest part of night, Benny was there, developing his talents, playing trumpet as well as anyone his age, creating paintings that pulsated with color and energy, dancing on the stage to the music of the great ballroom era, arm-in-arm with a beautiful girl, joining his friends in their own creative cross-dressing skit to the music of the 70's for the annual variety show. Now I could listen to Clark with pure pleasure, feeling that we belong. Although it seems as if it had been only moments since Benny entered the building for the first time, a wobbly, red-cheeked five-year-old, who could barely respond to his own name, I knew that he was ready for more. Each morning as he would enter Boulder School, I saw his long, lanky body walk carefully alongside the children so small they seemed like toys, and I could hardly catch my breath as I realized again and again how far he had come. He was outgrowing the confines of elementary school. I knew he would relish the independence that middle school would bring, the chance to walk into town after school, use a cell phone, and explore subjects in more depth.

Despite my successful career in education, I was woefully ignorant about inclusion. At the time of our move I feared that we were taking a huge risk. My mind was full of misconceptions, such as we were outsiders trying to impose a child with disabilities upon other children. These thoughts have slowly been replaced over time. I was sure inclusion was fueled by pity that I would be left with great gratitude if it worked for Benny. I had no idea how much Benny would contribute to a community independent of his delays. Importantly, I had little sense of the way that my own education had contributed to narrowing my focus, forcing me to aim only for a certain type of limited success that I expected to come solely through a predictable chain of events.

Subtle and overt directions on how we must categorize and label our fellow human beings are pervasive throughout our culture. One of the largest culprits in the transfer of these messages to society is our educational system. It does not take an advanced degree to realize that education is on a state of crisis in this country. High stakes testing is taking over. Teachers are under enormous pressures and often do not know how to respond to seemingly conflicting demands made upon them by federal and state governments, along with their local education authority. How can a teacher differentiate instruction, create glorious projects which tap on all talents, while ensuring high scores on state exams, the results of which factor into their own evaluations?

Curriculum is changing faster than textbooks can be published. Sadly, teachers have less and less autonomy to react to the needs of their students. School communities across the U.S. are now plagued with crises including shootings, pervasive bullying, and unconscionable rates of suicide. Despite these horrors, we hear mainly about the need to raise standards, and little, if anything, about the power of schools to shape emotional growth.

Boulder provides an excellent academic curriculum, but this is not what makes the school stand out. It only takes a glimpse down the block during early morning to see the energy that pulsates into the neighborhood from this school. Children run, breaking away from the grasp of their loving caretakers, to get to school quickly and greet the teachers who lined up each morning in front of the building. They run with crazy hats, funky socks, posters, and circus toys. They run with an enthusiasm for school that is unequaled to any I have seen. They run right into their principal, who gives them high fives and then hugs their tired parents, as he stands on the street waiting to start the day. Clark has at least once been mistaken for a hired "plainclothes" clown.

When I moved my family out of New York City in search of an inclusive classroom for Benny, I had no idea that I would find an educational oasis unequaled by any other I have seen. The Boulder School is indeed a family, a haven where teachers speak to parents like friends and the principal insists on being called by his first name. Boulder has given Benny a chance to find talents and skills that no one could have predicted he had, and it also given Adam opportunities to develop sides of himself that might have lain dormant for years, if not for a lifetime. The school has taught me more about education than any course, readings, or research. Boulder has re-energized my own teaching, made it possible for me to educate in new ways with a passion I thought could not be regained.

It has taken me several years to really begin to understand the mission and to appreciate the way it is reflected in both everyday routines and special events. In the hopes of sharing some of the magic, I take you with me on a journey through the pivotal moments in my relationship with Boulder. My appreciation and understanding have deepened over time and no doubt will deepen even further. This book is a snapshot at best, a cross section of experiences that have helped me understand Boulder in its glory.

The school is a dynamic community of several hundred students, staff, and families. It is a place where equality and equity reign, manifest in ways that turn academic tradition upside down. While I spent years looking for evidence of expertise in fields related to disabilities, I found little. Instead, at Boulder I find a community where difference is *valued*, where staff and students are allowed to be themselves and encouraged to extend themselves, to grow and change as they connect with each other. It is for this reason that what they have to offer is a lesson for us all, for every school and community. It has taken me years to understand what makes it work and I expect it will take many more for me to truly appreciate the immensity of its reach. I see now that in order to embrace inclusion, to truly create spaces where everyone can contribute in meaningful ways, we must be open to changing ourselves. When we do, we find that the world becomes a place of incredible opportunity and beauty.

***

Diane's sentence, "I knew that he was ready for more," struck a chord with me in its directness, simplicity, and honesty. It also encapsulated a form of parental knowledge that is quite distinct from professional expertise. That it supersedes professional knowledge—in cases like this—upsets the epistemological order of things. Plainly put, how can a mother know more than top doctors, often with their decades of studying, research, and practice? It has been noted in DSE literature that parental knowledge, specifically a mother's knowledge about her child with a disability, is not valued within the field of special education, particularly when weighed against a professional such as a teacher, principal, psychologist, or doctor, let alone a combination of all four (Valle, 2009). Mothers are often charged with being too emotional, too close, too subjective, and in denial about their child's dis/abilities. It is worth considering another way to characterize mothers: to recognize their primary disposition is to believe in their child's abilities, potential, and growth. In other words, they do not wish to impose a limit of expectations upon their child. While a doctor is with a child for perhaps an hour or less, and a teacher for six hours, parents are with their children almost all of the time, and have studied them intently since birth. In this way, Diane's family contrasted "medical, scientific, psychological understandings with social and experiential understandings of disability" (Connor et. al, 2008, p. 448), and trusted themselves over the knowledge shared by experts that was meant to guide them in their decisions about Benny. I share this point without wishing to be overly simplistic, realizing this is a delicate subject, and there are many factors to consider in contemplating what's "right" for a child. However, in most circumstances that I have been privy to, it strikes me that the mother is asking for an opportunity, a chance, a possibility of keeping the door open to encourage growth. We can never be one hundred percent sure of if, how, when, or why growth happens. I am wondering right now, if Boulder had not provided space and time for playing music, painting, dancing, and theater performance, would Benny have grown so much? Yet it was these opportunities that made an impression when Diane and her husband walked through the school that first time. They were *felt*, a somatic reaction, leading Diane to realize that it was "instinct" not "science," that made her know she was making the best choice.

At the same time as possessing deeper knowledge of their child than anyone else, parents also experience a sense of flux in terms of expectations: shoot for the stars, while recognizing and accepting what is the current reality. An area of interest for me, revealed in this chapter, is how career-long educators often have such limited understandings of disability (including special educators who graduate with master's degrees). Diane's initial understanding about inclusive education was that it was fuelled by pity. She also felt her family's desires for Benny could be construed as an imposition upon others. These feelings, carried deep within, typify cultural knowledge about disability within highly limited and misinformed tropes, including disability's relation to charities that blatantly invoke pity (such as Jerry Lewis's telethons) and the general notion that people with disabilities are a "burden" (Diane uses the word "imposition"). These tropes are the root of stereotyping people with disabilities and can be seen throughout our culture (Fleishner & Zames, 2001) and in the media that both reflects and helps construct our cultural values and beliefs (Haller, 2010), pervading all aspects of society, including education.

There is much work to be done within the field of education when it comes to the topic of disability. One of the reasons why an informal network of critical special educators began to cultivate a different theoretical framework for "disability" that eventually became formalized into DSE were the overwhelmingly deficit-based understandings of human differences that our culture had determined that has also permeated education. Starting with the professional fields of science, from which grew medicine, from which grew psychology—all three conceived of disability as an abnormality that excluded those determined as such from the realm of "normal." What became problematic for we who began our careers in special education, is that the discipline is unquestioningly rooted within science, medicine, and psychology, fields that hold perspectives that there's something missing, sick, wrong, incomplete, aberrant, about a person so labeled. It is as if the person is considered incomplete or fully human, and in need of a fix, cure, or intervention. In DSE, this phenomenon is what we work against, instead, asking: What are better ways in which we can understand and accept the diversity of people as natural? By focusing primarily, rather, on the social, cultural, and historical aspects of disability, we believe educators come to understand disability as a form of human variation, and in the process question, and hopefully "unlearn," some of the damaging knowledge accrued through their educational programs. Diane herself alludes to the limited ways in which teacher education prepares us to understand human variation, and trains us to value certain forms of seeing, doing, and being, sharing: "I had little sense of the way that my own education had narrowed my focus, forced me to aim only for a certain type of success which I expected to come solely through a predictable chain of events." What Diane initially experienced dissonance with were the unexpected directions in which Benny's interests grew, his academic growth spurt (varied across content areas, like most children), and a blossoming social life—all which defied "a predictable chain of events," that is the template of teacher expectations.

In the traditional fields of special and general education, inclusion has often been conceptualized as something a child with a disability had to "earn" the right to enter. The child did this by approximating the "normalcy" expected within general education classrooms (Anastasiou & Kauffman, 2011; Kauffman, 1999; Kauffman & Hallahan, 1995; Fuchs & Fuchs, 1995). In contrast,

DSE sees entry to general classrooms as the civil right of a child (Kiuppis & Hausstatter, 2014), and therefore children with disabilities in class should be a normal occurrence. This sentiment is echoed in the documentary film, Including Samuel (Habib, 2007), primarily about a young boy with multiple disabilities, and featuring half a dozen portraits of children with various other disabilities. Samuel's father comments upon how until he had a disabled son, he could not believe his failure to see the erasure of disabled citizens from our cultural consciousness. Like Habib's narrative and those of other families he features, Diane's story is very much in tune with DSE research in several ways. First, "Disability is primarily recognized and valued as a natural part of human diversity," (Connor et al., 2008, p. 449). Second, DSE states it "Recognizes and privileges the knowledge derived from the lived experience of people with disabilities" (p. 448). Given the theme of this book, as I have already mentioned, I believe that the latter can also be done via a family member who is able to articulate the lived experiences of their child, sibling, or parent.

In transitioning to another related topic, this chapter also raises how narrow the scope is of current education. In the climate of inflexible standards, incessant testing, and teacher evaluations, the pleasure has gone out of teaching for many teachers I know. When I ask what keeps them in the profession, they invariably respond with, "the kids." This makes sense as it was likely the reason why they entered the profession in the first place. However, as a career-long educator, I have a deep concern when I continue to see approximately fifty percent of people leave the profession, most within less than five years (Ingersol & Smith, 2003), and hear seasoned university educators say, "If I had to go into teaching today, I don't think I would do it." There's something terribly wrong with this picture, of a profession in which half of well-motivated people leave, and most others are unhappy unless they can eke out a supportive school or find reasons to feel successful, amid the constantly shifting demands, and negative media portrayals (Goldstein, 2011). These issues are related to inclusive education in many ways. If standards are the only measurement, while many students with disabilities will be stretched and "succeed," there is a larger group of students with disabilities that may never be able to do so. This makes students feel inadequate, and teachers feel pressured, lest they be held personally accountable for not getting all students to fit into the mold. In sum, such policies can set students, teachers, and principals up for failure—when student "scores" are tabulated and reign supreme in policy decision-making. Such policies have side effects, too. I know of instances where students with disabilities are not welcome in some schools, or their entrance is delayed in start up schools, or they are "cherry-picked" by charter schools to fit their minimum quota.

What's clear about Boulder is that, even in this climate, the principal and staff have found ways to maintain a commitment to a happy and healthy environment in which academics are taught, opportunities are provided to socialize and grow, and interests, talents, and skills are discovered and encouraged. To state the obvious, the principal's vision is strong, clear, consistent, and authentic. He states, "Any school can teach reading, writing, and mathematics...I want my children to learn about themselves, to develop confidence, to discover talents and interests, and to become courageous and proud." In the spirit of gentle critique, I'd amend his first statement to, "I know we can teach your child reading, writing, and mathematics... but I also want my children to...," because we know—by Diane's experience alone—that not any school can teach reading, writing, and mathematics. However, the success that Clark desires for all children encompasses, from the beginning, who they are, and who they can come to be. His philosophy is reminiscent of other highly successful principals interested in the whole child, including the child's family (Meier, 2002; Monroe, 1999; Hehir & Katzman, 2012). Given the forceful presence of a principal whose gentle imprints can be seen all over the school, the theme of a strong, committed leader is woven throughout several chapter commentaries in this text.

In keeping with the topic of principals, I would like to share some current observations on inclusive practices in urban high schools. As previously mentioned, the majority of my work in a previous position within the Office of the Superintendent of Manhattan High Schools, was to design and implement support for inclusive classrooms. In this position I had access to forty-four schools, and spent a lot of time over nine years working with principals, assistant principals of general and special education, general and special education teachers, paraprofessionals, parents, and students. During this time, among other things, I provided monthly professional development for team teachers, visited many schools and observed teachers at work, spoke with concerned union members, took assistant principals to visit "model" schools in other boroughs. I share this information because during that time I was able to unofficially compare all schools, and I saw that for almost all of them, shifting to develop more inclusive practices was two-steps forward and one step back. I'd say approximately five or six did what I'd consider an effective job at inclusion and the link between them all was the principal's belief that this was the right thing to do. Back then, when asked by people, "Can you show me where inclusion is effective?" I could take them to these sites where it was always a work in progress, involving a lot of hard work by the teachers. Once, I was asked to provide three hours of professional development to all of the high school principals about developing more inclusive classrooms, and subsequently wrote up that experience into what was my first publication (Connor, 2004). During the planning stages with the superintendent, I asked to use DSE as part of the lens through which I wanted them to re-think the concept of disability and its connection to inclusive practices, as long as I could spend sufficient time on practical suggestions and options that had been successful in some schools. In short, they allowed me to do so—and since then, when possible, I have used DSE in any inclusive presentations. One of DSE's strengths is that it has the power to destabilize people's thinking about fundamental issues such as: "What does it mean to be human? How can we respond ethically to difference? What is the value of a human life? Who decides these questions, and what do these answers reveal?" (Kudlick, 2003, ¶1). In terms of schooling practices, Kudlick's thoughts trigger further questions such as: Who belongs? Who does not? Who decided who belongs and who does not? Who benefits? Who does not? Who did not have input into these decisions? On basis were the decisions made? What are the implications for a democracy of the inclusion and exclusion of citizens within its public institutions, including general education classrooms?

I have focused on this topic of urban high schools because recently I was asked by a superintendent to provide two hours of professional development for principals on the topic of developing and supporting inclusive classrooms. When I went to the superintendent's office for the first meeting, I experienced a level of shock. It felt like déjà vu; I had been here before. I was asked to do the same things I had been asked over a dozen years earlier. It seemed like few schools were confident or comfortable in inclusive practices. The "good" inclusive schools I knew from a previous professional life were now struggling with these issues. Team teaching was being cast as the model to create an inclusive environment. I must say that I was saddened by this experience. I realize that inclusive education in urban high schools is challenging for a variety of reasons including disparities between expected and actual academic performances, content-driven classes, multiple teachers, the sheer size of some schools, class sizes of thirty-four students, and so on. However, to state the obvious, it did strike me that insufficient progress had been made as a whole within New York City. Despite a career of pushing an inclusive agenda, for a moment, I felt I'd stood still.

The presentation to contemporary principals went well. Grounded in a DSE framework, they pondered the issues of inclusion as primarily moral and ethical considerations rather than how they have been trained to approach them as technical and managerial. How they proceed this year will determine what progress can be made. The experience, though, did affirm what I have seen during my career. A school is an ecological system that grows and functions because of its particular climate. Each school is unique, and the most important person in creating the climate is the principal. To be a successful inclusive principal, a person must not only possess the knowledge and skills needed to be a strong leader, s/he must also have a disposition that fights for the equal rights of disabled students. Until this occurs, we will continue to have cyclical growth and decline of effective inclusive schools.

References

Anastasiou, D., & Kauffman, J. K. (2011). A social constructionist approach to disability: Implications for special education. *Exceptional Children, 77*(5), 367–384.

Connor, D. J. (2004). Infusing disability studies into "mainstream" educational thought: One person's story. *Review of Disability Studies, 1*(1), 100–119.

Connor, D. J., Gabel, S. L., Gallagher, D. & Morton, M. (2008). Disability studies and inclusive education--Implication for theory, research, and practice: Guest editor's introduction. *International Journal of Inclusive Education, 12*(5–6), 441–457.

Fleischer, D. F. & Zames, F. (2001). *The disability rights movement: From charity to confrontation.* Philadelphia, PA: Temple University Press.

Fuchs, D., & Fuchs, L.S. (1995). Inclusive schools movement and the radicalization of special education reform. In J. M. Kauffman & D. P. Hallahan (Eds.) *The illusion of full inclusion* (pp. 213–243). Austin, TX: ProEd.

Goldstein, R. A. (2011). Imagining the frame: Media representations of teachers, their unions, NCLB, and education reform. *Journal of Education & Educational Research, 25*(4), 543–576.

Habib, D. (Producer and Director). (2007). *Including Samuel.* [DVD]. Available from http://www.includingsamuel.com/home.aspx

Haller, B. (2010). *Representing disability in an ableist world.* Louisville, KY: Advocado Press.

Hehir, T. & Katzman, L. I. (2012). *Effective inclusive schools: Designing successful school-wide programs.* San Francisco, CA: Jossey Bass.

Ingersol, R. M., & Smith, T. M. (2003). The wrong solution to the teacher shortage. *Educational Leadership, 60*(8), 30–33.

Kauffman, J. M. (1999). Commentary: Today's special education and its messages for tomorrow. *Journal of Special Education, 32*(4), 244–254.

Kauffman, J. M., & Hallahan, D. P. (1995). *The illusion of full inclusion*. Austin, Texas: Pro-Ed.
      Kauffman, J. M., & Sasso, G. (2006a). Toward ending cultural and cognitive relativism in
      special education. *Exceptionality, 14*(2), 65–90.

Kiuppis, F., & Hausstatter, R. S. (Eds.) (2014). *Inclusive education twenty years after Salamanca*.
      New York: Peter Lang.

Kudlick, C. J. (2003). Disability History: Why We Need Another "Other." *American Historical
      Review, 108*, 763–93.

Meier, D. (2002). *The power of their ideas: Lessons for America from a small school in Harlem*.
      Boston, MA: Beacon Press.

Monroe, L. (1999). *Nothing's impossible: Leadership lessons from inside and outside of the classroom*.
      New York: Perseus Books.

Valle, J. W. (2009). *What mothers say about special education: From the 1960s to the present*.
      London: Palgrave McMillan.

· 3 ·

A FREE AND APPROPRIATE
EDUCATION (FAPE):
HOW APPROPRIATE IS MISERY?

October 2007

It was a refreshingly crisp fall day. The leaves were achingly beautiful, hung by silken threads to the trees, some falling fast, pushed along on a rather gentle breeze, spinning up before dropping down, creating dizzying displays of shimmering lights before settling in crunchy piles at our feet. A complex concoction of emotions ran through me as David, Benny, Adam and I made our way by foot from the railroad station to several elementary schools in this suburban town. While the cautions of top developmental doctors replayed in my head and threatened to weaken my resolve, hope pulled me along in search of an inclusive classroom, in which Benny might thrive.

At that time Benny had been in his self-contained 12-1-1 classroom in NYC for six weeks. He was already in his second such placement and neither teacher seemed to feel she had the skills to "reach" him. Benny had shown, to them, no indication that he had "academic readiness." He had been a disturbance in each class, making noises, running out of the room, hiding in closets and setting off fire alarms. Nevertheless, I remained unconvinced that a more restrictive setting would have been helpful to him in the long run. I found it particularly heartbreaking to think of sending him to a school other than the one that his brother

would eventually attend. I knew that when the time came I could not look into the eyes of either of my boys and tell them that one of them was so different, so disabled, that he could not be educated in the same building as his more able brother. Deep down I knew also that Benny was at his best when he was beside typical children, who drew him out like no one else ever could.

In addition to the dismay of his teachers, Benny himself had been absolutely miserable since the start of kindergarten. Most mornings began with a major tantrum in the house and once out of the house, he would often plaster himself to the sidewalk on the way to school, sometimes flopping his whole small body right down into the chilly muddy puddles. When we finally got to school I would walk him into the cafeteria where the special education children gathered together. It was a horrific sight, three tables of boys, often finger-painting the tables with ketchup, bits of breakfast soaking under their feet in pools of milk, spilt by a combination of carelessness and outright disobedience. What was most striking to me, though, was the sadness in the faces of these children. While the children at other tables had a light in their eyes, these children looked lackluster at best. The lifeless look in their eyes, combined with the stench of school cafeteria food created a scene that bordered on the grotesque. Before the first bell even rang, their teachers would begin to scold the class, reminding them of the ways they had failed to behave the day before. One day Benny's teacher recreated a scene in the cafeteria. She used a chair to represent a toilet, to train a child to go to the bathroom instead of wetting his pants, as he had done the previous day. The entire training session was done in public. Had I witnessed this today I would have found the words to express my horror. That day, in shock, I stood passively on the side. However, I did promptly contact and inform the parents of that small child, and within the year, his parents had found another placement in a special needs private school, at the expense of the school district.

While I was routinely witnessing these atrocities, administrators kept telling me that Benny needed a more restrictive setting. There was no need to argue. I had no desire to keep him in this school. The days rolled into one another like a nightmare from which I could not wake. The only bright spots were the few moments when Benny would shock me with a gesture so lucid, so hopeful, and so profound that I was forced to believe in him and follow that glimmer of light wherever it might lead.

One morning Benny was a little late to school and I was asked to walk him to class. Along the way I was privy to one of those moments of great lucidity. In the New York City schools, many of the special education classrooms are housed far from the other rooms. Benny's classroom, tucked behind the auditorium on the fourth floor is a small dark room with only one set of small windows. The walls are bare, so as not to "over stimulate" these children with disabilities. Along the way we passed a general education kindergarten classroom. It was bursting with color, artwork done by the children strung along string, held there with multicolored clothespins and the walls were overflowing with posters and pictures. Benny tugged my hand hard and began to walk into that classroom. I told him that he could not go in because it was not his class. He looked at me with wise and sorrowful eyes and asked, "Why?" Within his question I saw possibility, I saw a child who struggled with so much but had great insight and knew he deserved more. I explained that this was not his classroom for now and I asked him if he would like to be in a classroom like this one, larger and more colorful than his current classroom. The tension drained from his face momentarily and he smiled. I resolved in that moment to find him a classroom that would shower him with joyful activities, and a healthy variety of materials with which to create drawings and poems that would sail across the room on strings. I wanted nothing more than the chance for him to be in a setting with a mix of children and with a chance to grow. I heard in his question, in the music of the way he asked, "Why?" the resolve of a child who knew what he needed in order to function and eventually to flourish. As I promised myself that I would follow his lead, a part of me was still plagued with insecurities. I admonished myself for dreaming, for irrationality, and as I had heard myself described by many "professionals" in regard to Benny, for being in denial.

While I expected to be able to converse with Benny's teachers, and to work together on a plan for his success, that did not happen easily in these city schools. I was completely taken by surprise by the negativity stemming from Benny's teachers in the city. They were angry that I wanted him educated in what they saw as a setting that was above his abilities. In turn, I wondered how he could learn if the bar was so low. Their suggestions to find another setting were imbued with a threatening quality. Every day, after drop off or before pick up, they would stand together telling me how badly the day had gone for Benny, and how inappropriate his behavior had been. We did not sit down, like adults, to make a plan for a child who struggled. Instead they tried to bully me into accepting the need for a more restrictive setting by humiliating me publicly, day after day. One day they even threatened to take legal action in order to force us to move him to a 6–1–1 class outside of our district.

Instead of accepting their recommendations, I began to research school districts around the country. I was ready to relocate, when the assistant director of Benny's former preschool found for us the names of four districts within an hour of New York City that had some degree of inclusion. Since David and I both had local jobs and aging parents nearby, the chance to stay "local" was greatly appreciated. I had already called over 20 nearby districts at random and found that few offered even a small chance at the type of educational opportunities I envisioned for my son. I had not spoken to any districts that were able to promise me "full" inclusion as I learned it was called. Most districts, including three of the four my friend had found for me, described complicated tiered programs which they assured me would be tailored to Benny's needs. I sensed that inclusion should be simple, that if it could work, Benny's day should be very similar to that of his peers.

Programs with many bells and whistles made me nervous. Some districts promised me so many extra supports and such a constant stream of evaluation that I felt he would still be imprisoned by the labels. I envisioned inclusion as an opportunity for him to be with his peers for almost all of the day and likewise to have all the opportunities that they had academically and socially. I was not sure he would be successful, but that was my dream. I was not convinced that anything less would offer him substantially more than that of in a fairly restrictive setting in the city. Some districts offered part time inclusion. Administrators assured me that if my son could not handle much time with his peers that was okay, they had flexibility, they could remove him for most of the day if need be. Many districts cautioned that they only had room for a certain number of inclusion students; in other words, inclusion was not really for all, just for some. Those districts only opened a few classrooms up for inclusion, creating a reason to compete for those spots. These options made my head spin. I thought inclusion meant that my child would really be included all of the time, not half the time, not when he behaved like his peers, not only when he was able to score reasonably well on all of their measures.

It was as if some districts held out the possibility of inclusion as a reward for good work, or progress, not realizing that inclusion ought to be a right and not a privilege. I did not think that spending half a day in a regular classroom would work for him. How was a child to succeed if he spent his time in two different classrooms? How was a child going to feel that he was part of a community if he was only there part-time? How would a child going in with transition issues, social issues, ever become a part of a classroom if he were removed for hours at a time? Would other children embrace a child already a little different if the teachers did not believe he would benefit from a full day in their classroom? It did not make sense to me and I was not willing to gamble and give up a life I enjoyed in the city I was also terrified of putting Benny in another situation in which he would fail.

At the same time as I researched the details I became fixated on the bigger picture as well. Friends and colleagues directed me to several textbooks and articles about special education laws and some consequences of special education policies. My good friend Jennifer, a disability rights lawyer, suggested I read about the School to Prison Pipeline, as well as the dismal graduation rates for students in self-contained settings in New York City. In the course of my study, I came across the Individuals with Disabilities in Education Act (IDEA), which promised all students a Free and Appropriate Education (FAPE). Apparently the word appropriate is subject to interpretation. I began to wonder how we measure "appropriate"? Is this something we can quantify easily? Don't we have to look ahead and see how these students are faring ten years down the line, when they have a larger chance of dying than graduating HS with a usable diploma? Is that appropriate? Is it appropriate for a child to be moved repeatedly in a constant downward spiral landing each time in a more restrictive environment? How is a child to ever establish a sense of comfort or community in that kind of system? Although I had been in education for many years, I had inadvertently shielded myself from these issues by working in elite private schools, where only a handful of children showed any signs of difference. As I read more about the dangers of segregation I became alarmed at the ease with which I accepted his placement in a self-contained classroom. Had Benny and his teachers been happier, he might have stayed in that setting, and when he failed to make academic progress we would have blamed his disability and not the inadequacy of the school placement. It is not easy to flag a deficiency in the educational program when the children targeted have a bar that is held so low. While the administrators at Benny's current school were saying that he needed a "more restrictive setting," I was quite sure that there was nothing "appropriate" about his current placement. I also was aware that—like most parents—I did not have the time or resources to fight this battle.

Benny's tremendous academic success, whose trajectory began within hours of our decision to relocate, was a complete surprise for me. Even as a teacher I had no idea as to how far he could progress. I was used to children who follow a predictable growth curve. I realized there was a huge problem brewing, that in the city I loved, and in many districts around the country, our most vulnerable population of children was being cut off from the opportunities they needed most. While my instincts told me inclusion was the answer, my misunderstandings of the term prevented me from embracing the opportunity with confidence.

Disillusioned, I spoke to many districts and after I had all but lost hope until I spoke to Gina, the chairperson of the Department of Special Education in the district to which we moved. Gina answered the phone herself and understood our plight. She reached out with an outstretched arm and led us to her town. Gina even followed up my call to her with a call to me a few weeks later. She wanted to make sure we were following through because instinctively she knew this movement would give my son a chance to succeed in school and life.

It was only days after our first conversation that we came out by train on that glorious fall day and walked to not one but two elementary schools that were possible options for Benny. I wanted to see these schools and I wanted the principal and administrators to see Benny before I turned our life upside down to move. The first school we visited was within walking distance of the town and train line to New York City. The Principal offered Benny a choice of an empty gym in which to play or a busy Kindergarten classroom to visit. Benny surprised us all by choosing the classroom. He slipped inside with a graceful step and took a seat in the circle with all the children seated together on the carpet. The classroom was filled with laughter and light. The girls were still in summer dresses that twirled as they walked across the room. The class was listening to the teachers reading aloud. The teacher spoke with warmth and enthusiasm. The Kindergarten children were cooperative but never quite quiet, a rustle here and there made it sound like a meadow, with movement from somewhere, though everyone seemed still. The classroom was full with sensations, busy walls and windows, the sort some expert warned me would be over stimulating to Benny. This was not the case; instead, Benny sat with rapt attention, drinking in the sounds and sights of a rich and varied classroom experience. The mere sight of him sitting appropriately was a comfort to me. I desired nothing more than to know this could be his each and every day.

David, Adam and I stood in the hallway and spoke with the Principal. He gave us some information about the school, mainly trivial, which might matter to a parent with less at stake than their child's entire soul. When I pressed him about the chances of success for my son he sighed, drew in a deep breath and told me that most of the time inclusion works, but if the time comes when he felt that the school could no longer accommodate my son, then Benny would be sent to an alternative special education school nearby. His words were spoken with kindness, warmth, and sensitivity, but they brought me down to a place of misery. While the district supervisor, Gina, described to me a total commit-ment to inclusion, the words from the lips of this principal suggested to me that Benny might not in the end be able to benefit from their program.

I wondered how it could be that the district administrator described such a complete commitment to inclusion, while this principal did not seem to embody that level of commitment? Yet his words were sensible and kind, and I wondered how I could really have believed that someone would promise me that he would succeed with typical peers, without ever having met him, or even read the voluminous reports about his potential or lack thereof. I felt too close to what I knew was right for him, but too far yet for comfort, and the dichotomy plunged me into a terrible state of despair.

We walked on to another school within the district. As a New Yorker and one with an addiction to public transportation, I had all but ruled out this second stop. The zoned area for this second school was a full three miles from the railroad. I could possibly make peace with the suburbs if I were close to a town, a supermarket, and my daily newspaper. The further we walked from the town, the heavier my footsteps felt, as if I were fighting a horizontal sort of gravity. Benny was immediately reactive to my mood and began to whine incessantly. Like me, he wanted nothing more than to go home.

By the time we arrived at The Boulder School, Benny was in full-blown meltdown mode and he flopped his tired body on the sidewalk. He had no interest in this or any school, though I suspected that had we left him in the kindergarten classroom we had just visited, he would have been happy all day. Leaving Benny with Adam and David, I walked in alone to meet Clark. He struck me right away as a somewhat eccentric and personable man who seemed to have some nervous energy. I felt an immediate comfort with him and was able to get straight to the point. I no longer had patience for data that was not vitally important to my decision. I needed to know if Benny could function there and where he would go if he could not. I explained why Benny was not with me, that he was outside and upset. With a pounding in my head and little time, I feared my words would turn this man against my family. At any moment Benny could erupt into a full-fledged tantrum, so I spoke quickly as if overseeing a ticking time bomb. Clark perked up like a man on a mission of the utmost importance. He grabbed his jacket and walked right out of the school and he knelt down beside Benny. I could hear the leaves crunching beneath his fancy tan pants. There was not a note of insincerity as Clark began a conversation with my son. With face still to the sidewalk, Benny answered and then within minutes picked himself up onto his knees and finally his feet. Benny then introduced Adam, who rested in his stroller. Clark stood up and in a gesture with great tenderness took both of my hands in his. He looked straight in my eyes and with an intimacy normally reserved for close friends promised me that he will make this work. Although Clark had read no reports on Benny and has had minimal contact with him, I trusted him with my heart and soul. Throughout my body I felt shivers of excitement that made my knees weak and my hands tremble. I felt as though I was falling in love. I no longer cared about proximity to a New York Times, or the ease with which I could buy a bagel. David and I went down the block and put a bid on a bungalow, a little house that over the next few months would reveal itself to be quite frail and run down. On that day, though, with the glistening leaves tucked in the gutters, and the voice of Clark still ringing in my ears, the house transformed itself into a glorious palace worth any price.

**

As has been noted elsewhere, the field of special education is rife with paradoxes (Connor & Ferri, 2007; Danforth & Rhodes, 1997; Gallagher, Heshusius, Iano, & Skrtic, 2004; Skrtic, 2001; Ware, 2004). The intent of the Individuals with Disabilities Education Improvement Act (2004) is for professionals to work closely with parents, developing partnerships in which consensus is built. Like all relationships, sometimes those between parents and professionals can become strained, and eventually not work out as intended. Bearing this I mind, it is worth commenting upon (1) some of the assumptions within the law, (2) mechanisms to operationalize the law, and (3) the professionals that facilitate the operationalization of the law.

First, few people would challenge the idea that the law is well intentioned in its protection of children with disabilities, including its assurances of a Free and Appropriate Public Education (FAPE). As Diane points out, the word "appropriate" actually opens the door for justifying any kind of placements. Like beauty, appropriateness is in the eye of the beholder; only in this case, the beholders are professionals who are encultured within deficit-based conceptualizations of disability. They actually become professionalized through learning such discourses, and are rarely able to see beyond them.

Second, between the idea of the law and its desired impact, lie mechanisms to broach theory and practice. The concept of FAPE has become inextricably linked with placement of students in the Least Restrictive Environment (LRE). This particular mechanism has reified a stepladder type mentality in which students can be placed on any point of a continuum of service placements. The concept of LRE serves as a way to contain students unless they can operate at certain normed academic, social, and emotional levels. Rarely can a student "skip" a step in moving to a less restrictive environment. This continuum is frequently invoked as a reason to why not to more fully include students with disabilities. It can make a parental decision appear "too fast," or "too soon," as a student has not proven him or herself sufficiently capable in the currently assigned step.

The professionals employed to work within a system rarely question it because not only is it their reality, it is also their job security, source of income, and their sense of identity as a professional. In brief, they are invested in maintaining the system in which they are the power brokers. It has always struck me as interesting that the professionals who work within special education systems, and who have a disabled child of their own, invariably have their child placed in a private school at public expense. On one hand, we must recognize that parents want the best for their children, and a private education with all of the benefits (smaller class size, more individualized schooling, closer ties between administration and families, etc.). On the other hand, as most of these educational professionals are white and middle class, we see how cultural capital operates, allowing a form of institutional racism to operate, leaving "other people's children" (Delpit, 1995) behind without choices within the public system.

I sometimes state, when teaching about Individualized Education Programs (IEPs), that it can be argued they are one of the best ideas, yet one of the most poorly implemented. I bring this up here, because it reinforces the point being made above, i.e. between the original intent of the law and its daily implementation within the lives of families of children with disabilities, a lot becomes lost along the way. The systems and structures that have evolved are overly bureaucratic, restricting the thoughts of those who work within them, reducing professionals to executors of rules and regulations who then work with parents that feel immobilized and without real choices, despite promises made within the law. As Diane mentions, "I sensed that inclusion should be simple, that if it could work, Benny's day should be very similar to that of his peers." Benny himself had indicated to Diane his desire to be within a general education class. He could see the difference between the art-filled room and his bare-walled smaller class, tucked away. This vignette captures a tenet of

DSE as it "recognizes and privileges the knowledge derived from the lived experience of people with disabilities" (Connor et al., 2008, p. 448). I am left wondering, why children are seldom consulted as to where they'd prefer to be. I know when I informally interviewed high school students receiving special educations services, usually four out of five told me they would prefer to be in general education classes (often with the proviso of having a "go to" special educator for help when they needed).

The "appropriate" term within FAPE is problematic for several other reasons. One of them is the tacit assumption that disabled students must approximate "normalcy" before being allowed into general education classrooms. This notion seems logical to many professionals who are currently unable to conceptualize teaching outside the mantra of standardization. I have, as an aside, sometimes heard visitors in some inclusive classrooms say things like, "It was great. You couldn't tell who the disabled students were." Again, while well intended, the point has been missed. Students with disabilities should consciously not be absorbed into homogenized normalcy; it is fine, actually desirable, for differences to be seen in appearance, ability, and behavior. Another problematic reason of FAPE is, because of its subjective nature, it inadvertently helps uphold institutional racism in terms of placements offered to students of color with disabilities. In their landmark publication, Racial Inequality in Special Education (2002), Losen and Orfield document how working class and poor African-American boys in particular receive different labels than their white counterparts with the same learning profiles. For example, Black boys are up to five times as likely to be given the label of Emotional Disturbance (ED) and Mental Retardation (MR, now termed intellectual disability, or ID) than their white peers. These labels in and of themselves are synonymous with automatic placements in more restrictive environments (Parrish, 2002). However, even if students are given the same label—such as learning disability (LD), ED, or ID—research has revealed more restrictive environments are given to students of color (Fierros & Conroy, 2002). Such disturbing knowledge has led some DSE scholars to seek different ways of calling attention to, and responding to, issues of disability and race simultaneously (Annamma, Connor, & Ferri, 2013), as both special and general education have failed to do this.

In regard to disparities in race and class, the special education "system" within education, can wear parents down—particularly those who disagree with decisions made by professionals around labeling and placement. We can easily see how parents who are working class or poor, immigrant, and/or speak another language, usually do not have the knowledge or confidence to dis-agree with a group of middle-class professionals who have already made their decision about the label, placement, and services of their child. In addition, parental experiences may range anywhere from recalling having their own "bad" experiences in the system (including not graduating), to one of unques-tioning reverence for educators found in may non western countries. On the other had, while never assured, there is more likelihood to challenge the edu-cation system if one is middle class and white (Gillborn, Rollock, Vincent, & Ball, 2016). This is not meant to detract from the reality of emotional inten-sity and feelings of despair experienced by middle-class white parents and their children with disabilities, but rather to illustrate that having a certain amount of resources—provides an option not available to most families.

In my experience, many middle-class families are willing to move city or state to find the best school "fit" (or the most appropriate placement, in their eyes) for their child with a disability. Over the years I have come across numer-ous families who physically uprooted their lives to make sure that their child received what he or she needed, whether it was in a specialized school in the suburb of Philadelphia or a full inclusive public school in the city of Syracuse. It is widely known that many families moved to the state of Vermont because it historically had the best national reputation for inclusive education (Roach & Caruso, 1997). Diane writes of Benny, "I found it particularly heartbreaking to think of sending him to a school other than the one that his brother would eventually attend. I knew that when the time came I could not look into the eyes of either of my boys and tell them that one of them was so different, so disabled, that he could not be educated in the same building as his more able brother." Many other families deal with exactly the same issues. Diane's story may be new for some readers of this book, but it is not uncommon. It does, however, illustrate the depths to which a family must go sometimes, to find a place of basic safety and comfort for their child. The family's drive is emotion-ally charged, fueled by both love and desperation, with an awareness that they are giving up so much for what is, in essence, a gamble they are willing to take. Families of non-disabled children are not placed in these situations.

In contemplating some of the connections within this chapter to DSE, again, Diane's family "supports the education of students labeled with disabili-ties in non-segregated settings from a civil rights stance" (Connor et al., 2008, p. 448) as part of a larger agenda to "promote social justice, equitable and inclu-sive educational opportunities, and full and meaningful access to all aspects of society for people labeled with disability/disabled people" (p. 448). The theme of access is important and, as we have seen, mediated in part via a guaranteed Free and Appropriate Public Education in the Least Restrictive Environment. In the spirit of critique based on personal experience, Diane also began to raise questions about some of the detrimental impact of special education. On the surface, special education is often seen as rooted in benevolence—something that is beneficial, and socially just. For many children, it does manifest itself in these ways. For many other children, it does not measure up to the equality of opportunity assumed under a democracy and guaranteed within federal laws (Skrtic & McCall, 2010). For example, in comparison to their nondisabled peers, students in the special education system are likely to: have higher drop-out rates (Thurlow, Sinclair, & Johnson, 2002), and conversely, lower graduation rates (Advocates for Children, 2005); take a longer time completing school (U.S. Department of Education, 2005); have less chance of entering college and a greater probability of leaving prematurely (Gregg, 2007); experience greater levels of unemployment or underemployment (Moxley & Finch, 2003); and have higher rates of incarceration (Children's Defense Fund, 2007). These are in addition to continued forms of segregation according to race and disability, mentioned earlier (Losen & Orfield, 2002).

To critique special education's knowledge base, and the practices that are inspired by it—including its resistance to inclusive education—provokes outrage and ire from traditionalists in the field (Anastasiou & Kauffman, 2011, 2012, 2013; Kauffman, 1999; Kauffman & Hallahan, 2005; Kauffman & Sasso, 2006a, 2006b). The unanticipated consequences listed above are either ignored, under-acknowledged, swept under the carpet, or minimized as things needing to be addressed while moving forward with the same agenda (Brantlinger, 1997). And yet, the systems and structures that Benny was placed into, the same ones that did him a disservice, are those that uphold special education as we have come to know it—a series of possible placements wherein services are then delivered. However, the emphasis on placement always seems to supersede the emphasis on service.

Of note is that the systems in place rarely change to a significant degree. Take, for example, New York City's response to New York State Department's pressure to provide more inclusive services to students with disabilities. After hiring Tom Hehir as a consultant, one of the country's top special education experts, and his team of researchers to ascertain the lay of the land and then provide suggestions (Hehir, Figueroa, Gamm, Katzman, Gruner, Karger, & Hernandez, 2005). NYC's Department of Education created collaborative teaching classes that could have 40% of children with IEPs. This then became known as "The 60–40 formula" and encouraged principals to rigidly program classes in this manner. This method allowed entire self-contained classrooms to be folded into a general education class. In other words, it kept the special education structures, but now within general education. This decision was seemingly premised upon existing funding formulas and budgeting needs. However, this is an example of a technical response to what is essentially a social and cultural challenge. Classes should reflect the natural proportions of disabled and non-disabled people in society—somewhere between 15–20 percent, depending on who is counting. New York City's formula has resulted in classrooms that have sometimes combined the remaining 60 percent to be comprised of English Language Learners (ELLs) and Long Term Absentees (LTAs), in essence, creating larger classes with specialized needs. I was once assailed by a seasoned, angry teacher from a school I was advising who kept saying, "This inclusion thing that you talk about isn't working." He was right about his context because what was being done under the name of inclusion actually was not.

Likewise, in Diane's story, she notes the limited authentic option of inclusive education, reduced to three or four choices in the suburbs of one of the world's greatest cities. The good news is that she found one of these schools, thereby changing the narrative of what could have came to pass. I cannot help but think in terms of Charles Dickens' A Christmas Carol (1843), in which the main character Scrooge simultaneously sees himself in the past, present, and future. In engaging with Diane's tale, there is a version of Benny past, present, and future. The "past" Benny is a ghost of who he would have become had Diane's family not moved. In some ways, he exists in an alternative universe, from which the family escaped. The "present Benny in the now, very much alive and enjoying his life with his sibling and peers. Finally, the "future" Benny is what he will become, borne from his accumulated history and current experiences, a symbol of hope.

That is appropriate.

References

Advocates for Children (2005). *Leaving school empty handed: A report of graduation and drop our rates for students who receive special education services in New York City.* Retrieved November 11, 2011 from *www.advocatesforchildren.org/pubs/2005/spedgradrates.pdf*

Anastasiou, D., & Kauffman, J. K. (2011). A social constructionist approach to disability: Implications for special education. *Exceptional Children, 77*(5), 367–384.

Anastasiou, D., & Kauffman, J. M. (2012). Disability as cultural difference: Implications for special education. *Remedial and Special Education, 32*(5). Retrieved on September 15 from: rse.sagepub.com/content/early/2010/09/21/0741932510383163.full.pdf

Anastasiou, D., & Kauffman, J. M. (2013). The social model of disability: Dichotomy between impairment and disability. *Journal of Medicine and Philosophy, 38*(4), 441–459.

Annamma, S. A., Connor, D. J., Ferri, B. A. (2013). Dis/ability critical race studies (DisCrit): Theorizing at the intersections of race and disability. *Journal of Race, Ethnicity, & Education, 16*(1), 1–31.

Children's Defense Fund (2007). *America's cradle to prison pipeline.* Washington, DC: Author.

Connor, D.J, & Ferri, B. A. (2007). The conflict within: Resistance to inclusion and other paradoxes within special education. *Disability & Society, 22*(1), 63–77.

Connor, D. J., Gabel, S. L., Gallagher, D. & Morton, M. (2008). Disability studies and inclusive education--Implication for theory, research, and practice: Guest editor's introduction. *International Journal of Inclusive Education, 12*(5–6), 441–457.

Danforth, S., & Rhodes, W. C. (1997). Deconstructing disability: A Philosophy for inclusion. *Remedial and Special Education, 18*(6), 357–366.

Delpit, L. (1995a). *Other people's children: Cultural conflict in the classroom.* New York: New Press.

Gallagher, D.J., Heshusius, L., Iano, P., & Skrtic, T. M. (2003). *Challenging Orthodoxy in Special Education.* Denver, CO: Love Publishing.

Gillborn, D., Rollock, N., Vincent, C., & Ball, S. J. (2016). In D. Connor, B. Ferri, & S. Annamma (Eds.) *DisCrit: Disability studies and critical race theory in education* (pp. 35–54). New York: Teachers College Press.

Gregg, N. (2007). Underserved and unprepared: Postsecondary learning dis/abilities. *Learning Dis/abilities Research & Practice, 22*(4), 219–228.

Fierros, E. G., & Conroy, J. W. (2002). Double jeopardy. An exploration of restrictiveness and race in special education. In D. J. Losen & G. Orfield (Eds.), *Racial inequity in special education* (pp. 39–70). Cambridge, MA: Harvard Education Press.

Individuals with Disabilities Education Improvement Act (2004), U.S.C. 1400 et seq.

Kauffman, J. M., & Hallahan, D. P. (1995). *The illusion of full inclusion.* Austin, Texas: Pro-Ed.

Kauffman, J. M., & Sasso, G. (2006a). Toward ending cultural and cognitive relativism in special education. *Exceptionality, 14*(2), 65–90.

Kauffman, J. M., & Sasso, G. (2006b). Rejoinder: Certainty, doubt, and the reduction of uncertainty. *Exceptionality, 14*(2), 109–120.

Losen, D. J., & Orfield, G. (Eds.). (2002). *Racial inequality in special education.* Cambridge, MA: Harvard Education Press.

Moxley, D., and Finch, J. (2003). (Eds.). *Sourcebook of Rehabilitation and Mental Health Practice.* New York City: Plenum.

Parrish, T. (2002). Racial disparities in the identification, funding, and provision of special education. In D. J. Losen & G. Orfield (Eds.), *Racial inequality in special education* (pp. 15–37). Cambridge, MA: Harvard Education Press.

Roach, V. & Caruso, M. G. (1997). Policy and practice: Observations and recommendations to promote inclusive practices. *Education and Treatment of Children, 20*(1), 105–121.

Skrtic, T., & McCall, Z. (2010). Ideology, institutions, and equity: Comments on Christine Sleeter's 'Why is there learning disabilities?' *Disability Studies Quarterly*, 30(2). http://dsq-sds.org/article/view/1230/1277

Thurlow, M. L., Sinclair, M. F., & Johnson, D. R. (2002). Students with dis/abilities who drop out of school—Implications for policy and practice. *Issue Brief*, 1(2). Minneapolis, MN: University of Minnesota, Institute on Community Integration, National Center on Secondary Education and Transition.

U.S. Department of Education (2005). *Comparative indicators of education in the United States and other G8 Countries: 2004*. National Center for Education Statistics 2005–021. Retrieved November 25, 2011 from http://nces.ed.gov/pubs2007/2007006.pdf

Ware, L. (Ed.). (2004). *Ideology and the politics of (in)exclusion*. New York: Peter Lang.

· 4 ·

FIRST IMPRESSIONS:
INSTANTANEOUS BEHAVIOR SHAPING

February 2008

On the day of our move, I watched carton after carton carried out of an apartment I loved, and saw Benny spinning in circles on the carpet, dancing beneath the overhead light for hours, mesmerized by the shadows he was able to create on the carpet. I began to fear that all the experts were right, that this move would be in vain, and began to weep. I cried for the life I was leaving behind in a city I adored, all the while painfully conscious of a tiny bubble of hope, deep within, that continued to fight tenaciously for survival. It was this fragile evanescent orb that made me feel simultaneously both hopeless and hopeful. I felt for Adam, who had a best friend living just a few blocks away. I worried for our future should the move have proven to be a waste of time and resources.

Though initiated and orchestrated by me, I suddenly saw the move as a tremendous gamble, a last ditch attempt to save my soul by turning over *every possible stone* before agreeing to educate Benny in a segregated classroom. In exchange for my own redemption, through proof of my unending belief in my son, I now felt that I was giving up too much of what gave my life stability. I was holding out for something that sounded theoretically possible, ideal in some erudite educational circle, but something that in reality I had been told

again and again was likely to fail. Every developmental pediatrician cautioned me against the move, suggesting that inclusion was the right idea for some, but not for Benny, a child with so many delays and such little academic promise. Although conflicted about his official label, almost all professionals agreed that his academic and social future was bleak. The few folks who suggested otherwise were not qualified to confer a diagnosis. I recalled the evaluations I ripped to bits because of the dire predictions they contained, only to pay thousands of dollars out of pocket to have new ones done. I then choose only the ones that held some hope, but now it seemed irresponsible at best, irrational at worst. At no point did I have a choice. I was driven by forces outside of my control.

While keeping one eye on Benny falling to pieces, and one eye on the jewel of a school in that suburban community, I was able to apply for a mortgage, sell an apartment I adored, and close on a house I would never have chosen to live in had it not been for the particular set of circumstances. On the day of our actual move, reality set in and I felt the earth give way beneath my feet, leaving me without a solid foundation on which to step. This created within me a deep and profound sadness, a terror that made my entire body tremble. I must have been quite a sight, sobbing on the railroad platform, taking boys to our new home, while David drove with the movers. New Yorkers came to me offering me support and comfort, as I stood with tears streaking my cheeks and my two small boys wide eyed beside me

The first few minutes in my new house confirmed the claustrophobia I had from the start. The entire house seemed carved out of a shoebox, rooms spread down a long hallway, alternating sides with little style. There was a dank smell as well, as if the house had not been taken care of properly for a while. Normally we would have cleaned for weeks before moving our family in, but there was an urgency to get Benny back into school.

It was only a few hours into our residence in this house, when I saw the light in Benny's eyes begin to shine again. As I scrubbed and scoured the floors in between the boxes had we piled just a few hours before, I saw a creamy pink color filling in his cheeks. I sensed a direction in his step. I saw my child standing with a confidence that I had thought was lost forever. Sure that it was a mirage, I kept my thoughts to myself. After dinner we decided to go for a short walk to a supermarket to get some milk. As we left the house, on this evening in early February when the sky had already been dark for many hours, Benny turned to walk in the direction of the school. We took his hand and led him the other way towards the main street and the supermarket. He pulled back, and with his few words and little conversational ability told us that he wanted to go to school "now." David and I looked at each other with questions in our eyes. I explained that it was too early for school, unsure how he could have changed so quickly into a child who wanted to go to school after all of these months of pure agony. We were shocked to realize how much he understood about this move and his new school, when all his evaluations suggested limited intellectual ability and receptive and expressive language processing in the decimal percentiles. His demeanor suggested an even deeper appreciation of the situation than we were able to have at the time. While we anticipated difficulty getting him to try a new school, his behavior that evening told us we would need little prodding. We walked to the store and then back home. Benny went to bed early, and we all slept easily and deeply for the first time in months.

Morning came complete with the largest sky I had seen in a long while and with sunlight that seeped into our room with a determined focus. Benny, who had been until this day unable to dress himself, stood beside our bed completely clothed for the day. He announced with just a few short words, that he was ready for school. We ate a quick breakfast and then David, Adam and I walked beside Benny who needed no encouragement to make his way down the block to his new school. I recalled the days I spent prying him off the sidewalk and couldn't quite believe his optimism today. I had warned Clark that Benny might need some prodding or time to feel safe again walking into a school. He suggested we come a little after the day began for the other students and he would be waiting with the team to welcome Benny and to do whatever they needed to do in order to make him comfortable. Benny walked with the pride of a highly successful student, not at all like a child who had failed within two special education placements. Benny opened the door to his new school and walked in with a skip in his step I had not seen for quite some time.

We heard the voice of the administrative assistant, who saw us through the security camera. "The Bermans are here," she announced over the loudspeaker with a lilt and lightness in her otherwise raspy and authoritative voice. Suddenly, out of nowhere, like actors making their first appearance on a Broadway stage, we saw: Clark the Principal, Cara the Occupational Therapist, Marina the Special Educator, and Donna the Kindergarten Teacher. Together they danced down the hallway, like they were making their entrance onto a Broadway stage. They swept Benny into their outstretched arms and whisked him into his classroom. Cara and Marina spoke at the same time interrupting each other's words with excitement, as good friends might, trying to find out from me what Benny enjoyed, and what made him laugh. There was a celebratory air in the school, as if this was a day in which to rejoice. Just a few weeks earlier, when we left his second elementary school of the year, the assistant principal had said to me on the last day, "I am so glad for all of us that this is finally over." How is it possible that these two worlds exist so near to each other? How is it fair that some students must stay in that kind of hostile environment while others can leave and enter as close to paradise as school can get? This is why I write. I cannot turn my back on the world we left. A part of us still lives there. Not a day goes by when I do not think of the contrast and wonder where we would have been had we stayed, and what kind of teenager Benny would be now after growing up in that environment.

Instead we are here transported to heaven and all the talk is about how to make him comfortable, on this day that could be overwhelming to any small child. I was so used to being asked about his deficits and then being told about how many milestones we must pass before we could breathe a sigh of relief, or receiving a list of ways he must change in order to succeed. This conversation was completely different. It seemed as though finally he had done enough, he was good enough the way he was now—to relax, to enjoy and to laugh. The emphasis on his comfort washed my anxieties away. The sight of Benny amongst a happy group of typical children at a desk with his very own name in brightly tinted bubble letters lifted the tension out of my body and I felt like singing. He fit right in with these beautiful children who were eagerly showing him around this most colorful classroom. In Benny I saw a deep calm and comfort rising up from within. He sat beside his new peers, as the same creamy pink I saw the previous night rose up and circulated upon his cheeks. Adam looked on with interest, absorbing his first moments in The Boulder School, though it would be several years before he would start kindergarten. He looked excited, proud, the way a younger brother might as an older brother began school for the first time. The stress of the last few months had taken its toll on him, too. He looked relieved, smiling the sort of smile that creates a glow around his tiny head. The strain of the past few months began to recede for him too, but I know it will never fade completely.

This became one very joyous day as David, Adam and I walked home and spent the next few hours cleaning and unpacking our boxes, trying to condense 1200 square feet into 800. The small, run down bungalow began to feel like home. Those first few moments at Boulder suggested to me that those in charge of his academic life would take good care of him. I still feared for him socially, wondering how the typical children would perceive and interact with him. It was only a few weeks into our stay in this new town that we had a chance encounter in the playground that turned around my entire approach. I had been working hard trying to elicit speech from Benny, often becoming quite frustrated. One morning a five-year-old showed me how to converse with my son.

It was a warm and sunny Saturday afternoon. We were in our local playground where the equipment bursts with color, as it twists and turns in fanciful ways. There are bridges made of ropes to cross, animal forms to ride, boards which bounce on springs designed to help practice balance, and bright tubes in which to appear and disappear. The playgrounds are nestled in parks and surrounded by trees.

I was used to the metallic slides planted in rectangular arrays between the buildings and stores of New York. In my city, these slices of refuge pulsated with people in every season. Older folks sat on benches, playing chess on the sidelines, while children created fantasy games that enlivened the grey, linear landscape. Though duller in color, I find myself yearning for the slides in the city.

Adam found friendship easily and he was running around with a few small boys. Often Benny sat alone, sometimes under the slides, studying the metal bolts that hold the equipment together. One morning, however, a classmate from his new school called to Benny. They ran together for a while, Benny laughing hard and smiling long. David and I delighted for a few moments in this until we heard the other child say to Benny, "Come on Benny. Let's sit down and chat for a bit."

Upon hearing those words, that invitation to talk, I froze inside and filled with a panic that came on quickly. My legs wobbled and my stomach churned. Benny was still not, to our knowledge, conversational. He had many words; he could answer some basic questions but I had never heard him engage in a spontaneous give-and-take conversation. I called to David and we stood nervous together within earshot of the boys. I was delighted to hear them laughing. Benny was telling his new friend how his father broke a bowl in the sink the week before and how several years ago his Daddy spilled tomato sauce on the CD player. The boy was laughing so hard he could barely catch his breath. Benny grinned with a mischievous twinkle. David and I stood huddled together behind a tree, eavesdropping, mouths hanging open in surprise. I was absolutely floored.

It was frightening to realize that I had no idea how well Benny could converse when in a natural setting. I realized that it had been a long time since I spoke to him expecting a full and spontaneous response. I quickly ran through the past few days' conversations with Benny. I had initiated them, not in full voice, and not freely. The questions I asked of him were not steeped in curiosity, did not reach out with true yearning for his response, but rather were rhetorical, simple questions designed to open a dialogue, but not to truly engage. They were mechanical exercises instead of invitations to relate. During the years when Benny was doused in years of therapy, I unconsciously imitated the interactions I heard between Benny and his therapists. I had learned to speak to him in the same tone, asking questions that were staged and rarely spontaneous. I had lost hope in his abilities, and this loss of hope colored every interaction I had with him. Benny seemed exquisitely attuned to this, and had no interest in more talk that went nowhere. His therapy was necessary, but this therapy was not enough. It enabled him to learn skills and vocabulary, but Benny desperately needed the music of the real world in order to involve himself in meaningful expression. This one small boy who invited Benny to chat made me see what was possible. From that moment on, my own interactions with him grew and grew. Not long after, my conversations with Benny became sparkled with nuance and humor.

***

The beginning of this chapter remains deeply connected to the theme of parents of children with disabilities following their own instincts. The drive of such parents, the constant fight against many odds and questioning bleak predictions by experts, is a phenomenon that merits further attention because it speaks to a form of personal faith (that is not necessarily aligned with religion). Diane never gave up, being "painfully conscious of a tiny bubble of hope, deep within, that continued to fight tenaciously for survival." Despite fear and misgivings, she recognized "… the move as a tremendous gamble, a last ditch attempt to save my soul by turning over every possible stone before agreeing to educate Benny in a segregated classroom." In sum, Diane could not live with herself unless she's tried everything she knew. This involved making significant sacrifices. In many ways, it can be argued that the quality of her family's life was "downsized" in terms of living space and neighborhood, along with cultural and leisure opportunities—although of course these things are all relative. (Of course in retrospect the family's choices ultimately yielded benefits that exceeded all expectations). It did seem, however, that everything felt "on the line," and I can only imagine the pressures of feeling hope and excitement on one hand, and the fear of feeling "I know this is as far as we can go" on the other.

I must confess at first being uncomfortable with some of Diane's diction to describe Boulder. Word choices such as "heaven" and "paradise" seemed extreme, especially to anyone who knows the hard, practical work that goes behind the scenes in administrating schools and teaching classes. However, upon reflection, I can imagine her feeling, after such a long, arduous, and unsure journey, that the situation in which she found herself provided a level of exhalation akin to an awakening of religious experience. As she reminisced, "Just a few weeks ago, we left his second elementary school of the year and the AP said to me on the last day- 'I am so glad for all of us that this is finally over.'" It is not a stretch to see Boulder as a contrast to the hellish experience of previous placements, with bullying teachers, and unsympathetic administrators. Ultimately, as a mother, Diane wants for Benny what other children have. She and her husband are pleasantly surprised at the simple steps taken by the school to welcome Benny and all of his family members. Diane can immediately see how much the faculty care, collaborate, and have a genuine interest in what makes Benny tick.

A change of school and a change of house also changed the script. Reminiscent of a Shakespearian plot, Diane and David "accidentally" overheard social arrangements being made by their son and his friend that prompted them to hide behind a tree and eavesdrop. What comes to mind immediately is that this opportunity would not have occurred, because it could not have occurred, in Benny's previous school where all children considered to be autistic were placed together. Here, the everyday interaction of children—that many take for granted—talking together naturally and spontaneously, is highly appreciated and valued. Perhaps most importantly is Diane's realization that her own interactions with her son had remained largely in the discourse utilized by service professionals. She shared, "I had initiated the conversations, not in full voice, not freely. The questions I asked of him were not steeped in curiosity, did not reach out with true yearning for his response, but rather were often rhetorical, simple questions designed to open a dialogue but not to truly engage. They were mechanical exercises instead of invitations to relate." In other words, Diane's interaction with her own son, despite a level of consciousness on her part, was still predominantly lodged within an "intervention" mentality that structured conversations as directions, didactic in nature, more akin to being a clinical professional than a family member. In many ways, this realization illustrates a medicalized versus socio-cultural understanding of the purpose of language and its power to create and maintain authentic connections, rather than be "more talk that went nowhere." Interestingly, Samuel's mother Betsy Habib, in the documentary Including Samuel (Habib, 2007) came to the same realization. She recognizes that if she did and said all of the things the experts were telling her to always do in her relation with her son, she would actually be more of a therapist than a mother. However, she wanted to take the pleasure of being Samuel's mother and spending time with her child, instead of perpetually working on "improving" or "fixing" him.

Another compelling aspect of this chapter is the ability of children to be with each other and develop their own communities without being overly supervised. Diane's epiphany happened because of a small boy's reaching out to Benny with the expectations that they would communicate about a shared experience, having clumsy fathers (or, to give David the benefit of the doubt, fathers who had clumsy moments). This invoked laughter on both of their parts, further encouraging a rapport that Diane and David did not think possible. From this experience, Diane changed her disposition toward conversing with her own son. She had to "unlearn" the limited ways she had seen professional specialists work with her child, in order to cease having him answer as expected, and to connect with him in ways he could identify and respond to, based upon his personality and interests.

The immediate absorption of professional discourse, I have noticed, occurs with teachers too. For years I taught "incoming" graduate students, and although my disposition was rooted in DSE, I observed that their enculturation in special education knowledge gained from other classes happened very quickly. I sometimes overheard one new teacher instructing another in joint-the-dots approach to writing an IEP and managing a "caseload" of children. In professional conversations between my college and the NYC Department of Education, the latter emphasizes the need for new teachers to hit the ground running in terms of generating IEPs. The situation calls to mind the old adage, "a little knowledge is a dangerous thing," because invariably, these approaches to an IEP are very much based in student deficits and are invariably mechanistic, as if children are being trained to perform discrete tasks devoid of context and meaning, measured in simplistic, unidimensional terms. Such occurrences evoke the work of scholars like Lous Heshuisus, who had a DSE disposition "before DSE had a name" (Taylor, 2006, p. xiii). As far back as the 1980s, Heshusius called for the field to question its positivist scientific frameworks of disability because of the limitations she saw in subjectivizing and dehumanizing people with disabilities within school and society. In her thoughtful and innovative article, *The Newtonian Mechanistic Paradigm, Special Education, and the Contours of Alternatives: An Overview* (1989), she suggested the field find different ways of thinking about human difference. This is what we have endeavored to do in DSE, otherwise the only discourse pre-service and in-service educators have access to is largely composed of pseudo-science (Gallagher, 1998) within a technocracy (Skrtic, 1991). Parents, in contrast and unsurprisingly, tend to see the individual child, particularly the social and cultural dynamics of the context that contribute to the disablement of their child. Historically, parents have felt estranged from the professional discourse in special education that they find alienating (Kalyanpur, Harry, & Skrtic, 2000; Valle, 2009). Recently, to combat the above critiques of the system, the government of New Zealand instituted much more nuanced IEPs that are narrative based, designed to capture the child, the context, and the child's growth within that context, with these efforts being developed in conjunction with DSE researchers (Millar & Morton, 2007; Morton, 2014).

In returning to the initial theme of this response—parents of disabled children who follow their own instincts to engage with, and often fight limitations within the education system—it is worth noting how dear this topic is to several researchers in DSE. The work of Van Hove and colleagues recognize what they call "parents on the margins" (Van Hove, DeSchauwer, Mortier, Bosteels, Desnerk, & Van Loon, 2009, p. 187). In analyzing metaphors used by parents on the margins to describe themselves, the authors discuss "the traveler," "the warrior," "the builder of bridges," "the discoverer," "the strategist/diplomat," "the tight-rope walker" "the trainer/teacher," and "the manager," as example of how parents constantly negotiate their lives in relation to their children and their children's needs, concluding that "We can learn a lot about parenting in general" (p. 187) from such advocates and strategists. The metaphors used by these parents are in sharp contrast to those described by Ferguson (2001) as examples of parents that professionals came to know through their induction into the field, such as "the neurotic parent," "the dysfunctional parent," "the suffering parent," "the powerless parent," (pp. 379–384) and so on. Similar characterizations of parents by professionals have been found in the work of Valle although, interestingly, the overwhelming majority of these negative descriptions appear to refer to mothers, with fathers largely perceived as more rational figures who are far less emotional (Valle, 2009). Ferguson's (2001) observations that school clinicians sometimes conceptualize, and often refer to, "a family with a disability" (in Van Hove et al., p. 187) further reveals ways in which family members are perceived by professionals and subsequently subjected to their expertise.

Hostile treatment can occur in different ways, including the refusal to listen to a parent's point of view, unwillingness to try a certain educational setting for a child, and the initiation of more restrictive environments, which can be intimidating enough in and of themselves. Without wanting to blame or scapegoat teachers, as there is already enough of that in the popular press, I would still like to address the topic that hostile environments within some schools exist for many students. Historically, before the passage of Public Law 94–142 in 1975, all children and youth with disabilities were not welcome in schools. Many are still not welcome in inclusive classrooms today, as can be seen from Benny's early years. For students who struggle to learn in traditional ways, including those identified as LD, ADD, ADHD, ED, school environments are often unhappy places, especially if access to the curriculum is not provided. On related note, not only the academic, but social realms, can prove to be the primary reason why some students do not succeed in schools. For example, when an atmosphere of intolerance and bigotry toward Lesbian Gay Bisexual Transgender and Queer/Questioning (LGBTQ) students exists, it has been shown that those who drop out experience a greater degree of mental health, including a stronger self-concept (Bidell, 2015). Of course, we must remind ourselves that students with disabilities and LGBTQ students are not single issues, as many students are both (McRuer, 2006), along with having other (sometimes marginalized) markers of identity. Although the ethic of caring in schools has received some attention, particularly through the consistent work of Noddings over the years (1988, 2002, 2013), I believe it would be worthwhile to look at it in depth specifically in relation to inclusive education primarily conceived of as an ethical project (Allan, 2005). After all, schools not only teach—both formally and informally—society's ethics and values, they also reflect them. Like the conversation initiated by Benny's friend, until we, too, have one, we do not know what we are actually capable of doing, and the sky could be the limit.

References

Allan, J. (2005). Inclusion as an ethical project. In S. Tremaine (Ed.), *Foucault and the government of disability* (pp. 281–297). Ann Arbor, MI: University of Michigan Press.

Bidell, M. (2014). Is there an emotional cost of completing high school? Ecological factors and psychological distress among LGBT homeless youth. *Journal of Homosexuality, 61*(3), 336–381.

Ferguson, P. (2001). Mapping the family: Disability studies and the exploration of parental response to disability. In *Handbook of disability studies*, .in G. Albrecht, K.Seelman, and M. Bury (Eds.) (pp. 351–372). Thousand Oaks, CA: Sage Publications.

Gallagher, D. J. (1998). The scientific knowledge base of special education: Do we know what we think we know? *Exceptional Children, 64* (4), 493–502.

Habib, D. (Producer and Director). (2007). *Including Samuel*. [DVD]. Available from http://www.includingsamuel.com/home.aspx

Heshusius, L. (1989). The Newtonian mechanistic paradigm, special education, and the contours of alternatives: An overview. *Journal of Learning Disabilities, 22*(7), 402–415.

Kalyanpur, M., Harry, B., & Skrtic, T. (2000). Equity and advocacy expectations of culturally diverse families participation in special education. *International Journal of Disability, Development, and Education, 47*(2), 119–136.

McRuer, R. (2006). *Crip theory: Cultural signs of queerness and disability*. New York: New York University Press.

Millar, & Morton, M. (2007). Bridging two worlds: Special education and curriculum policy. *International Journal of Inclusive Education, 11*(2), 163–176.

Morton, M. (2014). Using DSE to "notice, recognize, and respond" to tools of exclusion and opportunities for inclusion in New Zealand schools. *Review of Disability Studies: An International Journal,* 8(3), retrieved from: http://www.rds.hawaii.edu/ojs/index.php/journal/article/view/89/307

Noddings, N. (1988). An ethic of caring and its implications for instructional arrangements. *American Journal of Education, 96*(2), 215–230.

Noddings, N. (2002). *Educating moral people: A caring alternative to character education*. New York: Teachers College Press.

Noddings, N. (2013). *Caring: A relational approach to ethics and moral education*. Berkeley, CA: University of California Press.

Skrtic, T. M. (1991). The special education paradox: Equity as a way to excellence. *Harvard Educational Review, 61*(2), 148–206.

Taylor, S. J. (2006). Before it had a name: Exploring the historical roots of disability studies in education. In S. Danforth and S. L. Gabel (Eds.), *Vital questions facing disability studies in education* (pp. xiii-xxiii). New York: Peter Lang.

Valle, J. W. (2009). *What mothers say about special education: From the 1960s to the present*. London: Palgrave McMillan.

Van Hove, G., De Schauwer, E., Mortier, K., Bosteels, S., Desnerck, G., & Van Loon, J. (2009). Working with mothers and fathers of children with disabilities: Perspectives on diversity in early childhood education. *European Early Childhood Education Research, 17*(2), 187–201.

· 5 ·

BEHAVIOR:
ADDRESSING IMPULSIVITY

Kindergarten proved tricky for Benny. While at first his issues seemed to evaporate with the move, it was not long before they resurfaced. Benny could not sit still for very long. At school he would jump up on the desks and then leap from one to the other. Other times he would take to the floor and crawl under the desks, sometimes resting his head beneath the desks. One day he toppled a fan, another day, a radio. He had numerous sensory issues that were addressed in occupational therapy but nothing seemed to curb his habit of licking the dust off the computer screens. Those were among the more unusual of his behaviors but even in-between these more outlandish acts, the day was filled with the more garden variety disruptions we see in children with mild and moderate disabilities.

The teachers would report some of these events to me but not in a threatening manner. In the same breath they would also tell me how he was progressing nicely with reading and writing. They found that with large chart paper he could better control the shape of his letters. Donna was excited to see that within a few days he was already progressing with his reading of sight words. Benny was spending most of recess under the playground equipment, but he was rarely alone. Other children, one boy named Mark in particular, would huddle there with him and gently try to coax him out. The teachers

would tell me daily that the other children liked him. I was delighted. I began to wonder what was at work in this place that enabled Benny to attract other children, when in his previous schools he remained so isolated?

While some districts designate one school to be the inclusion school and some schools designate one class to be the inclusion class, Boulder has a more equitable model. In this district, every school is an inclusive school and at Boulder School, any classroom could be an inclusion classroom. Clark likes to keep the number of children with a disability in any classroom to between two and four. Each classroom has a full time general education teacher and one full time teaching assistant (TA). These TA's are most often certified teachers looking for full time jobs. They are motivated and eager to work hard, taking their position very seriously. Their role is to assist in all areas of the classroom, but they have a responsibility to look after the children who come into the class with IEPs. There is also an inclusion specialist who dedicates two periods a day to the children with IEPs, working in both the "push in" and "pull out models," depending on the activities of the day and the needs of the children. The inclusion specialist also helps guide the teacher and the TA towards appropriate accommodations, modifications, and offers suggestions and ideas for differentiation.

During my sleep, night after night for several weeks, I would have the same bad dream, that upon pickup I would be told that Benny could not be supported in this setting. They would say with a smile that his behavior was too distracting to the other children. I had already learned to accept that the needs of the typical took precedence over the needs of the disabled, and I accepted that he might be rejected from this setting, should his behavior remain problematic. Once morning came and the bright suburban sun streamed through the window by our bed, I knew this would not materialize. Benny was always happy to go to school, and Clark, standing on the corner most mornings, greeted us with hugs and high fives. I trusted in the promise Clark made to us that very first day we met. I accepted his words at face value and interpreted them to reflect an unconditional guarantee. There was symmetry between each of us in this complex triad of connections. Clark, Benny, and I were bound in a circle of trust, an unquestioned refreshingly irrational confidence. Clark trusted in Benny's ability to adapt and learn, and in my ability to support his growth. I trusted in Clark's promise to support our family at all costs. Benny trusted us both enough to shed his fear of school immediately and to try his hand at challenging tasks many of which he knew would initially result in failure. The covenants that bound us in this endeavor were made with that firm handshake on the first day and a genuine desire to

believe in each other. In this day and age of educational accountability, this
alone is virtually miraculous. It was in this nexus of connection that we found
the fuel to persevere. It is not easy for a child to step into the world of the
typical when you come with massive delays. It is not easy for the parent or the
child. We must face our differences daily and in public. I wonder if it is fear of
this reality that causes so many parents to choose segregated settings that do
not place high demands on their children.

Nevertheless, despite Clark's support, things were not going well for Benny
in the classroom. There was already an assistant teacher in the room, before
Benny joined the class, a lovely experienced woman who tried her hardest to
keep Benny in check, but her efforts were not enough. Benny routinely ran
from her and she seemed powerless to stop him. He had developed a habit in
his first and second kindergarten self-contained settings of running clear out of
the classroom. I imagine the habit began because he was truly trying to get away
from the classroom, which offered little in terms of joy to him. Even though he
was now in a school he loved, the habit had stuck, and when he wanted to avoid
some task, out he went, fast as can be on his strong little legs.

The assistant teacher in his current room was assigned loosely to all the
children with disabilities but began giving most of her attention to Benny.
It was not enough. The inclusion specialist, Marina, began spending extra
time in the classroom, using her free time to chase after Benny. Lunchtime
was especially problematic. Without the classroom structure, Benny was even
harder to contain. Several teachers began giving up their lunchtime to take
turns monitoring Benny.

One day, upon pick up, a young handsome man with a strong handshake
came up to greet me. He walked beside a beaming Benny and told me his name
was Tony, he was now the teaching assistant assigned to the class, and he would
take responsibility especially for Benny. They had an immediate connection.
Benny looked up to Tony with sincere respect and admiration. It wasn't until
years later, when the relationship between Clark and me had turned to friendship, that I learned what I had suspected: Clark had changed assistants to better
accommodate Benny. This was the first time I saw the climate change for a child
so dramatically. Benny, who could learn to read and write, had little control
over his behavior. Instead of waiting for his behavior to improve, the school did
what it could to find the best fit for him within the classroom.

Once again, Benny's behavior improved for a few days, and then he
became comfortable. One day I came to pick up and could see from Benny's
face that it had been a difficult day. Tony told me Benny had kicked him

during a reading session. I was mortified, but Tony was calm and told me it was because Benny was frustrated by the task and that he would find a way to approach it with him another day, in a new way, and that Benny would master the skill. I was perplexed. The emphasis was not on my son's act that might have led to suspension, but on finding another way to teach Benny without extreme frustration. This moment broadened the trust that Benny had for Tony and that deepened the bond that I felt for the school.

It was apparent that Benny needed a one-to-one aide for the following year. From previous experiences, I knew that districts are reluctant to give him this support, arguing that the placement of a less restrictive environment is not right, that the child needs a more restrictive setting. It is cheaper in the short term to transfer a child to a class with a smaller teacher-to-student ratio that to add another aide to a classroom. The request for more supports, and a 1:1 aide, in particular, required walking a very fine line. We had to make the case that this was indeed the right setting, but that Benny needed more support to be able to take advantage of the education that was within his reach. His teachers had to make sure they gave support indicating that he was growing academically, while at the same time, they had to provide evidence indicating that he needed more 1:1 support than the classroom could provide. Their generosity in providing this support, before it was mandated, enabled us to make the argument at the IEP meeting with great clarity. They proved for us and for the district that Benny could learn grade level material with 1:1 support. When it came time for his IEP meeting to prepare for 1st grade we were easily able to make that claim. I realize now that if they had not given Benny what they felt he needed, we would not have been able to fight for it as effectively at the meeting. The typical protocol followed by a school when trying to build a case for greater support, is to document off-task behavior. The typical response of the district is to move the child to a more restrictive environment, rather than being given a chance to succeed. Instead Boulder provided the support Benny needed, out of their own free time, and built for us the very best case they could for Benny.

His teachers proved for us all that with support, Benny could be safe and could function in a general education classroom. They demonstrated that Benny could learn grade level material. These teachers gave up their prep periods for several months for Benny, but in return they proved the point that is so hard and often impossible to argue effectively. Most importantly, they never made me feel guilty for this. In fact, Marina still says she is grateful to us, between missing lunch and the running she did to chase Benny, she lost eight pounds that spring!

Had they let him flounder and allowed his behavior spiral out of control, the district would have been within their rights to move him to a special setting, in a special school, dooming him once again to a life in exile of his typical peers. Meryl and Tony gave up their free time to support Benny. They reaped their reward the next year when the district gave them funds for a 1:1 aide and when they saw how quickly Benny was able to grow.

Often my graduate students ask me how it is possible to do all one should do for students within the limitation of a 24 hour day. I think of these months when two teachers gave up their preps every day to keep Benny safe and I tell them they must give 150%, and sometimes more. They look pale because they are already overworked and overtired. Yet it comes back to them. Today, as I write, I am getting texts from my boys' 3rd grade teacher who also went above and beyond. She just saw both of them (who are entering grades 6 and 8 shortly) in a camp show and had to tell me right away how amazing it was to see them sing and dance. We have become part of each other's lives in ways that transcend the typical relationships between teachers and families. When you care about your students and their families as you care about your own, time is no longer measured the same way. We give not according to our contracts but from our hearts and then it no longer feels like a job. My own teaching has changed by the Boulder example and while I work harder, I am happier by far than I ever was in this profession.

It was not long before we got another sign, as clear as the proverbial white dove flying above, that we had landed in the right place. Just a few weeks into our first spring, I was walking Benny to school when a small kindergarten classmate jumped out of a car beside us and grabbed his hand. She looked up at me and, with a twinkle in her eye, pulled him ahead. No sooner had she walked ahead did his backpack fall off his shoulder, and she scooped it up. "I can walk him in, Ms. Berman," she said, "I can help him with his bag too, I do it all the time."

I was dumbfounded, and not quite sure where to go. So I walked slowly behind them, the distance increasing between us ever so slightly with each step. Then a teacher stopped me and with her hand on my arm began to speak, slowly. She told me he was fine and that I should turn right around and walk home. I expressed my concern that this little tiny girl was carrying my son's backpack, and she laughed. "Yes, she looks after him like that, she unpacks it for him too in the classroom." I was stunned; it seemed unfair. The teacher sensed my discomfort and intuited why I felt that way. She continued to explain to me that it was fine and that they had a deal, an exchange, a friendship of sorts. In return for her help with his backpack, Benny pushed her on the swing throughout all of recess.

This was all I needed to hear to know unequivocally that we had made the right choice to move here and place Benny in a general education class. Benny had never had a friendship, spontaneously with another child, other than with his brother. Back in the city, one of the teacher's constant complaints was that he could not even unpack his own backpack. Here that problem was gone, erased, replaced with a friendship, with a natural exchange of support between five-year-olds, worked out without the help of adults. All I had to do was step away and let Benny walk down the block with this little girl. This was my first lesson in the power of the peer group, the intelligence that lies within cooperation. That moment provided a window into all the growth that was to come for Benny and his peers as they were allowed and encouraged to find ways to build each other's strength and learn to cooperate in a world that is complex for all of us. All I needed was to see this one exchange to know that momentous growth was in the future, waiting to develop as a tree grows from one tiny seed. The joy of that moment, watching Benny hand in hand with that girl continues to usher in waves of happiness, even today, many years and many milestones later.

All that said, it was about this time that the question of medicating Benny came up with the neurologist. David and I were set against it but seeing Benny thrive in some ways and fall apart in others led us to consider it. Clark told us we should not feel pressured, that they would work with the behavior medication or not. If we tried it and it did not help, Clark assured us that Benny was where he belonged and that he was personally committed to Benny's success. At the time, as much as I needed to hear these words, they went against so much of what I had learned to expect as a parent and as an educator. We never made promises we might not be able to keep. We were not supposed to sacrifice the safety and comfort of the typical to nurture those that were different. There was an unquestioned assumption that we could/should educate those with disabilities in the same classroom so long as the needs of the typical took precedence. In other words, if the needs of those with disabilities were small and quiet, it was fine. It was acceptable (although illegal) for schools to pressure (even threaten) parents into the use of psychotropic drugs.

Ultimately, toward the end of kindergarten, due in large degree to the insistence of his neurologist who felt we had put him in a situation with huge challenges without giving him the tools to handle the expectations, we tried giving Benny a low dose of a drug to address Attention Deficit Hyperactivity Disorder (ADHD). The immediacy of his response, both positive and negative, was startling. His demeanor changed. He was able to concentrate on reading and he began to draw voraciously. In the classroom, he could sit longer during circle time and did not run out other door. On the other hand, his limited speech seemed to retreat even further. He became quiet and less engaged. At home he lost his appetite, grew angry and sullen as the medication wore off, and slept restlessly. During the summer we took him off the medicine, and put him back on it at the beginning of the first grade. Benny learned to read and write. He was able to control his behavior better, but his language and social skills seemed to have plateaued.

I was unhappy to think that we were resorting to drugs, in part to sustain his placement in a general education classroom, and in part to achieve relative normalcy. Would we have resorted to drugs had he been in a class for the severely disabled? I began to question whether it was fair to place him in a setting so rigorous when his potential seemed so limited. Still, deep down I knew that no one really could effectively predict his potential. I knew the reality of his desires and his abilities would take years to become apparent. Placing him in a restrictive setting would become a self-fulfilling prophecy. Clark's repeated promises that he would support Benny with or without medication enabled me to uncouple the use of medication with the fact that we had placed him in an inclusion classroom. This uncoupling alleviated some of the pain associated with the use of a drug.

The use of medication became a constant focus of conversation between the staff of Boulder and our family. The teachers themselves began to question the use of medication, because of the flat affect it engendered in Benny. Over the next year or two, we experimented with smaller doses. However, the teachers preferred Benny's animated self, felt it easier to shape his lively albeit impulsive behavior than to try to draw out a child who was already quite remote. By the end of grade two, he was not taking the drug. Medication is often a topic that teachers are told is off limits for discussion. At Boulder the conversation was allowed to happen and, as a result, we were able to get an accurate portrait of our child on and off medication and, at their suggestion, we were able to try him without it. I know despite the illegality, many schools resort to threats in order to pressure parents into medicating their children. At Boulder, the exact opposite occurred. We were pressured to take him off his medication despite the fact that some of his impulsivity returned.

***

It has been said that the interrelated topics of behavior and classroom management are always in the top three areas of interest for in-service teachers throughout their careers. Without structure, there can be chaos, even anarchy. I have witnessed it when observing numerous classes. However, overly regulated classrooms can also be oppressive, with the regimented control masquerading as learning, creating soul-destroying environments for children and youth who come to hate school. This chapter allows us to reflect upon behaviors—what is expected, and what is not—and most importantly, how educators understand and respond to them.

Benny's behaviors, sometimes predictable, sometimes not, indicate that he makes great efforts to adapt, and then regresses. For many students identified as disabled, this can be a common pattern of two steps forward, and one step back. What becomes apparent in this particular story is the teachers' understanding of Benny in their accounts of him. They see Benny from a strength-based perspective, an idea at the core of DSE, and simultaneously are aware of and concerned about, behaviors that are not "normal" (a concept that is, of necessity, woven throughout this book). His teachers want to find ways to build on his strengths, while helping him unlearn behaviors that can be harmful to himself (e.g. licking dust) or others (e.g. kicking people in the legs).

Diane shares her thoughts around these issues openly, stating, "It is not easy for a child to step into the world of the typical when you come with massive delays. It is not easy for the parent or the child. We must face our differences daily and in public. I wonder if it is fear of this reality that causes so many parents to choose segregated settings that do not place high demands on their children." Here we see the additional challenges for parents of children, and of course the children themselves, who do not conform to normed expectations. Might it be easier for parents and their children with disabilities to keep them segregated? It seems for some that the answer may be yes. District 75 has a very politically savvy, vocal group of parents who do not wish to see it dissolved or reconfigured into more inclusive environments. I realize that these are very difficult issues, and highly individual decisions that must be made by families. That said, the lack of generally known effective alternatives to more restrictive environments is troubling. Also, perhaps, the ableism that permeates society on so many levels may have influenced some parents toward viewing segregation as primarily a form of protection, rather than containment. Many adults with disabilities, while deeply grateful for their parents' love and support, have shared that they felt over-protected when growing up (Fries, 1997; Grealy, 1995; Rodis, Garrod, & Boscardin, 2001) a phenomenon that can adversely impact self-advocacy and lead to general underachievement (Sanders, 2006). Others have shared their preference for a specialized school where they were supported in the development of a positive disability identity (Lehrer, 2015, personal communication). There is no singular response to this situation, and I am always interested in the preferences of people with disabilities. However, I do wonder about several things, including the potential of a school's receptivity or hostility toward including a student with a disability. Already, we have seen the difference that this can make in Benny's case. Another thing I am aware of, as alluded to in a previous chapter, are the choices available for some families, but not others, to have their child with a disability included into a receptive environment.

What emerges in this chapter are some of the structures, systems, and policies in place at Boulder that create and maintain a supportive inclusive environment, changeable in relation to the need of the students. Diane notes that this school has an "equitable model," meaning that it is flexible enough for every classroom to become an inclusive environment in terms of accommodating students with significant needs. The teachers and other staff members know that they are eligible to shift from a class that, broadly speaking, supports "typical" students to one in which they may come to work with students with specific needs. There is no negotiating between administrators and union members to not teach "inclusion classes," that sometimes occurs in NYC. Because of these observations, Boulder's structure is worth discussing as it is in contrast to more familiar models of supporting inclusive classes through co-teaching, such as those developed by Marilyn Friend and colleagues (Cook & Friend, 1995; Friend & Bursuck, 2000; Friend, Cook, Hurley-Chamberlain, & Shamberger, 2010). Friend's models are widely used, and consist of following configurations, depending upon the context and classroom ecology: one teach, one observe; one teach, one drift; station teaching; parallel teaching; alternative teaching, and; team teaching. These valuable models provide a much-needed framework through which to conceptualize and operationalize the possibilities of more than one educator working in a classroom providing support to all students. At the same time, they have arguably become reified into the only options available.

Boulder is an example of a school that has developed its own system that seems to work, by all accounts, quite well. As overseen by the principal, here's what they do:

(1) Each teacher is highly qualified, and dedicated to the profession. There is a level of stability in place, with long-term commitments to the school by teachers. It is also an attractive place to work due to the positive environment, high level of collegiality, and shared sense of purpose.

(2) Each classroom has an assistant teacher. The assistant teachers are actually certified teachers, and therefore serve in the capacity of additional teachers. The system can be seen as an apprenticeship model, allowing the principal to see if the assistant teachers are a good fit with his vision, the children, faculty, and families in the community. Nobody enters as a head teacher; everyone first works as an assistant, earning the right to become head teacher.

(3) The inclusion specialist is a constant resource in terms of consultation about the particularities (and perhaps peculiarities) of situations involving students with IEPs. This specialist, in collaborating with the teachers, can "push in" to classes, which is the ideal for inclusion. However, on occasion, she can be flexible enough to use a "pull out" model, short term, for a reason professionals involved believe to be valid, based on a child's needs.

(4) A 1:1 paraprofessional can be obtained if the circumstances merit. In Benny's case, they did. Tony was chosen with Benny in mind, and he came into the job knowing the learning and behavioral needs of his charge.

(5) The ratio of disabled to non-disabled people in a class broadly reflects that within the population. Having two to four children with disabilities is more manageable than higher numbers.

Let me now articulate a counter-point for each of the above elements that support inclusive education. In NYC:

(1) There is a large percentage of teachers who are not highly qualified, as they are in the process of obtaining certification as they learn to teach. Approximately twenty percent of all new teachers are sponsored through programs such as Teach for America (TFA) and NYCs Teaching Fellows (TFs) (Goodnough, 2002). Supplying the neediest schools with inexperienced teachers has been severely critiqued by nationally prominent educators (Darling-Hammond, 2008; Darling Hammond, Hotlzman, Gatlin, & Julian Vasquez, 2005; Meier, Kohn,

Darling-Hammond, Sizer, & Wood, 2004; Ravitch, 2000, 2014). TFA in particular funnels teachers who are often committed only for two years, who then go on to other professions having served in the capacity of a form of domestic peace corps (Foote, 2009). The local rival to TFA, TFs, fares better as they are of local origin, and more tend to stay in the profession for longer periods. However, the point remains that first serving a school within an apprentice-type model allows teachers to come to know the children and the culture, making them more ready for being the lead teacher. Otherwise, feelings of being overwhelmed experienced by first year teachers (Schilchte, Yssel, & Merbier, 2010), impact how effective they are in general, including the degree to which they support students in inclusive settings.

(2) There are no assistant teachers in the general education classrooms of NYC schools. However, there has been an increased number of collaborative team teaching configurations designed to support inclusive practices. In best-case scenarios, the senior teacher helps "show the ropes," and teaches some "tricks of the trade" to the rookie teacher. In worst-case scenarios, the teachers do not want to work together, or the experienced teacher treats the new teachers as a paraprofessional, rather than having equal status. The latter has very bad implications for inclusive education as teachers need to trust and rely upon one another, be problem-solvers, have shared responsibilities and therefore shared status.

(3) There are very few inclusion specialists per se in NYC schools. A small number exist, including those who work in the NEST programs, but they are for the most part absent in schools.

(4) Paraprofessionals who are dedicated to assisting one child do exist but, because of the expense, are rare. While acknowledging there has been rightful criticism about the overuse of 1:1 paraprofessionals in the inclusion of children with disabilities (Giangreco, Edelman, & Broer, 2001), it is also clear that this model is needed for some children and can work—until a child has transitioned into behaviors and skills that allow support to be scaled back, and/or have the supporter additionally work with all students in the room.

(5) Programming for a more accurate representation in classes of the number of disabled people in the population is such a simple idea that should be incorporated into educational systems. Simply put, having NYC's forty percent of students with disabilities as the "norm" for "an

inclusion class" is an unacceptable metric if inclusion is to be done meaningfully, responsibly, and effectively.

The five elements we have listed reveal how inclusive education can be done in the context of one school. With full respect for the teachers of NYC (and, according to literature in our field focused on elsewhere in the country), these professionals are rarely provided with adequate circumstances, support, and continuity for them to see noteworthy successes the value of inclusive education.

Another element that Diane refers to supporting the success of Benny is the circle of trust between herself, her child, and the principal. In some regards, it appears more like a triangle of trust among them, although the word circle holds the promise of having room for more people to enter as needed. I have also seen, and admired, this level of trust and concern in principals of urban schools who earnestly seek the collaboration of the family and student in order to make situations work. However, in schools with large numbers of students, the individualized knowledge of a child or youth is less likely to occur, unless it is for those "in trouble" (Pas, Bradshaw, & Mitchell, 2011). By making a demonstrable difference through an action, rather than only words, a principal helps students and their families trust educational institutions as partners, rather than potential adversaries. Diane's realization that Clark had enabled a level of support customized for Benny confirmed that Boulder was the right place for her son. She could see the changes in Benny immediately, writing, "This was the first time I saw the climate change for a child so dramatically. Benny who could learn to read and write had little control over his behavior. Instead of waiting for his behavior to improve, the school did what it could to find the best fit for him within the classroom."

Diane's recollection of this episode reveals ways in which schools can actually have a solid system of resources in place, yet still have to rethink them based upon the needs of a single child if need be. Of note in this situation is finding the right match of people. The teaching assistant who supported Benny, as Diane acknowledges, understood the nature of the child. A kick is still a kick, and unpleasant to receive, but Tony did not take it personally as he knew it came from a place of frustration that had not yet been tapped and channeled into a form of expression. The incident illuminates how punitive measures for children who respond violently as part of their struggle in school are rarely the answer and often serve to exacerbate the problem—such as zero tolerance policies. As the fit was a good one, the relationship between the supporter and the supported grew to work—allowing Benny to participate in the general education classroom.

And yet, Diane still revealed the depth of her anxiety in the omnipresent fears that manifested themselves during sleep. What would be the tipping point, she wondered, when it all would implode, as it had before? As previously mentioned, she shares concerns about Benny having "massive delays." In special education language, delays are a paradoxical term as they assume that, like a late train arriving at the station, the journey will go on as originally anticipated, back to normal. However, "delays" are often a euphemism for being behind, with the fear of not being able to catch up. At the same time, in education we always want to keep an open mind about an individual's potential and actual growth, as otherwise there's an imposition of a ceiling of expectations. Even so, lived experience has informed all of us that everyone will never be able to do what's expected at school—if age and grade level standards are rigidly enforced, and also are constantly being raised over time. We are all very much restrained by the expectations always required and the language we use.

The very language of our profession, with terms like Behavior Disorders, and Emotional Disturbance, can misrepresent a student—who, although prone to behaving antisocially or in unacceptable ways—becomes seen purely as the BD or ED label, losing their personhood behind the professional inscription. Several scholars in DSE have sought reframings of how the field of education perceives students with troubling behaviors (see, for example, Annamma, 2015; Danforth & Smith, 2005; Harwood, 2006). What their work has in common is their urging of a shift to understand the student in his or her life circumstances, including past history, present situation, and the future envisioned by the child or youth. In doing so, this approach seeks to understand the reason for the behaviors and the need to work with the student toward changing those behaviors. In my own experience of having taught adolescents labeled BD or ED, I found most of them to have lived their lives in very difficult circumstances, and a sense of survival often superseded unquestioned acquiescence to the demands of schooling—as is expected of all students. In another instance, stories of young women labeled ED documented by Annamma (2014) revealed the conflicting demands placed upon them with family loyalties trumping school expectations.

We know that a DSE approach "assumes competencies" (Connor et al., p. 448), so this should be the grounding principle when working with all students, including those with troubling behaviors. Interestingly, the work of Graham (2010) on ADHD provides much food for thought as she chronicles the birth and reification of the term into a catch all for students who do not conform to classroom expectations. The identification (or to use medicalized language, the "diagnosis") of ADHD has grown into an enormous industry. In the case of Benny, Diane and David were ambivalent about using medication, and in their pursuit to make things work as best as they could—were open to the idea, although it always made them somewhat uneasy. Diane writes, "I was unhappy to think that we were resorting to drugs in part to sustain his placement in a general education classroom, to achieve relative normalcy. Would we have resorted to drugs had he been in a class for the severely disabled?" Here, we see raised again the double-edged sword of normalcy. It is important to move toward achieving desired academic skills and exhibit certain behaviors, yet at what cost? This is never an easy question, and it is never a simple "yes" or "no" answer. For some children and adults, medication has an affect that results in greater concentration and productivity in terms of academic work (Connor, 2013). On the other hand, for others it dulls the senses, robs them of who they are, changing them into another person entirely. One young woman with ADHD explains,

> There are so many positive aspects of ADHD. For example, I can do many things at one time successfully...My main goal is to be able to control my ADHD in certain settings and to use it as an advantage, rather than taking drugs to suppress my creative energy...The problem is that most of the literature is by people who do not have ADHD. They generalize ...and say the symptoms are concrete. This is extremely offensive to me... [As] my situation can be totally different from another person with ADHD (O'Connor, 2001, p. 71).

With Benny, medication had mixed results. On the upside, Diane notes, "The immediacy of his response, both positive and negative, was startling. His demeanor changed. He was able to concentrate on reading and he began to draw voraciously. In school he could sit longer during circle time and did not run out of the classroom." On the downside she observed, "...his limited speech seemed to retreat even further. He was quiet and less engaged in the classroom. At home he lost his appetite, became angry and sullen as the medication wore off, and he slept restlessly." Benny came off the medication in summer, and it was resumed for the start of first grade where he "...learned to read and write... control his behavior better," yet "his language and social skills ... plateaued." I imagine this to have been a very difficult call, seeing simultaneous progression in some domains while flat lining and regression in others. Ultimately, once Benny appeared to be better adapted to the school, and gain proficiency in reading, his family took him off the medication—even though the psychologist urged otherwise. In this case, cautious experimentation allowed Benny to function better in some ways, but his family members and teachers came to see he was better off not taking medication permanently.

Of course the bigger question that confronts us all is the vast expansion of drugs utilized for children and youth with ADHD. For some families, it presents itself as the first resort, rather than the last, as we live in a culture that is saturated in the notion that there is a pill for everything, an industry that promulgates such thinking for its own benefit, with doctors complicit in over prescribing (Seducing the Medical Profession, New York Times, 2006). In addition, children who are naturally active, effusive, outgoing, insufficiently engaged or bored by school are often perceived by teachers as to be in need of medication, with this phenomenon also linked to race, particularly male children of color (Blanchett, 2006; Collins, 2003). It is worrisome that so many children are medicated, as it is the quickest and easiest way to "control" them. However, in doing so, as can be seen in the case of Benny, there is a risk of losing who the person actually is, and it seems as if it's best to err on the side of no medication, if at all possible.

References

Annamma, S. A. (2015). "It was just like a piece of gum": Using an intersectional approach to understand criminalizing young women of color with disabilities in the school-to-prison pipeline. In D. J. Connor, J. W. Valle, & C. Hale (Eds.) Practicing disability studies in education, acting toward social change (pp. 83–102). New York: Peter Lang.

Blanchett, W. (2006). Disproportionate representation of African American students in special education: Acknowledging the role of white privilege and racism. Educational Researcher, 35(6), 24–28.

Collins, K.M. (2003). Ability profiling and school failure: One child's struggle to be seen as competent. Mahwah, NY: Lawrence Erlbaum.

Connor, D. J. (2013). Actively navigating the transition into college: Narratives of students with learning disabilities. International Journal of Qualitative Studies in Education. 25(8), 1005–1036.

Connor, D. J., Gabel, S. L., Gallagher, D. & Morton, M. (2008). Disability studies and inclusive education--Implication for theory, research, and practice: Guest editor's introduction. International Journal of Inclusive Education, 12(5–6), 441–457.

Cook, L., & Friend, M. (1995). Co-teaching: Guidelines for creating effective practices. Focus on Exceptional Children, 28(3), 1–16.

Danforth, S., & Smith, T. J. (2005). Engaging troubling students: A constructivist approach. Thousand Oaks, CA: Sage.

Darling-Hammond, L. (2008). A future worthy of teaching for America. *Phi Delta Kappan*, 89(10), 730–733, 736.

Darling-Hammond, L., Holtzman, D., Gaitlin, S. J., & Julian Vasquez, H. (2005). Does teacher preparation matter? Evidence about teacher certification, Teach for America, and teacher effectiveness. *Education Policy Analysis Archives*, 13(42) [51 pages].

Foote, D. (2009). *Relentless pursuit: A year in the trenches with Teach for America*. Vintage Books: New York.

Friend, M., & Bursuck, W. D. (2002). *Including students with special needs: A practical guide for classroom teachers*. Boston, MA: Allyn & Bacon.

Friend, M., Cook, L., Hurley-Chamberlain, D., & Shamberger, C. (2011). Co-teaching: An illustration of the complexity of collaboration in special education. *Journal of Educational and Psychological Consultation*, 20(1), 9–27.

Fries, K. (1997). *Body remember: A memoir*. Madison, WI: University of Wisconsin Press.

Giangreco, M. F., Edelman, S. W., & Broer, S. M. (2001). Paraprofessional support of students with disabilities: Literature from the past decade. *Exceptional Children*, 68(1), 45–63.

Goodnough, A. (2002, May 15). Half of new teachers lack certificates, data say. *The New York Times*, p. 8.

Grealy, L. (1995). *Autobiography of a face*. New York: harper Perennial.

Harwood, V. (2006). *Diagnosing 'disorderly' children: A critique of behavior disorder discourses*. New York: Routledge.

Lehrer, R. (2015). Personal communication.

Meier, D., Kohn, A., Darling-Hammond, L., Sizer, T. R., & Wood, G. (Eds.) (2004). *Many children left behind: How the No Child Left Behind Act is damaging our children and our schools*. Boston, MA: Beacon Press.

O'Connor, G. (2001). Bad. In P. Rodis, S. Garrod, & M. L. Boscardin (Eds.), *Learning disabilities and life stories* (pp. 62–72). Needham Heights, MA: Allyn & Bacon.

Pas, E. T., Bradshaw, C. P., & Mitchell, M. M., (2010). Examining the validity of office discipline referrals as an indicator of student behavior problems. *Psychology in the Schools*, 48(6), 541–555.

Ravitch, D. (2000). *Left back: A century of failed school reforms*. New York: Simon & Schuster.

Ravitch, D. (2014). Hoaxes in educational policy. *Teacher Educator*, 4(3), 153–165.

Rodis, P., Garrod, A., & Boscardin, M. L. (Eds.). (2001). *Learning disabilities & life stories*. Needham Heights, MA: Allyn & Bacon.

Sanders, K. (2006). Overprotection and lowered expectations of persons with disabilities: The unforeseen consequences. *Journal of Work*, 27(2), 181–188.

Schiltchte, J., Yssel, N., & Meiber, J. (2010). Pathways to burnout: Case studies in teacher isolation and alienation. *Preventing School Failure: Alternative Education for Children and Youth*, 50(1), 35–41.

Seducing the Medical Profession (2006, February 2). [Editorial] *New York Times*, p. 22.

· 6 ·

CREATING CLASSROOM COMMUNITY:
EMBRACING DIFFERENCE

There were many instances, large and small, throughout Benny's time at Boulder School when his classmates contributed in an integral way to his therapy. At first, this made me uncomfortable, but ultimately I was able to appreciate the genius of this natural design. I began to see that the relationships developed through the involvement of the entire community were truly symmetric. While at first it seemed as though the children were involved for the sole purpose of helping Benny overcome some limitation, in fact they were all engaged in purposeful activities that enabled everyone to grow in valuable ways. The constant emphasis on creating a community is, to a large degree, what enabled Benny to find comfort academically as well as socially. When he eventually left for middle school, Benny understood that his individual strengths and his unique abilities that could enhance a classroom.

We have close family friends in a nearby district, a district that time and again outranks ours on various scales. These friends have two children and the oldest child (let us call him Jon) is a boy with somewhat similar issues to Benny, except that from birth until recently, he seemed to be "higher functioning" than Benny, in several ways. He was a stronger academic student, and his language skills developed earlier. At gatherings he never seemed, to my admittedly judgmental eye, as impaired. He spoke easily with friends and

appeared to be comfortable in his skin. Benny, on the other hand, still struggles with academics and speech, and while those who know him, adore him, he still is hesitant in social situations. While his district is one of the nation's top ranking districts academically, it does not value inclusion. Had Benny attended that district, he would have been placed in a segregated classroom. They accommodated our friends' child, Jon, in general education, because despite his disability, on the outside, he appeared "normal." Discussions over the years with these friends always made us grateful for the way Boulder school spent time, thought, and money on activities and experiences that promoted social acceptance. We were grateful from the start for our district that truly invested in children with disabilities and did so in a celebratory manner.

Over the elementary years, Jon progressed well academically, but never quite fit in socially. Jon's parents did not feel valued or appreciated the way we did. In contrast to our own experience, they felt they had to fight the district for every service their son needed in order to function. Ultimately, social issues at school became a major challenge for Jon during the middle grades. In the end, this family chose to sue the district and send their son away to a residential school for children on the spectrum. Although they explored self-contained programs locally, they found what existed did not hold up to the high levels of academic work that they wanted for their child. Other private schools were located far from home, and would have necessitated hours of commuting time for their son. These are among the reasons our friends chose to send Jon away to a segregated program, albeit one that offers a high level curriculum. Since that move, suddenly, Jon seems more impaired than Benny, and is far less communicative. The family as a whole is saddened and broken by the move. There are clearly many dynamics here, and numerous factors that went into the decision of his recent placement. Nevertheless, the reality is they tried to make it work for eight years in the public school, and had it worked, they would have kept their son in the general education program in which he was excelling academically. This is not the only story I can share with a similar ending. Another family friend saw their son, also on the autistic spectrum, through five placements in a neighboring district before home schooling him for a year and then sending him away to a residential school. He began in a collaborative class for the first few years, then to a segregated class within the home school. When that placement did not work, this child was moved to the local Board of Cooperative Educational Services (BOCES) program that specializes in educating disabled students, but there he was severely bullied and beaten up by classmates. The parents then tried home schooling again for a year, but the social isolation was devastating to Billy. Finally, they tried one more segregated placement within a public school before suing the district and moving the child to a residential center by middle school, once again fracturing a family, and choosing a setting as far from inclusion as one can get. Let us also consider the amount of money the home district is now investing in these children sent away. For that price tag, how many teachers or TA's could the district hire in order to better support the students within their own schools?

While we may associate a good school with a solid academic program, we must also pay attention to the social dynamics. A child who is not happy socially most likely does not succeed academically. I know that Boulder teachers had their eye on that reality long before Benny left for middle school. The following endeavors illustrate how, beginning in grade one, teachers were aware of the need to integrate Benny into the social dynamics of the school, to make his goals part of the shared goals of the classroom. All of his teachers' work insured that Benny's peers understood his needs and that he could learn to relate fully to his classmates, even with the limitations of his language and processing.

While these opportunities were woven throughout the tapestry of his time at Boulder, in large and small ways, I will highlight a few instances which had great visibility and which took substantial time and attention from the traditional academic events of the day.

First Grade: Starting Conversations

Benny began grade one on solid footing. Marina, the inclusion specialist, had given him a proverbial "toolkit" to help him with his behavior and he was working hard on trying. Benny was told how to do the job of a first grader, in just a few simple ways. He was reading and writing with relative fluency, although still lagging somewhat behind his classmates. His teacher Ann had spent a lot of time over the summer preparing for Benny, by differentiating many of the activities and lessons. She found that she had watered things down too much, and in the end, preferred to adapt on the spot, finding a way to help him access more of the regular curriculum.

Ann was a teacher with both experience and a youthful glow. She was the prototypical "good" teacher who could have stepped out of a fairy tale. Her handwriting also came with a bounce, as loopy letters would cascade into positive phrases as they offered support and praise on each and every workbook page. Ann radiated a protective shield around her class and was the kind of teacher with whom students feel comfortable from the start. In a determined yet soft spoken way she was able to move the class from one activity to the next unable to suppress the delight in working with her charges.

Benny's greatest challenge at this time was expressive language. As he was still scoring in the decimal percentages on the tests administered, we wondered if he would ever be able to have a conversation that flowed. He was able to use words to communicate but not in a spontaneous way. Yet, we saw humor and sensitivity in him, through his gestures, his play, and his drawings. We yearned to know him through his spoken words, but it was with a great sadness that we were beginning to accept that this might never be possible.

At the time he had speech therapy three times a week. His speech therapist, Sandy began allowing him to invite a typical peer to his sessions. Initially, this seemed inappropriate to me, but the teacher and therapist explained that they often did this. After all, who better to elicit conversational speech from a delayed child than a peer who knows exactly what is interesting to speak about? I recalled the incident when David and I stood eavesdropping behind a tree during our first few weeks at the school. Although I was persuaded that this would be helpful for Benny, I still felt uncomfortable with the arrangement.

Sandy also decided to push into his classroom for one of her weekly sessions using laminated cards featuring conversation starters. These were simple at first and then worked up to more complex questions as the year progressed. This activity was so successful that Ann decided to begin every day with a 20-minute conversation starter. When Ann explained this to me, I objected at first. It seemed unethical to me to use other children in a somewhat therapeutic relationship with my son. I suggested that other parents might feel uncomfortable with this setup, expecting their children should be doing more math or reading instead. Ann explained that every first grader needed time to learn to listen, and to take turns, therefore, this activity benefitted everyone. I was puzzled; my experiences in education had been so different. I had grown up in NYC in an era where classes were routinely homogeneously grouped in fear that "weaker" students will hold the faster ones back. Not only did Benny now share a classroom with all of these on-level learners, suddenly they were being used to support his development. Additionally, the level of importance that was placed on Benny's social and conversational growth surprised me. I had thought that once he was a quiet and well-behaved member of the class, attention toward him would wane. That was the model I had witnessed for so long as a teacher myself. Maybe inside I was looking forward to less visibility.

Parents did comment to me about these arrangements, but--to my surprise--it was always very positive. Often they would share how happy their child was that Benny picked him or her to go with him to speech. The teacher would tell me how grateful she was to Sandy for introducing the conversation circle as it turned out to be a great benefit for all of her students.

Second Grade: An Accidental Opportunity

In grade 2, Benny had a very seasoned teacher, Barbara, with 30 years of experience when she met him. Admittedly she had never had a student quite like Benny and initially felt that perhaps she did not have the right skills or training to help him. (Note that I feature many struggles of that year in chapter 8, but for now I would like to focus on the role of peers in Benny's development and eventual success in this classroom.) Barbara was in some ways a traditional teacher and felt the responsibility to do it all for all of her students. She wanted Benny involved and engaged in every activity and spent hours planning ways to accomplish that. Around the holiday time she brought in small looms for the children. They had been studying the 1800's and had visited a restored village. She wanted them each to create a woven potholder for their parents. Since Benny could not yet tie his shoes or place a button through its hole, it seemed unlikely that he could create a potholder on a small plastic loom within an hour's time in the classroom. Instead, Barbara prepared a sorting activity for him. He was to sort the colored bands of fabric and then color in a bar graph relating to the numbers of each color.

Benny wanted nothing to do with that task and knocked the bands to the floor. Barbara tried to redirect him to the loom but he seemed to be all thumbs. She was frustrated and left for a while to assist some other students, many of whom were also struggling. When she returned, barely ten minutes later, Benny was working away, weaving orange and white together, creating a potholder with the utmost of dexterity. Barbara looked right at Benny and asked him where he learned to do that. Benny just smiled and the girl next to him, a lovely red head, looked up and said, "Gee, Mrs. Roberts, it was not that hard, I just showed him and he picked it right up." Barbara was floored. She took the potholder all around the school to show his other teachers, therapists, even Clark, and called me that day to explain and then sent the magnificent square home in his book bag. Barbara learned inadvertently that day that she did not have to be the only agent for Benny's growth. She had

26 students who might know different, even better, ways how to get him to produce, that just might take him to a place no one expected he would get to. This experience enabled Barbara to relax a bit and let go of the tension that was interfering with relationship she was trying to build with Benny.

Grade Four: Drop Everything and Converse

Once Benny reached grade four he was, for the most part, on track academically. He still needed supports but the supports that were in place were working well. His behavior was exemplary and he was polite and happy in school. Sophia, his teacher, was a young and hip with a great deal of enthusiasm. While Benny had been accepted socially, grade four brought new dynamics to the table. The children were becoming more involved in their own cliques. Conversations were moving faster, becoming quick more complex while Benny still had a hard time processing language. Sophia felt he was being left out, not intentionally but as a result of the changes that took place in these pre-teen years. While Benny had mastered basic conversation, suddenly there was a whole new language developing around him and he was getting lost. The lunchroom was always crowded and noisy, and Benny had a hard time sustaining even a short conversation in that setting. She was concerned, and decided to think of a way to help him bridge this new gap that was growing between him and his peers.

The entire fourth grade had a 30-minute time period every day called DEAR time, which stood for "drop everything and read." She suggested to me that Benny be given this time to partner up with another classmate just to "hang out" instead of reading. Sophia's plan was to assign each week a different student to be Benny's DEAR time partner. They would go out into the hallway, take a game or two, a small whiteboard, some books and just play together for the time. My initial reaction was surprise. Playing instead of reading seemed contrary to what I had learned about education, especially in grade four, a high stakes testing year. Still, I had already learned to accept the wacky and wonderful ideas that germinated in the minds and hearts of these Boulder folks and so I said "Sure," despite a certain hesitation in my heart and mind. Once again I feared the resistance of other parents.

The idea was a hit from the start. Benny came out smiling every day, eager to tell me first about the time he was able to spend with a classmate. While I worried about how parents would feel, afraid that they would resent the time their child spent away from reading, parents told me their children looked forward to their time with Benny and often prepared ahead. One boy taught him all about football while another girl taught him how to draw animals. Other teachers commented on how lively and happy Benny seemed out in the hall with his friends. Benny began to call his classmates on the phone, to continue conversations he began during DEAR time. Genuine friendships grew from this time together. Sophia had told me this would last until March, with each student spending one week with Benny, after which she would find another activity for him. However, so many children had already requested extra time with Benny- recalling a missed day when they were absent or when there was a rehearsal, that accommodating all of these requests, Benny was booked through June.

DEAR time became a time when the Benny's classmates could see what really made him tick and they saw his humor and intelligence. Sophia said she did it as much for Benny as she did for the other students. She knew Benny had a lot to share and wanted to give him an opportunity to do so. Sophia also wanted the other students to know that it is worth the extra effort to get to know a student who might seem more remote at first. She hoped this would carry over to middle school and enrich their lives as well. In our district, elementary school goes through grade five. Benny had one more year after grade four within the cozy sanctuary of Boulder. Sophia knew middle school was on the horizon, and wanted him to go off with confidence. She also wanted the other students to realize that inside his quiet demeanor was a creative, funny and passionate child. It was a lesson for everyone, a time to realize we all have parts of ourselves that can lie hidden in certain situations.

Boulder believes that the social is as important as the academic. A child who is unhappy and unrelated to his peers is not a child who will learn well how to live, work, and participate in society. The emphasis we place on academics can only work if we conjoin it with an equal emphasis on community. This is magnified for students who may struggle socially but it is true for each and every student who does not struggle. Perhaps this is where educational reform is heading most astray. The single-minded pursuit of academic excellence will not work because we need to work together to create positive change and societal growth. I still marvel at how amidst the stress of Common Core and new state tests, fourth grade teachers across the country are cutting out all sorts of extras from their classrooms, while Sophia, here at Boulder, is rethinking reading time and listening for laughter.

Of all the many reasons I wanted inclusion for Benny, the most compelling was for the chance to find friendship. I was not sure that simply moving him into a general education classroom would enable friendships to form, but that was my deepest wish for Benny. I could envision a life without the ability to read or write or even to speak, but I could not imagine a life devoid of companionship.

It was these formal and informal actions that enabled Benny to grow in his conversational skills. He is now fully conversational. I do not think placing the nexus of his development solely in the hands of the speech therapists would have brought on this tremendous development. He needed the input of all of his peers and by involving his classmates, Boulder build a community of learners.

***

The sentence that lingers in my mind the most is Diane's simply expressed thought: "I could envision a life without the ability to read or write or even to speak, but I could not imagine a life devoid of companionship." There have been many critiques of inclusive education claiming that it is primarily, even only, for social reasons, and actually detracts from the academic growth of students with disabilities and their nondisabled peers (Fuchs & Fuchs, 1995; Anastasiou & Kauffman, 2011). This issue is, indeed, a divisive point for many educators. However, if we are to conceptualize learning as social activity, as many prominent theorists have (see, for example, Bahktin, 1986; Dewey, 1997 Gutierrez, 2012), then we see the artificiality in a forced, and false, dichotomy between social and academic skills. What we actually recognize in the vignettes within this chapter is the ability of teachers to create classrooms in which Benny, along with all of the other students, can have access to learning.

Universal Design for Learning (UDL) has been in existence for decades, and I have always found that thoughtful, effective teachers tend to adhere to the principles of UDL without necessarily identifying them as such in a conscious way. As many readers will know, Universal Design originated within architecture of the 1960s and began with the premise of, "If we construct the building right from the start, allowing all people access to all parts, then we won't need to exclude people, retrofit spaces and internal structures, or place limits on some citizens." When this same principle is applied to learning, classrooms and lessons can be constructed with view to providing all students access to both the information within the curriculum and the physical space of the room (Burgstahler & Corey, 2008). Similarly, the formalized literature on Differentiated Instruction (DI) has been around for almost two decades (Tomlinson, 1999; 2001), yet since schools began, thoughtful and effective teachers have provided different opportunities for students in the same class to develop academically and socially. In fact, it could be argued that this was the premise of the one-room schoolhouse associated with small towns across America. Again, the teachers in the vignettes shared by Diane reflect examples of differentiated instruction at work without them necessarily explicitly describing them as such.

When teaching inclusive practices to pre-service and in-service teachers, I am often asked, "Isn't Universal Design for Learning more work?" or "It's overwhelming! Where do I begin and where do I end when thinking about differentiation?" These are good questions to openly discuss with a class, and explore educators' conceptions of what these two compatible approaches actually are. My responses, to paraphrase, usually are that UDL is not necessarily more work it's really more about how we begin our thinking, planning, and selection of materials. It is a habit of mind rooted in making sure that everyone is welcome, and provided with "entry points" to the lesson. Once they're "in" the lesson, students can be engaged in similar or different ways in the content, process, and product, depending on many factors such as readiness, interests, and learning profile of the students (Tomlinson, 1999). In brief, effective teaching can be complex, but organized planning, flexible pedagogy, and having a disposition that accepts and welcomes the range of natural human diversity helps educators become effective.

Several scholars within DSE have written books that describe ways in which to build inclusive communities, including: Shapiro's *Everybody Belongs: Changing Negative Attitudes Towards Classmates with Disabilities* (1999); Baglieri's *Disability Studies and the Inclusive Classroom: Critical Practices for Creating Least Restrictive Attitudes* (2012); Danforth's *Becoming a Great inclusive Educator* (2014); Udvari-Solner and Kluth's *Joyful Learning: Active and Collaborative Learning in Inclusive Classrooms* (2008); Sapon-Shevin's *Because We Can Change The World: A Practical Guide to Building Cooperative Inclusive Classroom Communities* (2010), and *Widening the Circle: The Power of Inclusive Classrooms* (2007); Lawrence-Brown and Sapon-Shevin's *Condition Critical: Key Principles for Equitable and Inclusive Education* (2014), and: Valle and Connor's *Rethinking Disability: A Disability Studies Approach to Inclusive Practices* (2010). Each one of these books advocates for approaches to teaching similar to the day-to-day practices at Boulder that support the academic, social, and emotional growth of all students.

In first grade, the development of conversation starter cards arose from two teachers working together who wanted to encourage Benny's speech while realizing that all of the class could benefit from an increased opportunity to talk. We can imagine the scenario in some schools to be met with protest for a number of reasons (or excuses, depending upon your point of view), including Diane's observation, "Other parents might feel uncomfortable with this setup, expecting that their children should instead be doing more math or reading." Interestingly, it was Diane who objected at first, stating, "It seemed unethical to me to use other children in a somewhat therapeutic relationship with my son." Here I'd like to call attention to the word "therapeutic" as an example of medicalized language dominating the discourse of education for students with disabilities. Benny's situation can also easily be looked at as the need to practice an underdeveloped skill, and teachers have the ability to recognize that and the power to do something about it. As the teacher explained, "Every first grader needed time to learn to listen and to take turns," making this activity meaningful for everyone. Using conversation starters between peers also exemplifies how academic and social skills are inextricably meshed in very natural ways.

In the vignette shared from second grade about Benny and the potholder, we are reminded that all teachers cannot always reach all of the children in their classrooms in ways they wish to. The pressure, the responsibility, the very real limits of our knowledge (in this case despite being an educator for three decades) can result in an impasse between teacher and struggling student. Worth noting is that the teacher had initially differentiated instruction with good intent, assigning Benny to sort and count the colored strips of fabric. He rejected that work because he was desirous of doing what his classmates were doing, despite his (then current) inabilities. Although the phrase is somewhat clichéd, we see that teachers, by necessity, are life long learners. By stepping back when things were not quite working—instead of continuing to force the issue—the teacher inadvertently created a space for an observant student to step into and show Benny how to do what was being required. DSE encourages the cultivation of such classroom ecologies because it accepts that people are actually interdependent, rather than independent. Help and support can be requested when and where it is needed, including exploring options related to space, time, amount, and complexity of work assigned. Each child in a class can potentially hold the answer to the question that the teacher cannot always have at her brain tips. In this case the opportunity of another "milestone" for Benny was created by his classmate; a situation that could not have occurred in his original school.

In fourth grade, the modified use of Drop Everything and Read in Benny's class is another demonstration of how a teacher can develop arrangements within a reading class that benefit all children. Although Benny does read and would benefit from the 30 minutes devoted to reading, Sophia realizes that at this point in time, it is crucially important for him to communicate with his peers. By the teacher's promotion of conversation time, Benny comes to know all of his classmates, their personalities, and their interests. The act of reading is about communication (albeit in a limited way), and in order to get there, Benny has to understand the value of communication in a larger sense, among his peers and about their interests. Then, reading makes more sense because people tend to read about what they are interested in. The opportunity to share likes, dislikes, skills, questions… makes for a rich experience for both students, and for Benny to understand the concept of peers/friends and for peers/friends to understand an atypical student like Benny.

It is precisely at junctures like this that teachers often feel stymied for the right thing to do—being restrained by an unimaginative curriculum, and fearful of not always following the "official script" for all students, regardless of whether that script is within reach of a student's current capabilities. However, by opening up the format of the class (allowing 1:1 for Benny, and likewise, the peer), and broadening the concept of independent reading to interdependent talking, the teacher actually provides what students need. All students in that class came to primarily see Benny as Benny, not the student with a disability called Benny. The social, emotional, and academic are entwined in lessons like this, permitting all students to be who they are and contribute to the collective class knowledge. These situations also demystify disability as difference that is sometimes noticeable, and sometimes is not, yet is a natural part of human diversity. In reflecting upon Diane's desire for her son to have camaraderie with peers, she knew moving Benny to a general education class would not automatically result in friendships, but it was the first step in the right direction. Between the targeted attention of speech therapists and coming to understand all of his peers within the general education classroom, Benny eventually shifted from having little or no conversational skills to being fully conversational, thus averting Diane's fear of "a life devoid of companionship."

The examples above also testify to a tenet within DSE that states, "Disability is primarily recognized and valued as a natural part of human diversity." Generally speaking, Benny was accepted and understood to be Benny, even though the "right" way of doing things for teachers was not always immediately clear-cut. What all these teachers have in common is their own observations of Benny—made across time and verified with other colleagues—as the basis on which they then developed their decisions to instruct, modify, and assess, in an ongoing way that was open ended. Part of inclusive education must be organic, as the predictability of research-based practices do not neatly and tidily generalize to context-specific situations.

Contrastingly, in the shadow of these successful examples of inclusive practices, stand the stories of Jon and Billy. These students live in "one of the nation's top ranking districts academically" that does not value inclusive education and would have placed Benny in a segregated classroom. The more the child approximates academic normalcy, and the superficiality of behavioral norms, the more likely he or she will be included in this academic top-ranking district. Yet the very concept of "normalcy" comes into question when we see ways in which school environments either enable or disable children who are atypical in terms of "expected" levels of academics and behavior. The policies, practices, and procedures within Boulder are sharply juxtaposed with those in the adjacent school district. Again, we see ways in which highly limited options within school systems adversely effect the educational and social experiences of students with disabilities and their families in ways that are neither recognized nor fully understood by families with "typical" children.

Diane also raises the topic of public expense. Cynics of inclusive education have often said, "It's being done to save money." Depending upon the circumstances, this may possibly be true. However, in most circumstances, if inclusion is done well, it can be supported by the same budget, or cost less than spent on supporting segregation. When I worked as part of a professional development network funded by New York, at State Education Department meetings I heard that funds to support students in special education students were out of control and no satisfactory mechanisms were in place for the justification of such expenditures. For example, there were extreme instances of children and youth being flown weekly from one part of the state to another in order to receive services. This not only meant plane fare, but boarding school Sunday night through Friday afternoon. All of this was at public expense.

Diane's comment about ways in which money can be better spent toward creating and maintaining more authentic inclusive placements is well taken.

Restrictive environments cost far more money than general education placements for students with disabilities. Even the ratio of per capita spending is usually three times as much for a student with an IEP (Hehir et al., 2015), with decades of research-based evidence revealing poor outcomes for students receiving special education services (as have been articulated in chapter 3). The choice of Diane's friends, parents of Jon and Billy, were whittled down to a forced choice between either a local placement with low academics or a school far away. Being able to hire lawyers and sue the local education authority, claiming the need for highly specialized school services that are not provided by a public system is the legal right of all parents. However, as we have noted, only those who are sufficiently wealthy and informed are able to leverage the law in this way. I am always left asking: Why doesn't the public school system offer these services if private ones can? Isn't it an obligation of the public school system to do so?

It is the instance of inclusive education working in Boulder's setting that holds promise for other schools and districts that struggle with the issues. All of the other themes we have addressed so far—the least restrictive environment, school climate, the appropriateness of placements, ways in which schools shape behavior, and the systems in which professionals collaborate— all feed into creating and maintaining a learning community in which all people feel safe, and preferably happy. As Diane notes, "A child who is not happy socially most likely does not succeed academically," underlining the importance of the social realm of schooling. As we have seen, the social and the academic domains cannot be parsed from one another when creating a nurturing classroom environment.

References

Anastasiou, D., & Kauffman, J. K. (2011). A social constructionist approach to disability: Implications for special education. *Exceptional Children, 77*(5), 367–384.

Baglieri, S. (2012). *Disability studies and the inclusive classroom: Critical practices for creating least restrictive attitudes*. New York: Routledge.

Bakhtin, M. M. (1986). Toward a methodology for the human sciences. In C. Emerson & M. Holquist (Eds.), *Speech genres and other late essays* (pp. 159–172). Austin, TX: University of Texas Press.

Burghstahler, S., & Corey, R. (2008). Moving from the margins: From accommodation to universal design. In S. L. Gabel & S. Danforth, (Eds.), *Disability Studies in Education: An International Reader* (pp. 561–581). New York: Peter Lang.

Danforth, S. (Ed.) (2014). *Becoming a great inclusive educator*. New York: Peter Lang.

Dewey, J. (1997). *Experience and education.* New York: Touchstone.

Fuchs, D., & Fuchs, L.S. (1995). Inclusive schools movement and the radicalization of special education reform. In J. M. Kauffman & D. P. Hallahan (Eds.) *The illusion of full inclusion* (pp. 213–243). Austin, TX: ProEd.

Gutierrez, K. (2012). Re-mediating current activity for the future. *Mind, Culture, and Activity, 19*(1), 17–21.

Hehir, T., Figueroa, R., Gamm, S., Katzman, L. I., Gruner, A., Karger, J., & Hernandez, J. (2005). *Comprehension management review and evaluation of special education submitted to the New York City Department of Education.* Cambridge, MA: Harvard School of Education.

Lawrence-Brown, D., & Sapon-Shevin, M. (Eds.) (2014). *Condition critical: Key principles for equitable and inclusive education.* New York: Teachers College Press.

Sapon-Shevin, M. (2007). *Widening the Circle: The Power of Inclusive Classrooms.* Boston, MA: Beacon Press.

Sapon-Shevin, M. (2010). *Because we can change the world: A practical guide to building cooperative inclusive classroom communities.* Thousand Oaks, CA: Corwin Press.

Shapiro, A. (1999). *Everybody belongs: Changing negative attitudes toward classmates with disabilities.* New York: Routledge.

Tomlinson, C. A. (1999). *The differentiated classroom: Responding to the needs of all learners.* Alexandria, VA: ASCD.

Tomlinson, C. A. (2001). *How to differentiate instruction in mixed ability classrooms* (2nd ed.). Alexandria, VA: ACSD.

Udvari-Solner, A., & Kluth, P. (2008). *Joyful learning: Active and collaborative learning in inclusive classrooms.* Thousand Oaks, CA: Corwin Press.

Valle, J. W., & Connor, D. J. (2010). *Rethinking disability: A disability studies guide to inclusive practices.* New York: McGraw-Hill.

· 7 ·

FRIENDSHIP:
REVERSING THE STATUS QUO

Of all the many reasons I wanted inclusion for Benny, the most compelling was for the chance to find friendship. I saw that even at the age of three, the fact that he rode a bus to a preschool far away, which had the right collection of therapists for Benny, impacted our social life within our neighborhood. I could not take part in the conversations, which sprung up in the local playground, as they often revolved around the happenings at the nearby preschool. Even more surprising and depressing was that within Benny's special education class at preschool, I felt like an outcast. Even within the world of the "special needs child," there was a hierarchy. Parents and some therapist spoke in terms of "levels of functioning," and it seemed Benny was "lower functioning" than most of his disabled peers with whom he'd been grouped. I recall a low point for me, when I tried to exchange phone numbers with a mother of a boy from Benny's class. He happened to live near to my mother and we had run into each other accidentally in a playground near her house a few times. Adam played nicely with this boy and Benny expressed more interest in this boy than he usually did. However the mother denied my request to arrange some more play dates, telling me that her son would be moving to a higher-level class the next year. Implicit in her rejection was the idea that children of disparate levels should not mix. I began to accept that even in the presence

of these parents of other children with disabilities, there was no equality and no inclusion. Actually, it seemed that those who also lived in the world of the special needs child judged Benny is a harsher manner.

That realization was one of a few of the very lowest points for me on this journey. If my son could not secure a play date with another child with a disability, with whom he had a rapport, then what options would he have with any other more typical child? Fortunately within a few months of our move, Benny began to benefit from friendships with peers that formed with relative ease. While I had anticipated that his issues might make him stand apart from his peers, instead I found that when his behavior was not scrutinized, he blended in more easily. Benny's differences were seen as novel. Aspects of his personality that were initially flagged as symptomatic of his disorders, were instead seen as interesting quirks, that more likely drew in friends rather than pushed them away.

Early in kindergarten Benny was invited to a birthday party with a sports theme. My husband took him to this party and waited on the side. David called me early on with worry in his voice. It seemed Benny was running around acting like a puppy while the party organizers were trying to organize a sports game for the children. David was anxious and asked me what he should do. We both knew that Benny did not do well with redirection when he was stressed. I suggested that David hang back and see what happens next. He called back in a few minutes, relieved to an extent. It seemed that now many of the children were running around like dogs and cats; Benny was no longer alone. David told me that the other parents were laughing and the only folks who were bothered by this were the party planners. As a teacher, I knew even then, that had his unusual behavior been made an issue of, the children would have shunned him rather than joined in. There is a fine line between shaping behavior and allowing children to be themselves, without calling negative attention to their behavior. Children tend to model their behavior by watching their teachers. Here we see an example of the way Benny was allowed to change the community, rather than being forced to be the one to conform. Is it okay that these five-year-olds adopted what might have been considered inappropriate behavior? In the end, some of these children became his good friends, and all of these children, including Benny, went on to become productive helpful members of the school community despite their occasional modeling of what we might term inappropriate behavior.

Spring 2009

It was Ann, Benny's first grade teacher who suggested to us that we initiate a play date with a child who had become friends with Benny in school. I was a little nervous because Benny had not really had a play date yet and was still struggling with expressing himself verbally. I worried that he would not be able to ask for what he needed in someone else's home. I was afraid he would look rude when he failed to respond to a question. We had been rejected so often, I was afraid to try again. David was the one who actually reached out to Mark's mom, Sara, resulting in Benny having his first play date at Mark's home. Sara did not want to hear much about Benny's issues, she was more concerned about having the right kind of cookie on hand. The play date went well and when summer came, we invited Mark over to our house. I cleaned for days on end. Our home is small and run down. We live with peeling tiles in the bathroom and walls in need of fresh paint. I was determined to have it shine. Mark was to come for lunch and Sara suggested a simple meal of pasta with some melted butter. I tried to coach Benny for days about which games he might like to play, knowing that spontaneous play did not come easily. When the day came, Benny was beside himself with excitement. He waited by the window all morning and then made what seemed like a million tiny jumps when he saw Mark walk from his car to our door. Nevertheless once Mark walked in the door, Benny retreated to his room. I feared that Mark would feel rejected and then turn away from Benny. Nervously I tried to make conversation with Mark, to keep him company. He was calm and cool and did not seem at all disturbed by the fact that Benny had run into another room saying that he did not want to play at all. Mark sensed my anxiety and said to me, "Don't worry, Mrs. Berman, this is how Benny is, it is okay. In a few minutes I'll go get him to play with me. He is like this all the time in school." Just as promised, Mark let Benny have a few minutes alone and then raced into his room arms outstretched, fingers wiggling and then dove on top of Benny with enormous of energy and a good deal of tickling. When this did not get Benny out of his room, Mark flipped his body upside down and walked on his hands. Bingo, that did it and Benny finally followed with eagerness. I wondered even then, long before I knew how much we all had to learn from these children, and if there was any play therapist out there in the world who would have walked on their hands for my son?

Benny and Mark went to the basement and took out brushes and paints. Soon I heard a commotion. Mark was crying, sobbing actually, with an intensity that made me fear a major injury. I ran to the basement to find Mark wiping his arm furiously with a paper towel. I saw no blood, just a few drops of green paint on his elbow. I took him to the bathroom and examined him further for wounds. I found none. He told me through his convulsive sobbing that he got paint on his arm and I tried to console him. I told Mark that it was only paint and that it will wash away, but he did not want to hear my words of consolation. Benny pushed me away and stood beside his friend, furiously handing him slightly dampened paper towels every few seconds. Benny, too, looked quite concerned. He hovered right over and around Mark, helping him wet the towels which he then used to wipe away the remnants of the paint, which luckily was washable and non-toxic. Benny understood exactly what Mark needed; he needed a friend to take his pain seriously.

They had no need for me; they had it all under control. When all the paint was wiped clean, the boys had a snack. They ate pretzels, rice cakes, and water. As they ate, the tension drained from their bodies, but they each looked worn out and needed to rest for a while on the couch. I asked Mark if he wanted to go home, fearing the certain end to this first play-date in our home, but he says no, he is okay now.

A few minutes later they went back down and this time I followed closely, making sure all the paint was away and the table was clean. Mark took out some glitter glue. I dove to take it from him before it spilled or got on his arm but he held onto it tightly. I suggested he find another activity in light of the paint incident and he looked up at me with his earnest, big brown eyes. "Don't worry, Mrs. Berman, I am not afraid of glue at all…only paint." His wide eyes remained fixed on Benny, not me, so I slunk upstairs and prepared dinner. The world is filled with quirky children; I saw that Benny was not alone. He may have flagged a few diagnoses, but these labels did not define him. Despite dismal scores on measures of social awareness Benny knew just how to be a friend to Mark.

A few months later, still early in the friendship between Benny and Mark, I ran into Sara at the preschool Adam was attending with her younger son. She was, as usual, surrounded by other moms and conversing freely while I stood apart in my own world, not unlike the professional evaluations of Benny. She reached out to me, pulled me into the circle and said: "This is Diane, her son Benny is Mark's best friend." I tried to act nonchalant, as if these words were ordinary to me. In fact--inside my head was spinning with joy, hearing the words "Benny," "friend," and "best" mingling together for the very first time--creating a melody of intense and novel beauty. Over the next few days I played the words over and over in my mind, trying to hold onto them, to hear them again and again exactly as they sounded in the hall amongst others, a glorious and very public declaration of Benny's ability to form a friendship. I would have been elated to hear any two of those three words strung together, and to hear all three made me feel as though I had won the jackpot. Somehow I kept wondering if the words Sara used were earned through some misperception, something she did not yet know about my son. It was then I realized I still carried some sort of darkness within me, a remnant from the days when I was told my son was causing others to regress, and of when I could not secure a play date even with another child with disabilities. While I tried to pin the darkness on others, and perhaps it originated with them, I could not escape the fact that I was guilty too, that there still existed a part of me that did not yet believe that my son deserved to have a best friend.

November 2011

Third grade parent conference day came in late November. I was always a little nervous on this day. It was hard for me to tell where Benny was as his progress was still uneven and often chaotic. It seemed to me that Benny had been doing nicely with his schoolwork. He had been able to complete his homework, but apart from a few smiles from his teacher, I had little other contact. The news delivered by his teachers and therapists was good, and then, because I knew that he was often alone in grade two during recess, I asked how he was doing socially-- especially at recess. Lucy lit up; she was excited to tell me Benny had a large group of children he played with regularly. She explained that they divided the large suburban field into two stations. Penn station was over by the soccer field and Grand Central was out by the baseball field. The children divided into two groups of ten or so each and ran between the two, imitating the 1, 2, or 3 train to 42nd street, located by the fence and then the S train which completed the journey to Grand Central in one direction and Penn station in the other. They would shuttle like this for the entire 30-minute time after lunch. The children enjoyed learning about NYC. When Benny first came to Boulder school, his teachers recognized his interest in trains and suggested he bring in train and bus maps and schedules to share with the class.

Trains and buses had long fascinated Benny. Even as a toddler he would stand sometimes for hours over subway gratings in the city, waiting for the rumble beneath our feet. Efforts to move him along would result in major tantrums. He would also stand for similar periods of time studying bus maps in our living room and cry out when we tried to move him into another activity. His first team of therapists suggested that this was actually perseverative activity and we should not let him engage in this behavior. They pointed out that obsessions with transportation often went hand in hand with an autistic spectrum diagnoses, as if that alone justified trying to get Benny to abandon his passion. We tried in vain to re-direct him but intuitively we recognized that by withholding his passions we were only damaging our relationship with him. Instead we found that by engaging him through his interests we could build his interpersonal strengths as well as his communication skills. At the time we had no idea that these obsessions would grow into an area of strength. We did not imagine that the hours he spent studying train and bus schedules would ultimately translate into real events with his peers, and that his friends would look up to him because of the knowledge he possessed. They saw this as an area of expertise, rather than a symptom of his disability.

Grade 4 Play Date, March 2012

One Friday afternoon in grade four, Mark came over to play with Benny and his new Lego set. Here is a snippet of how I recall their conversation.

Benny:	Come Mark, let's make a city. I have the police station here and the gas station there, and a few tall buildings over here.
Mark:	Great Benny…I will work on the school down the block.
Me:	Do you want a snack, boys, cookies, apples?
Mark:	Ms. Berman, look how Benny plays with me now? Remember a few years ago when it took him a while to get used to me?
Me:	Yes Mark, I do. I am so glad you are still in our lives.
Mark:	I will never forget when Benny first came to Boulder school…remember Benny, when you were in kindergarten?
Benny:	No, I don't. Let's just work on the city, Mark.
Mark (to me):	Ms. Berman, when Benny first moved here he was very shy. He would sit under the playground equipment at recess, and I wondered how to get him to come out. I would go under and try to talk to him but he would not look at me. (Mark sighs and stands up, walks closer to me, smiles a bit). I would go under and tickle him and he would just sit there. I did not like him sitting under there. I wanted him to come out. (Mark pauses, smiles some more).
Benny:	Vroom vroom…here comes a bus…watch out Mark…crash…
Mark:	(moving toward me) I tried *everything* I could. I made jokes, I poked and prodded. Nothing seemed to work, at first. After a few weeks or maybe months…one day he came out. That is when we became friends!

	(Broad beaming smile under his curly dark hair, dark brown eyes shining, while Benny busies himself with his city).
Me:	Yes Mark I remember. I am so happy you found each other.
Mark:	Hey, Benny, I see you got the training wheels off your bike- that is great news!
Me:	Yeah…it took awhile but we got them off.
Mark:	Ms. Berman, don't speak like that. It does not matter how long it took, it matters that he got here.

Once again I learn the most from a child. What happens to us as we get older, when do we lose this positive and supportive outlook?

Birthdays in the City

It was not long before Benny's interest in the city transportation systems spread throughout his circle of friends in real and tangible ways. When he turned eight, instead of a birthday party, he asked to take his friends to Central Park, all the way by train, bus, and subway. At 9 AM we tackled the Brooklyn Bridge, 10 was the Highline Park, 11 Riverside Park up to 125th and then down through Harlem to Columbia University for cupcakes on the campus. At 12 we went through lower Manhattan, and 1 PM took us back to Central Park to walk the reservoir. Each year we take between 10 and 15 folks along for our tour. His friends enjoyed the events so much it has become a tradition over school holidays as well. I imagine as he grows, one day he will lead his friends around the city without us. They look up to him for his skill in navigating the metropolis marveling at his ability to find several ways to connect two points within what appears to some as ordered chaos. It is interesting to note that while his reaction time to general questions is still somewhat delayed, in this setting he can provide a frustrated commuter alternate routes faster than most MTA employees. This indicates the extent to which disability is context-based, and the strength to which interest can drive success. Benny says now he wants to work for the MTA. He has ideas about new subway lines and ways to improve safety. He wrote up some of these ideas for a project last year in English class and he received a grade of A. The school understands that through interest we can develop strengths and talents, integrating them into literary and communication skills. This kind of teaching brings out the best in everyone, not only those who come to the table with differences. That is the part of the power behind using differentiated instruction as the basis of everyday teaching.

April 2013

One of the most poignant moments came during his birthday walk in 2013 when he was turning 10 years old. We led a group of 18 friends, parents and a grandpa of one of the children over the Brooklyn Bridge. Any trip to New York reawakened in me my love for what I still call "my city." The first few steps in my city filled me with excited anticipation and an expanse in my lungs as if only in that air I do breathe fully. We are like lovers who have been parted, my city and I, and for the first few minutes of any city trip, we dance together. I become quickly intoxicated by all the smiles and nods I exchange with strangers in the space of a few short blocks. No matter how many times I walk through my city there is always more to see. It is a continual presentation, a dizzying array of options that my soul has come to equate with life itself.

Most of the group came from our new neighborhood, and our best friends from Queens met us at the foot of the Brooklyn Bridge. Smiles widened, faces glowed as we paused at the bridge's midpoint, stopped for water, snacks, and photos. Benny chatted happily with his group of friends who admire him for his knowledge of the city. I marveled at where we were, and how now we have it all. We have our city and we have our community.

We have moved on to a world where there are no boundaries. Benny can be friends with anyone and there are no limits placed on him of what he can learn. He has surprised us all. When we came I felt constant gratitude to the school for allowing him to learn among his peers. It was not long before the staff began to work consciously to rid me of this feeling, replacing it slowly but steadily with a new vision of a community that grew with us, becoming something new and beautiful.

I began to reflect on the many misconceptions about inclusion, some of which I harbored even after making this move. I see on the bridge that it is not a program that benefits only those with disabilities. It is a philosophy that drives a community and allows each member to become his or her own person. It is a school without categories, a class where children learn without labels, and a place where great moments happen because everyone is encouraged to develop individual talents. It provides rich and stimulating classrooms that are able to turn into new places, reactive to all the children in the room. It opens up to a world where a group of parents, children, and even a grandpa come together to celebrate a birthday over the East River, walking miles, sweating, discovering one of the greatest sights in the city, sharing stories and making memories. It is a world where Benny can share his knowledge of trains, subways and buses. It is a world that has grown larger, because Benny is a part of it and not in spite of it. Boulder did this, and it is a school that has enabled Adam to flourish as well.

It was a bittersweet moment there on the bridge, there together with our new community, overlooking a city of splendor. I realized that my city which, despite its riches, does not offer the simple gift of acceptance to students like Benny. Its school system still feels threatened by different children, despite their tremendous potential to influence the transformation of classrooms.

***

This chapter begins with the failure of friendships between Benny and other children, and ends with his success. The journey toward socialization with peers both inside and outside of school was long and unpredictable. Additionally, Diane highlights the related social ostracization experienced by parents of children with disabilities. There is a distinct parallel between how children are treated by nondisabled peers and how parents of children with disabilities are treated by their nondisabled peers, as if contaminated by association, a form of stigma identified by Goffman (1963). What shocks Diane is the hierarchy of stigma within special education, when another parent rejects the possibility of a play date in the park with Benny, because her own son was "higher functioning."

Hierarchies within minority identities are highly problematic as they ultimately oppress from within, reflecting a subscription into the master narrative of what is acceptable, desirable, and "normal." In brief, hierarchies within minority identities are paradoxical as they actually reinforce what is being resisted; in attempting to assert one's identity, the minority "group" fragments into layers of sub-categories, with those who approximate the oppressor's standards more likely to assert relative normalcy and attempt to assimilate. The assimilation will always be surface, however, as the fundamental ideology that upholds the hierarchy has not been challenged. For example, within African-American culture, there has been a historical privileging of lighter skin, with darker skinned people viewed less favorably, unsuitable for marriage than lighter-skinned counterparts (Hochschild & Weaver, 2007). The origins of these different layers of skin color are intertwined with the practice of slavery and racial apartheid, and still exist in contemporary times. Likewise, in the LGBTQ communities, historically, gay men distanced themselves from transgendered people, believing them to hurt "the cause" of equality recognized been homosexual and heterosexual people (Weiss, 2010). In both of these cases we see that in a desire for equality by a minority group, within that group some members are more valued than others. What is interesting within this phenomenon is the desire to approximate the existing "norm" or societal ideal. Thus, the closer to whiteness, the closer to heterosexual males, within African-American and LGBTQ communities respectively, reifies the ideal citizen and maintains oppressive ideologies and practices.

As noted disabilities studies scholar Garland Thomson has pointed out, the ideal American citizen is male, middle-class, Christian, heterosexual, English-speaking, athletic, and able-bodied (1997). Diane's attempt to reach out to another parent revealed hierarchies within the disability world, in which the mild, moderate, and severe/multiple categories of disability exist as if layers in an inverted triangle, with the largest group (mild) at the top, the smallest group (severe/ multiple at the bottom), and a middle space between (moderate). Those at the top are the closest to the norm or ideal citizen, and subsequently disassociate from those in categories "below" them (in addition to sometimes rejecting people in the same category, lest they are reminded of their disability). It is perplexing that our educational system is organized into such reductive categories. It is even more troubling that the labels given tend to determine how that child is looked at in his or her entirety, including future "performance." The descriptors such as "low functioning" strongly imply a predetermined capability. Like African-American community members who resist racism, and LGBTQ community members who resist hetero-normativity and transphobia, people who are disabled or have disabled family members should resist ableist discourses that, simply put, position disabled people as inferior. Of course we all should work against these forces. What Diane's recollection revealed are the fears of "My child is not like your child, therefore I am not like you." All of the prejudices mentioned, including ableism, create systems of denied potential, including possible friendships among all people. Diane shares the incident of being denied a play date was one of "…the very lowest points for me on this journey. If my son could not secure a play date with another child with a disability, with whom he had a rapport, then what options would he have with any other more typical child?" Here, we witness the insularity of Diane and David's world—and more importantly, Benny's world—created, in part, by other parents, and the segregated school system in which they are obliged to be in.

We also see the psychological toll placed upon parents as they come to self-inscribe into the limited roles assigned to them when positioned by others in the community. In these recollections of failed attempts to be with other parents and contribute to the socialization of each other's children, Diane describes feeling "a darkness," symbolizing what could be a host of things, including—sadness, isolation, an inability to see and understand in ways she hoped to, uncertainty about the way forward, and so on. She notes, "While I tried to pin the darkness on others, and perhaps it originated with them, I could not escape the fact that I was guilty too; that there still existed a part of me that did not yet believe that my son deserved to have a best friend." In this frank explanation, we see how perceptions of her son by people came to be internalized by Diane, eroding the belief and drive she had to educate Benny with typical children. No wonder she felt isolated and at a loss in the darkest hour

And yet, the friendships that evolved organically after Benny's changing schools is an integral part of this whole story. He became used to other kids; other kids became used to him. Mark is able to coax Benny out from his usual place under the slide examining the nuts and bolts, and he then comes to Benny's home. He knows Benny needs space and time; Mark appears to be a problem-solver by nature. And, like all of us, he has his own quirks. I have been given pause to think several times during this text, contemplating children's responses to difference. The phrase, "Out of the mouth of babes," or a variation, "From the mouth of babes," comes to mind. An example of it can be found in Mark's gentle castigation of Diane when she noted how long it took for Benny to ride a bicycle, "Ms. Berman, don't speak like that. It does not matter how long it took, it matters that he got here." He's supporting his friend because he knows Benny did the best he could do. And made it. Did the time it took really merit mentioning?

A tenet of DSE is to "promote social justice, equitable and inclusive educational opportunities, and full and meaningful access to all aspects of society for people labeled with disability/disabled people" (Connor, et al., 2008, p. 448). One aspect of society that we sometimes do not sufficiently articulate in the educational literature is friendship. When parents of children with disabilities are made to feel like pariahs, it can be anxiety-inducing when making efforts to be part of the larger school community of other parents and children (Valle, 2009). And yet parents of disabled children must, as without opportunities, their children's potential will never become known. When Mark's mini-meltdown occurred because he had paint on his clothes, Benny's response was apt, leaving Diane to concur, "He may have flagged a few diagnoses, but these labels do not define him. Despite dismal scores on measures of social awareness Benny knew just how to be a friend to Mark."

At this juncture I want to foreground a tenet of DSE that "Recognizes the embodied/aesthetic experiences of people whose lives/selves are made meaningful as disabled, as well as troubles the school and societal discourses that position such experiences as 'othered' to an assumed normate" (Connor et al. 2008, p. 448). In some ways, this is what I believe we are doing in this book. By studying the lived experiences of Benny and his family, we see ways in which he shifts from what 'othering' mainstream disability discourses may stereotypically view as "a burden" to the community to being a participant and contributor of knowledge within that community. His experiences, including how he has come to understand and move through the world, to problem-solve, to learn, and to socialize, helps us recognize that there are other ways of being and doing that have not been articulated and recognized within the field of education. These are actual situations for us to study and learn from, as we "recognize[s] and privilege[s] the knowledge derived from the lived experience of people with disabilities" (p. 448).

In Looking at "individual understandings of disability" as an example of DSE at work, we see the emergence of Benny's self-understanding. Diane's own knowledge of Benny also points to how family members come to their own individual understandings of disability that are highly contextualized, and in this case, open ended—without the imposition of a glass ceiling. Because of these factors, groundwork is being set for supporting Benny "in the development of a positive disability identity" (ibid, p. 449), something that will be discussed at greater length in a later chapter.

One of the major foci of DSE is that it "Predominantly focuses upon political, social, cultural, historical, and individual understandings of disability" (ibid., p. 448). By focusing on multiple realms, we see ways in which disability is impacted by, and impacts upon, various ways of understanding differences among humans. By contemplating the individual and social understandings of disability in particular, this chapter also reveals the politics of disability. For example, we see ways in which our systems are structured and the impact it has on people inside and outside of those systems, how power operates to further segregate within existing segregation, and how the environment enables or disables friendships between parents and between children. We also recognize the power that friendships bring. Among many things, they open up a world of possibilities in terms of gaining knowledge, self-confidence, and feeling part of a community.

Diane observes, "We have moved on to a world where there are no boundaries. Benny can be friends with anyone and there are no limits placed on him of what he can learn. He has surprised us all." Given the previous experiences within segregated settings, it is unsurprising that now, it seems as if Benny's life will be exponentially better—because of shifting from actual containment to virtual freedom. This chapter raises again the specter of the child Benny would be, had he stayed in District 75, most likely a child without friends or at best only having friends with other children "on the spectrum." At Boulder, the forging of a mutually respectful organic friendship, the acceptance of Benny's interests in transport, and access to a variety of typical children in class and on the playground, coalesced into providing him with opportunities to grow and develop socially in ways that nobody could have predicted.

The rituals of showing friends around Manhattan and explaining transportation systems, including how to get from point A to B on a map, place Benny in a leadership role. The annual trip to the city is an enjoyable ritual where his peers see Benny sharing what is valuable to him and of interest to them. It is these instances of inclusive education both within and beyond the walls of schooling that carry such importance for what is known as "The Hidden Curriculum" (Glossary of Education, 2014). In brief, the hidden curriculum is a concept that conveys all of the knowledge students come to learn within school that is outside of the formal curriculum, particularly the social dynamics of power, including who is valued and devalued in society. What Benny's peers are learning all the time by being with him is how humans can be noticeably different, and that is simply a part of diversity. Disability is therefore not something that is hidden, shunned, made fun of, placed into a hierarchy of worth. It has many faces. In this case, the face is Benny. He may be different in some respects, yet he is similar to his peers in many other ways. Those differences are not transformed into "a big deal" for his peers, who will be far less likely to be puzzled, embarrassed, or feel awkward, and much more informed when involved in other social situations with people who have notable differences.

As schools simultaneously reflect and shape society, there are some strong implications for the need to continue promoting disability as diversity, in ways big and small (Salend, 2007). As with many educators, Diane's constant thinking about inclusive education has left her refining those thoughts. She shares, "I began to reflect on the many misconceptions about inclusion, some of which I harbored even after making this move. I see on the bridge that it is not a program that benefits only those with disabilities, it is a philosophy that drives a community and allows each member to become his or her own person." Indeed inclusive education is a philosophy and has been claimed as such from its inception (Lipsky & Gardner, 1997; Skrtic & Sailor, 1996; Villa & Thousand, 1995), helping educators to understand the humanist rationale undergirding the ideology. While philosophy is important to keep us grounded, we also have to focus on the practice of what constitutes inclusive education, otherwise cynics dismiss it as merely an unreachable ideal (Kauffman & Hallahan, 1995). Perhaps it is, but then again, the same thing can be said about true democracy. In fact, it can easily be argued that inclusive education is part of a true democracy, as it will always be a work in progress, created by people in a specific time and place.

References

Connor, D. J., Gabel, S. L., Gallagher, D. & Morton, M. (2008). Disability studies and inclusive education--Implication for theory, research, and practice: Guest editor's introduction. *International Journal of Inclusive Education*, 12(5–6), 441–457.

Garland-Thomson, R. (1997). *Extraordinary bodies*. New York: Columbia University Press.

Glossary of Education (2014). http://edglossary.org/hidden-curriculum/

Goffman, E. (1963). *Stigma: Notes on the management of spoiled identity*. New York: Simon & Schuster.

Hochschild, J. L. & Weaver, V. (2007). The skin color paradox and the American racial order. *Social Forces*, 86(2), 643–670.

Kauffman, J. M., & Hallahan, D. P. (1995). *The illusion of full inclusion*. Austin, Texas: Pro-Ed.

Lipsky, D. K., & Gartner, A. (1997). Historical background of inclusive education. In D. K. Lipsky & A. Gartner (Eds.) *Inclusion and school reform: Transforming America's classrooms* (pp. 73–83). Baltimore, MD: Paul H. Brookes.

Skrtic, T., & Sailor, W. (1996). Voice, collaboration, and inclusion: Democratic themes in educational and social reform initiatives. *Remedial and Special Education*, 17(3), 142–157.

Salend, S. (2007). *Creating inclusive classrooms: Effective and reflective practices for all students* (6th ed.). Upper Saddle River, NJ: Pearson.

Valle, J. W. (2009). *What mothers say about special education: From the 1960s to the present*. London: Palgrave McMillan.

Villa, R. A., & Thousand, J. (1995). *Creating an inclusive school*. Alexandria, VA: Council for Supervision and Curriculum Development.

Weiss, J. T. (2010, July 20). Transphobia in the gay community. *Bilerico Report on LGBTQ Nation*. http://bilerico.lgbtqnation.com/2010/07/transphobia_in_the_gay_community.php

· 8 ·

COMMUNICATION: BALANCING HIGH
EXPECTATIONS WITH ACCEPTANCE

Second grade began for me with excitement and trepidation. The success of Benny in grade one put him in a position where the depth of his earlier delays was not so apparent. He ended grade one with great pride in his ability to function within the classroom. I had been intrigued with Barbara, Benny's second grade teacher, for years before he entered her classroom. She was involved with coordinating the district wide math program and led the math club. My experiences as an adjunct at the City University of New York taught me that few elementary school teachers had a passion for mathematics. She also had a reputation for transforming her students through the course of the year. Since Boulder has an open door policy, where parents are welcome and invited to come in whenever they want, I was often walked through the halls. Whenever I passed Barbara's class I was conscious of the distinctly different atmosphere that permeated her room and seeped into the hallway right out-side her door. Somehow from the first few minutes before the school day began until well after the bell ended the day, her students were actively pursuing their education. While other classrooms teamed with morning activities, kids jumping around taking off their winter hats, putting their lunches away, and sharpening their pencils, Barbara had already begun to teach. She might be huddled with a few students going over an essay or article, while others sat

quietly absorbed in some sort of activity. Many days the entire class would be sitting together in silence on the carpet listening to a story that tied into their math or science lesson and also reflected some current movement in the world. I saw her charges leaving at the end of the day with cakes and cookies they baked, and potholders woven on a real loom. I wondered how she had time for all of these hands-on activities with the pressure to teach more and more seemed to slice these extras right out of the curriculum. Barbara's classes appeared to exist in a parallel universe and I was excited that Benny would have the chance to be in them. At the same time I felt curious as to why they placed him, a child with so many delays, in the class of the most academic teacher in the school, if not the district.

With Barbara's reputation for academic excellence comes one for disorganization. Her desk is cluttered; she loses papers, doesn't keep track of the time, often dismissing her class last of all. Parents waiting for their children speak about her and wonder what she does with them from 3:26 when the bell rings until 3:45 when they finally emerge. They come out slowly, one at a time, as they pass lugubriously from the world inside her room back into the world where their parents whisk them off to their afterschool activities. People speak of these attributes as if they are independent mutually exclusive traits. It is only now that I have begun to appreciate them as, instead, two inextricably intertwined features of a teacher who is not hemmed in by tradition.

It was only the second day of school when I first realized that this would be a year of challenge for Barbara, Benny and me. Benny lumbered out of school looking drained. Barbara followed and caught my eye. She knew I was hungry for feedback and told me, with a certain amount of disappointment in her voice, that the days are long for Benny. Tempted to say that the days are longer in her class than in any other, I wore a complacent smile, silently fighting back, justifying, making excuses, missing the easy days of first grade. I felt as though the evenings should be a time for Benny to recoup. I was sure that the homework was too taxing and while we would sit a few minutes and look it over, as soon as he would tumble out of his chair and moan, I would close the books and pat his head.

While he still had modifications for length on his IEP, I noticed that Barbara sent him home with the entire sheet of math problems and the same number of spelling words as his peers. I made a mental note to discuss this with her, but somehow felt a little intimidated by her piercing eyes and penchant for speaking at length to parents. A few weeks into the year she sent a note home reprimanding me for routinely sending in Benny without his homework complete. I called her to discuss and mentioned his delays and long list of diagnoses. She was quiet. "Well," she said with an irrepressible sweetness in her voice, "He could probably do at least a bit more than he is doing...and maybe if he did he might be more engaged in class." She went on to tell me how listless Benny was, how he mainly stared out the window and did not pick up a pencil to do any work unless she or his aide was right by his side. I was not surprised or even bothered by this news. She, however, was stunned by my complacency. Sensitive to the delicate nature of relationship that we had already established, she did not let on the extent of her surprise, but through the periodic lull in conversation and the softness of the silence filled with unspoken questions, I could sense it.

Just a few days later we met by accident at the entrance to the school. We were both in a hurry. Nevertheless, we stopped for a long while and repeated the conversation we had had days before. This time I was prepared, able to expand and augment my case. I spoke with a confident air, a mother who loves her child but knows her child's limits and accepts the grim prognosis. Barbara spoke with airy voice, a tone searching for direction, for answers to questions about Benny, about me, and about how to best use his time in her classroom this year. Like an aria straight out of the great operatic literature, we spoke around each other for a while until we come together in an epiphany of sorts.

Barbara:	"I don't have time to chat; I am late to a tutoring job."
Me:	"And I am late to pick up my boys..."

We pause in the doorway, lingering for a while until we both start to speak.

Me:	"I want you to know I appreciate that you care so much...it is just that you probably don't really know how limited Benny is."
Barbara:	"Well, you mentioned that on the phone, I am just trying to make sure that he is growing within my class, that I am not wasting his time, you know. I have a responsibility to him, to help him grow in some way."
Me:	"Well he has been evaluated by several top doctors and they all agreed that he had little academic promise. I moved him here for the social opportunities mainly, to go to birthday parties, to learn to sit through a class. He is doing great in many ways."
Barbara:	"Okay...well, that is wonderful, but in class he just sits by the window and stares. Perhaps he can still be more involved in the class. That is all I am saying. Even when I give him modified work, he seldom even tries. I feel like I am wasting six hours a day for him. What can I do to engage him in something, anything, while I am teaching the rest of the children?"

Me:	"I am just afraid if we push too hard he will turn off to school completely or become a behavioral nightmare. He has a history of impulsivity, you know."
Barbara:	"His behavior has been exemplary, actually. Gary (Benny's aide since Kindergarten) and I even question whether he needs medication, at this point. Maybe if we take him off it he would be more involved. Maybe this is something we could try."
Me:	(Shocked) "Did you see him in Kindergarten, running clear out of the school into the parking lot?"
Barbara:	"He is older now, he has grown. It might be nice to try him without medication for a few weeks."
Me:	"That we should discuss with the school psychologist."
Me:	"I just think you need to know that he has already accomplished all I hoped for when we moved. He can read, write a little, and he can function in a group...that is more than I ever imagined for him."
Barbara:	"I hear you and I am impressed with your ability to accept his limitations. At the same time I wonder why this is enough for you."

And there in the doorway I finally was speechless. I had no response to this comment. Our short conversation had become long. She had accepted and understood me, and then challenged me with a few simple words. We each shifted in our shoes, turned toward each other, speaking with our eyes as there were no more words to be said at the moment. Inside my head I continued the conversation, speaking slowly and patiently to myself. The truth was I was elated that Benny had made it through two years in an inclusive classroom, defying the odds and the predictions of others.

Benny's success socially and behaviorally at Boulder seemed to be a gift. To ask for more seemed petty. After spending years hearing that he would never read or function in an appropriate manner, I was thrilled to pieces that he could make it through the day without a hitch. I was amazed that he could read at all, delighted that he could write his own name. I thought that I had no right to expect more and had no desire to raise the bar. He had come so far. All I wanted to do was to celebrate yet Barbara wanted to push him further. Barbara saw Benny as a young child filled with potential. I was tired and worn out, felt that he had eclipsed his potential. His first seven years seemed the longest seven years of my life. I was bruised, walking around with wounds still open and perceived her to some degree as a threat to Benny's happiness and the limited success that I deemed possible for him. I saw Barbara's optimism as dangerous and her hope for him as a failure to accept, but hope is exactly what was needed giving him a chance to learn.

The conversation we started that day went on for weeks. I began to understand my role and responsibilities. I did not want to face more disappointment with regard to Benny and wished only to love him and to cherish his abilities. Yet I had an obligation to keep pushing him to engage in life and learning. Barbara alerted me to the injustice we would be doing to give up on him so soon. She knew that a child craves a challenge that human nature is to learn and move forward. I recalled the words of a top developmental pediatrician who warned me that academic challenges would lead to behavior problems as frustration would inevitably ensue. Instead, what Barbara knew intuitively was that leaving him idle on the side of a classroom was the ticket to future disaster. She realized that we had to find a way to get him involved.

We considered her suggestion to take him off his medication for ADHD. Tony could attest to the extreme change in his behavior that he felt that could not be due only to medication. Together they appealed to me to try him without his half dose of Focalin. As a teacher myself I was aware at how monumental this request really was. Teachers often do not look to have hyperactive children in their midst. Usually, the opposite occurs as teachers push parents in subtle and unsubtle ways to medicate their child. Since Benny suffered few side effects, I was stunned by Barbara's willingness to deal with the impulsivity and hyperactivity that would inevitably result in exchange for having a more alert, involved child in her classroom. David and I decided to listen to Barbara and Gary's appeal and took Benny off his medication.

Within a few weeks Barbara invited me on a field trip to the Old Bethpage Restoration Village, in part, to help keep Benny safe. I rode a yellow school bus with the group, against district policy I am sure. Benny sat with Jackson and they laughed the entire time. Barbara was delighted to see Benny animated and came by my seat to tell me how lovely it was to see him engaged with a friend. I was trying to understand the Benny she saw each day and she was trying to understand the child I knew at home. She stood by my seat for the entire ride, swaying with the bus, hanging on to the seat ahead, which struck me as somewhat unsafe, as she teetered in the aisles], grabbing on to the seats on either side of the bus for balance. Barbara stayed even when conversation petered out, waiting patiently, for more opportunities to learn about Benny. I was unsure at first how much to share as I did not quite trust her yet. She asked me question after question about Benny and also about Adam. Barbara was interested in every aspect of our lives, especially about why we decided to move to this town. At the time I was surprised at her level of interest. It was a few weeks later that I realized she was determined to find a way to reach Benny and the more information she had, the better equipped she would be to find a stronger connection with both of us. She knew that without a connection there was little hope, that both she and I individually held an incomplete perspective on Benny, and that only by coming together could we integrate the pieces and move forward. Barbara was on a mission to bring about a transformation of momentous proportions. I felt I was cowering in the sand, but that day in the bus I saw the resolve in Barbara's eyes and began to open myself to the possibilities she had in mind.

A few more weeks passed and we convened for a parent-teacher conference. It was a cold winter day with a bright blue sky. We numbered eight people: Benny's entire team of therapists arrived for the 30-minute meeting. We had barely enough time for everyone to give a brief report without leaving time to discuss the issues that had been circulating for months. Barbara was still unhappy with Benny's output. She felt he could be doing more work and I sensed for a while that she was pushing him too far. I was sure that her insistence on connecting with Benny was pushing him away. I also felt that somehow while her expectations began too high, they were now falling too low, no doubt because of his failure to produce. Somehow I assumed she would be able to appreciate his intelligence even in light of the fact that in class he did virtually nothing. Barbara mentioned his inability to do simple math but I knew that he was catching on, and that he liked to skip-count by many different amounts at home. I also realized I was being completely contradictory. I wanted her to back off and let him be. Yet it irritated me when I realized she was beginning to accept what I had been telling her for months, that he had little ability academically. Despite my attitude, she expressed no desire and no inclination to stop the conversation and kept talking with no end in sight.

After the scheduled conference all of the therapists, except for Cara, left. She sat there with a quiet presence that told me she was in it for the long haul. At the time I had no idea how long this haul would actually be. Cara remained largely silent, casting a calm amongst the group even as she herself was filled with tension, betrayed in the way her arms would flit from one position to another. Cara's lips, too, would tighten and release as the conversation got stressful. Her eyes remained brown pools of calm, to into which I looked when needing to breathe. I knew then that she would not leave until we were done. My mother-in-law was watching the boys and called to see where we were and when we might be done. I told her that I did not know when exactly we might be home. The conversation was circling now and it seemed that we had little direction. Barbara sighed periodically. She tilted her head to the side as she tried to see things from my perspective. We spoke in contradictions as we twisted in and around each other's words. I wanted her to stop pushing, but to see his brilliance. She wanted me to raise my expectations and to support what she was trying to do in the classroom. Even though this conference was a difficult one for me and tension tightened my throat, I realized that I was in that timeless place I had circled around for years with no ticking clock and no end to this conversation in sight. Little else existed for me in the space of that room, and the world outside those walls whirled by in dull, washed-out muffled scenes. Clark came on the loudspeaker to tell us all that conferences had ended. Teachers went home, one by one. Their cars started up and flashing headlights streaked the windows as they drove by. The dark sky settled into a deep and icy purple. My entire world filled the classroom. David, Cara, Barbara and I worked towards an elusive prize. We were focused only on one goal, spinning in dizzying circles as we tried to reach toward Benny's growth in disparate and seemingly contradictory ways. I felt exhausted and even resentful. I realized that I was experiencing the magic of Barbara's classroom--the focus, the intensity, the way her students disappear into her room and enter another space to come out only when the time is right, not when the clock reaches a certain point, not when a bell rings, arbitrarily marking a boundary to which we have been conditioned to adhere. The students come out when their questions have been heard, when they have reached closure on the day's topic, or when somehow the conversation begins to taper as it finally did for us after what could have been any number of hours, the exact total of which I am still unsure.

When we finally lumbered out of the room, my legs felt stiff, my bones tired. As Cara walked alongside us down the hall, though undoubtedly as exhausted as the rest of us, she mentioned again how nicely Benny had been doing in Occupational Therapy how he spells long words while jumping on the trampoline. I asked Cara if she could possibly practice some math facts while Benny jumps, remembering how sensory stimulation helped him learn to speak. She agreed, her eyes now reaching out with tenderness.

We walked home on a bitterly cold and very dark night. I ached for Benny and the struggles that lay ahead for him. Here within one classroom, in the space of a few months, he had been both underestimated and also pushed too far. It seemed so hard to get the balance right for him even in a world where everyone was trying their hardest.

The effects of the conference were felt at the end of the very next day. Cara and Barbara were standing excitedly at the door, waiting to fill me in on the recent events. Cara did just as we discussed and found that Benny could skip-count by many numbers to 100 and beyond. Early in the day Cara had taken Benny to the trampoline and had him skip count first by 2's, and 3's, then 4's, 5's, and 6's. She called Barbara to come and see right away. Barbara could not believe it as she had suspected that perhaps I was exaggerating Benny's strengths. Seeing him skip count was not enough for Barbara, so she had him write several trains of numbers on the board in the OT room. When he completed that task she had him come back to the classroom and write them on the board there. As Barbara described for me these tasks, tension grew within. I was waiting for the part when Benny falls apart, fails to function. She relayed to me with a smile in her eyes that she wanted him to transfer the skill to the classroom, and eventually to his own workspace. Barbara had him open his notebook and then write the rhythmic patterns with his pencil, one of the first contributions he had made to his book. I was sure that at this point Benny broke down, but no she told me that he wrote all the numbers from 1–100 in sequence, by 2's and 3's, 4's and 5's and even 6's. Barbara was triumphant.

It was within days of that experience Benny began to work in all areas of the curriculum. Even though Benny had scored dismally on all measures of fine motor abilities, even though he could barely hold a scissor, he was able to use a loom. It makes little sense to our brains wired to expect linear growth, but it is one of the most powerful arguments for inclusion I have seen yet.

Second grade continued to be a year of unparalleled growth for me as well as for Benny. I learned that he was capable of academics. I saw that he could work hard and produce quality within that work. Barbara continued to question his medication and, by the end of grade two, he was off it completely. She preferred to deal with his impulsivity in exchange for a livelier child. As Benny's strength grew in the academic areas, he was able to sit and attend for longer periods of time. When he needed breaks, his aid was there to take Benny for brisk walks through the hallways.

When the year ended, I was worried, nervous about the demands ahead in grade three. An assistant teacher from another class saw the anxiety in my eyes at the end-of-year barbeque. She came over and put her arm around me, saying, "Don't worry about next year. Benny's growth is coming from within, and it will continue regardless of which classroom he happens to be in." To this day those words resonate within my heart and mind, and to this day those words continue to reflect the reality of his progress. The entire school was committed to Benny's success and that is why an assistant for another class felt compelled to speak to me. This shared vision, this way that the entire community shouldered responsibility for all of the children, is part of the magic of Boulder school.

***

Some years ago, a colleague who worked for New York State Education Department and supported inclusive education often had to present to what I'd consider hostile audiences comprised of educators. I say this with full respect for teachers and administrators who are asked on a daily basis to do too much with too little, and are always subjected to changes in educational policies, usually without their input. For many educators, inclusion becomes "the last straw to break the camel's back," as they sit listening to what should happen in their current environments that already overstretch them. I recall educators in these audiences having mixed feelings about inclusive education. In analyzing them, I'd always look at the proverbial glass as "half full," seeing dedicated professionals who would like to do more for students with disabilities (and, all students for that matter). However, they conveyed a desire to variously be given a roadmap, an instructional manual, a blueprint, or connect-the-dots approaches to inclusive education. As practitioners without enough time already, I understood their expectation and this request. At the same time, I know that the answer lies somewhere "in between" what's known about inclusion in general, and what's known about inclusion in their specific context. My colleague from the New York State Education Department explained this situation in a simple, memorable way. She said problem solving within inclusive classes was like finding the best way after trying several reasonable approaches, very much like a tired Goldilocks did when she entered the bedroom of the three bears. In trying to find the place where she'd be most comfortable, the first bed seemed too hard, the next bed seemed too soft, but third one seemed just right. The idea of trying to find the "best" way forward, the middle ground for the student, as agreed upon by parent and teacher is the heart of this chapter.

Although we can share examples of roadmaps, instructional manuals, blueprints, and connect-the-dots approaches, it should be understood that the methods identified as successful are all highly contextualized (Friend & Bursuck, 2002; Salend, 2007). This means that what works in some schools and classrooms may also work well in other classrooms, or partially, or not very well at all. This situation is a major sticking point for educational research interested in "what works" within inclusive education—all education actually—if we view research as scientifically replicable, transferable, and generalizable. It is a well-acknowledged fact that there is a major schism between what researchers claim is effective in terms of teaching and learning, and what educators know to be effective in terms of teaching and learning in classrooms (Ferri, Gallagher, & Connor, 2011). While this disagreement about what works is admittedly a major topic that challenges all stakeholders within educational systems, it is pertinent to foreground it here momentarily. Why? Because even the most rigorous and robust research can only take us so far, and is in essence bound by the limitations in which it occurs. In contrast, the social, historical, and cultural dynamics within classrooms are quite complex, and always in flux, a far cry from the scientific positivist framing of classrooms found in most educational literature. It is the ecology of each classroom that is studied, including the teachers, children, curriculum, expectations, and so on, that gives the most authentic understanding of what can be effective in terms of practices that support student growth academically, socially, and emotionally in inclusive settings (Speece & Keogh, 1996).

Barbara is a teacher who is very much aware of how to create a classroom ecology that encompasses all children and immerses them in learning. She is a highly respected professional, to the point of appearing intimidating to parents, even self-advocates such as Diane. What makes this chapter interesting is the intersection of two phenomena, (1) finding the right balance for Benny in terms of his learning and, (2) the teacher-parent relationship in agreeing upon what constitutes the right balance. In this case, the disequilibrium between the latter and the former reveals a watershed moment in both teacher and parent understanding of Benny.

It is somewhat ironic, although also understandable, that Diane's view of Benny had plateaued after what she describes as the seven longest years of her life. There is more than a hint of exhaustion, of being battered down by professionals' erroneous prognoses, of surviving a school system that negatively impacted her child, of clinging to "signs," managing hopes, facing accusations of being in denial and having false expectations. At this juncture, Diane is content in accepting where Benny is, as he has come so much further than she and David expected.

Enter Barbara with a reputation of being one of the finest teachers in the district. Barbara welcomes Benny to her class, and wants to connect with him more than is currently expected of them both, in order to expand his thinking. She does not accept the premise that Benny is doing well enough, stating, "… in class he just sits by the window and stares, perhaps he can still be more involved in the class, that is all I am saying." Diane feels defensive. Somehow, without her realizing it, the roles have been reversed. The teacher is now the advocate that is pushing Benny's academics, and Diane fears repercussions in the form of his returning meltdowns. She thus fortifies herself for the next interchange with Barbara sharing, "This time I was prepared and I was able to expand and augment my case. I spoke with a confident air, a mother who loves her child but knows her child's limits and accepts the grim prognosis."

Yet Barbara did not accept the child's limits and grim prognosis. Diane had closed the door, but Barbara wanted it opened. When she said to Diane, "I hear you and I am impressed with your ability to accept his limitations. At the same time I wonder why this is enough for you," Diane is stunned into silence. At that point in time, all that she had fought for had somehow evaporated, leaving her content with what she currently had for Benny, without wanting more. And Barbara was questioning why. It is an example of something we all have faced, I imagine. Challenging abelism, sexism, racism, and so on, is not a one-way street. Our prejudices can be unconscious, doubling back on us to seep in gradually, leaving us in places where we cannot see them, including our day-to-day habits of thinking. That is, until another person points them out, leaving us in shock, mortified at how we appear to that person. Diane states that Barbara, "had accepted and understood me, and then challenged me with a few simple words… The truth was I was elated that Benny had made it through two years in an inclusive classroom, defying the odds and the predictions of others." Tired from the seven-year journey, Diane had sat down. Barbara made her stand back up. In reflecting on this moment, it is worth revisiting Diane's words:

> I thought that I had no right to expect more, no desire to raise the bar. He had come so far. All I wanted to do was to celebrate, yet Barbara wanted to push him further…I was bruised, walking around with wounds still open and perceived her to some degree as a threat to Benny's happiness and the limited success that I deemed possible for him. I saw her optimism as dangerous and her hope for him as a failure to accept, but hope is exactly what was needed giving him a chance to learn.

In this description we witness an example of what could variously be called the complexities of, or in everyday terms "the messiness" of, inclusive education. It is a precarious balance that Diane is striving for—to push her child, but not to the point where the strain will make him repeatedly break down at school and at home, as it had done so in the past. At that particular time, she saw Benny as doing fine, and was resisting Barbara's suggestion to encourage further growth. It is a powerful and painful experience for Diane to realize that—at this moment in time—Barbara had more hope for her son's growth and development than she did. Among many things, I am left wondering, to what degree do our school systems promote or remove hope that then becomes internalized by parents?

I was always been taken by title of President Obama's book, *The Audacity of Hope* (2008) that offers an intriguing pairing of two concepts not usually brought together. Hope signifies what is wanted or desired, indicating a sense of optimism, a trust, confidence that things will "turn out for the best." Although things may not always reach the desired outcome, there can be satisfaction in striving toward approximating what is believed to be "for the best." Audacity indicates a form of boldness or daring so strong that is imbued with arrogance, shamelessness, and even insolence. In some ways, it is this degree of hope, this audacity—relentless and driving, in the face of what's socially accepted—that I also associate with inclusive education. While she would perhaps not identify herself in these exact terms, as a person possessing the audacity of hope, Barbara's disposition as a teacher conveys these sentiments. In her daily practices she seeks to engage all of her students, including what many teachers may term "the most challenging" children, in finding a way to move to their next level. As Diane states, "Barbara alerted me to the injustice we would be doing to give up on him so soon. She knew that a child craves a challenge, that human nature is to learn and to move forward."

Hope is a concept that does not seem to be sufficiently discussed within education. It is predictably viewed as unscientific. After all, how can hope be measured, controlled, predicted? Yet hope is what we hold each day in almost everything we do, and this has implications for both teachers and parents, especially when they come together to discuss learning possibilities for the child they hold in common. As this chapter has shown, the interactions between teacher and parent are not predictable. Each one has a certain understanding of the child, holding different pieces of the puzzle that need to fit together in deciding what's the best way forward for now.

The IEP meeting Diane describes, where she, Barbara, and six others, sit to discuss Benny's current progress and generate future goals and objectives, is a painful experience for her. The contrasting or opposing views to be processed and considered, the push-and-pull of negotiations, the accrued years of asking for services and placements that may or may not be approved, all have taken their toll. Despite these dynamics, Diane feels somewhat stationary, stating, "I realized that I was in that timeless place I had circled around for years with no ticking clock and no end to this conference in sight." Here we see the intensity of IEP meetings for parents, particularly those who disagree with what school personnel suggest. Barbara's gentle audacity disarmed Diane, a proven fighter who described herself during this period of time to be "cowering in the sand." Diane wanted time for Benny to decompress after school, to pursue his own interests and hobbies, rather than being weighted down by math homework without any modifications, and run the risk of regressive behavior. Yet this period of time, and the IEP conference, proved to be a major crossroads of sorts. It was the unexpected meeting of the minds between a mother who had been historically ground down—currently at a low ebb, yet content with her lot—and a teacher with unequivocally high expectations who encouraged that mother to open herself up "to the possibilities she had in mind." What comes to the fore in this episode is how parent-teacher relations are crucial in brokering the future fate of the child, and how important it is for these discussions to remain open and ongoing, an informed form of trial and error, to find the balance that constitutes the best support for students.

As is this case with Benny, while decisions about inclusive education can be influenced by roadmaps, instructional manuals, blue prints or connect-the-dots approaches, authentic responses are highly context-specific to individuals. There were no clear and readymade answers at Boulder, but with all stakeholders working together, the dots became connected. Skip counting while jumping on the trampoline served as a springboard (no pun intended) to Benny, revealing his existing knowledge and using that as the basis for his further growth.

In addition to hope, this part of the narrative also brings up trust. Barbara sought Diane's trust, and although Diane was reluctant to give it, she eventually did, witnessing Barbara's genuine desire to help push Benny academically, as well as socially. Diane notes, "…that day in the bus I saw the resolve in her eyes and began to open myself to the possibilities she had in mind." Barbara disposition is another example of DSE, as she "assume[s] competence and reject deficit models of disability," (Connor, et. al., 2008, p. 448). Furthermore, in Barbara's classroom, "Disability is primarily recognized and valued as a natural part of human diversity," (p. 449); she feels it her responsibility to advocate for, and facilitate each student's academic capabilities so they reach their next level, rejecting "functional" glass ceilings imposed upon them. Finally, teacher and parents come to agree to at least try Benny without his prescribed medication. It could have gone either way, but the result was that Benny did not need to be medicated. His teacher understood, and worked with, his ups and downs and energy flows, preventing environmental disablement. Being willing to try a solution based upon an informed, responsible decision shared by teachers and parents, and be agreeable to modify that decision if need be, exemplifies how inclusion should not be the straw that broke the camel's back, but rather a welcome, professional challenge to find what makes sense in terms of finding the best choice in supporting the student. That's the behind-the-scenes dispositions of educators working together that create the "magic" Diane refers to. It is also part of the intrinsic satisfaction of being a teacher.

References

Connor, D. J., Gabel, S. L., Gallagher, D. & Morton, M. (2008). Disability studies and inclusive education--Implication for theory, research, and practice: Guest editor's introduction. *International Journal of Inclusive Education, 12*(5–6), 441–457.

Ferri, B., Gallagher, D., & Connor, D. J. (2011). Pluralizing methodologies in the field of LD: From "what works" to what matters. *Learning Disability Quarterly, 34*(3), 222–231.

Friend, M., & Bursuck, W. D. (2002). *Including students with special needs: A practical guide for classroom teachers.* Boston, MA: Allyn & Bacon.

Obama, B. (2008). *The audacity of hope: Thoughts on reclaiming the American dream.* New York: Random House.

Salend, S. (2007). *Creating inclusive classrooms: Effective and reflective practices for all students* (6th ed.). Upper Saddle River, NJ: Pearson.

Speece, D. L. & Keogh B. K. (1996). (Eds). *Research on classroom ecologies: Implications for inclusion of children with learning disabilities.* Mahwah, NJ: Lawrence Erlbaum.

· 9 ·

SETTING GOALS: LETTING THE CHILD BE THE GUIDE

The Flagpole, November 2011

Shortly after school is out, children begin to play. The small playground is full and many kids spill over onto the front lawn, which stretches from the entrance of the school to the driveway, spanning the length of the auditorium. The flag waves in the center. This patch of land is not really meant for running feet, as the official field lies in the back of the school, and measures at least twenty times the size. A larger playground also stands in back, but it is hard to convince tired parents to make their way around to the rear. Also this space is bordered on two sides by bushes and rocks, creating nooks and crannies that become fantastical places like castles or ships in the fertile minds of these youngsters.

Today Adam, now in first grade, runs out, drops his book bag and breathlessly announces his plans to meet a friend, Rachel, at the flagpole. They arranged this impromptu play date in the last few seconds of school, and before I can respond he is running towards his friend. She is also in first grade and is wearing all shades of purple today. A certain confidence flows through Rachel's body, from her feet which run securely over the uneven terrain, to her hair which bounces around her head, carelessly flopping from side to side,

with just enough curl to give it character. Adam, while her equal in wit and intelligence, is still very much a child. His large eyes sparkle, and his cheeks flush, as he runs with a bit of a wobble. Some days she takes the lead and they play that she is the queen and he is her servant. He does not protest but his constant frown gives away his displeasure. Today they take the lead together. Half a dozen children gather around the pole with them and wait for Adam and Rachel to make a suggestion. They respond by dancing across the lawn, beginning to use their bodies to make letters that they have studied that day. Adam becomes an "X" with his arms reaching up and legs spread apart. Rachel becomes a "T" as she stands tall with her arms out straight. They warm up with letters and then pull some other kids in so they can spell words. Adam and Rachel patiently remind the others how to stand and create words like "CAT" and "BAT." Soon they are on the ground wiggling their bodies to make more complicated ones. Words with "S" and "J" are more easily done on the ground. Soon there are a dozen kids and together they spell an hours' worth of words, falling to the ground laughing and then rising up with shiny bits of grass decorating their sweaty bodies like confetti. Even the less patient parents with long lists of chores to get done cannot seem to pull their children away from this activity they designed for themselves.

2010–2011 Poetry Chairs

Lucy, Benny's new third grade teacher, is a quiet woman with piercing eyes and a gift for maintaining a highly organized classroom that at the same time throbs with creativity. In many respects similar to me, she is a teacher with 24 years of experience and has two young boys. Lucy had been an avid traveler and incorporates her experiences into her teaching. Her classroom is crowded; she and her students share the space with a collection of what she has termed "poetry chairs." Each year in spring, she rescues an old wooden chair about to be abandoned. She sands it down, makes necessary repairs and repaints the chair. Then each of her students is asked to pick an original poem written this year, type it on a small piece of paper, and paste it to the chair. Lucy then applies a clear lacquer and soon the chair is ready to join its comrades, who stand proudly along the sides of the room or tucked into cozy corners. Together these chairs tell a very personal story about every class that has passed through Lucy's room. This ritual is one that unites the class at the same time as it highlights the individuality of the students, a theme that replays again and again on many levels in Boulder. Even a passerby in the hallway cannot help but be drawn in by the colorful collection of poetry chairs as they resonate with the very same frequency that can be heard and felt year after year, over and over again throughout the hallways of the school.

Lucy began to get to know Benny well before the first days of school in September. She is an avid reader and holds a book club for kids in the district summer program. Even though Benny did not take her class, she spoke to him frequently that summer when they crossed paths. Often she would seek him out early in the morning when the children would line up on the hot and dusty tennis courts outside the middle school where the program was held. She seemed to be a little nervous about having Benny in her class and I yearned for the time when Benny would not arouse any feelings other than normal excitement in his teachers. Yet, I was glad that she was taking her responsibility seriously and not wasting a moment in getting to know him, making sure they were comfortable with each other. Lucy confessed early in the year her anxiety about having Benny is her class along with her delight as she found out quickly that it was easy to read him most of the time and that she was able to find ways to support and challenge him. Third grade progressed with remarkable smoothness. However, at home I began to see a sadness take root in Benny. Winter couldn't seem to turn into spring. A few moments of bright warm sun were followed by dark grey skies and hours of icy rain. Benny seemed sad all the time. He was moody and told me several times that he did not want to go to school. Instead of fighting with him, on a few occasions I took him to work with me, where I teach middle school math. Benny was bright and cheery there, surrounded by older students who were intensely interested in him. He answered their questions; he told them knock- knock jokes. When the time came for my class to get to work, Benny wrote most of my notes on the board and then read them to the class. He spoke with an intensity that I had not heard from him. Benny showed me a self-confidence and pride that pierced me to my toes. I saw a part of him come alive; a voice that demanded to be taken seriously, a desire to connect and to entertain that had lain dormant for years. I began to realize that Benny craved the spotlight in ways I never ever thought possible.

Benny's IEP meeting came in early spring and it was a celebratory event. His scores, while still far below average, rose somewhat in every area and his behavior had become exemplary. His therapists and teachers radiated delight as they reported their own stories of his progress. I knew that Benny needed something from us but I held back, wanting his teachers to enjoy the success he demonstrated on paper. When I picked Benny up after school that day, I told him how happy his teachers were with his progress. He began to cry, deep and heavy. It had been a long time since I had heard him cry like that, maybe not since he was a toddler struggling to imitate a sound. I recognized the sadness as similar to the sadness Benny felt when there was something he wanted to do but could not. His anguish suggested a weighty grief that I suspect touched on and reawakened his pain from the past. At the moment Benny was unable to tell me why he was so sad. I knew, though, that when I relayed the good reports to him, rather than bring him comfort, they triggered a feeling that he was not doing all that he wanted to do, all that he felt he could do.

Teachers and therapists had been able to see Benny tackle more and more topics with increasing ease. But he still was quiet in class. Although he continued to raise his hand as he had in grade two, he was seldom able to answer the questions when called on. Lucy was not quite sure how to handle this, and neither was I. She called on him anyway and gave him extended wait-time, but most of the time he was silent. Every few weeks we would discuss this behavior and neither of us understood it. It was clear that he desired to be called upon and so Lucy continued to do so, even though he seldom gave an answer.

While I strained to find some clues from Benny, conversations over the following few days brought little illumination. I had to wait several weeks until our first truly beautiful spring morning awakened not only our garden but also something inside Benny. One day when I walked into Benny's room and sat beside him on his bed, he looked at me with an intensity that I had grown to equate with some transformational event to follow. His body still droopy with sleep, his mind purred with a crystal clear clarity, he looked up with his eyes that have the power to embrace and asked: "Mom...why do all my teachers tell me I am doing so well, when I never am able to answer any of the questions?" I did not have the words to respond but that was okay as my silence allowed him to continue: "Do you know why I never answer the questions?" he asked, with eyes wide with the purest of insight, " I know the answers in my head.... but I do not know the words to use." I knew then that this was at the heart of his sadness.

Benny's demeanor lightened instantaneously. While I had no ready answer for him, he relaxed as soon as he knew that I had heard, and that I understood. I took him to school, already a happier child, as he knows we would find a way to help him. I found Dr. Ruby, the school psychologist who is obsessed with the color pink. Her room is filled with oversized flowers, pink patterned pillows and even Oreo cookies filled with strawberry cream. She often writes notes in pink ink, notoriously difficult to read on her red tinged paper. Nevertheless, she is a wellspring of positive energy, and is filled with constructive and positive ways to help her students fit in and grow. While busy at the moment she saw the determination in my face and we made a plan to chat later. I stopped by to speak with Dina, Benny's speech therapist, and all together over the next few days we came up with a few ideas. I remembered that earlier in the year Lucy had assigned them a project on sound where students had to create and present a poster board. Benny loved the project, compiling an extra large board and asking to use both sides. Already an avid computer user, he found photos online of thunderstorms, trains, planes, musicians, and machines. When the presentation day came, Lucy was prepared to let him do only as much as he could, but Benny surprised her by standing in front of the class and presenting with ease and with great pride.

We realized that with the prompts in front of him he was able to speak and to share. We also discovered that he craved these opportunities. Sitting quietly was no longer enough for him, and even though it was enough for us, we had to listen to his desires; his goals for himself had to be recognized and addressed. The IEP is a guide, but I saw that those static goals were insufficient for Benny. He desired something greater, something momentous. He wanted to be heard, to contribute fully and reflectively to his class.

Dr. Ruby, Dina, and I decided that he would prepare posters for several of the topics the class would be covering. Benny could use speech therapy time to prepare his presentation and Lucy would give him a few minutes to share. It worked beautifully, and Benny's sadness faded fast, his spark intensified and he dove into these projects with a great enthusiasm. His first poster presentation was on Kenya, and it is on that test that he got his first score of 100%.

The school had a club called Junior Announcers. I had not looked too closely at the clubs since the getting through the school day was enough for Benny, but I reconsidered knowing Benny was ready for more. Each morning and afternoon there are a series of announcements that need to be made on the loudspeaker. The students of Boulder did this task, announcing the weather, various events scheduled for the day, reminding peers of upcoming deadlines, and giving birthday greetings to students and teachers alike. Benny had been mimicking the announcements at home for a while and when I asked him if he wanted to join the club, he said it would be very hard and he was not sure. But as he spoke an irrepressible smile came up on his face, and I knew that we had found another part of the solution.

Speaking for all to hear was not something anyone could have predicted would appeal to Benny—a child with serious expressive language delays (in the decimal percentiles on most official tests), a child who mumbled most statements, a child who appeared quite shy—but it did. This was a challenge he was craving and delighted in, a challenge that revealed to us a child with a fire inside. Benny wanted to be heard and seen, and a child who was going to conquer his difficulties not only by speaking simply to his class but in front of his entire school community on the loudspeaker to be heard by over 300 people.

On the morning of his first announcement, which happened to be on his ninth birthday, the area outside the office was filled with teachers, therapists, school personnel, and one very nervous mother. Together we waited for the chimes that signaled the start of announcements. There was a hush upon the school, an eerie quiet had taken hold of the entire building. I was trembling and when I peered into the office I saw Benny, looking small and timid. His hands were wrapped tightly around the microphone. Then we heard soft chimes and suddenly a voice, strong and clear, a mature voice, a voice never been taken for granted, a voice that rose out from the microphone and filled the hallways and the classrooms. The voice was in control, in command, rich like a melody to my ears perhaps only Brahms could compose. : "GOOD MORNING BOULDER SCHOOL. TODAY IS MONDAY MARCH 15th, THE JUNIOR ANNOUNCERS THIS MORNING ARE BECKY, TOM AND BENNY…" The transition from silence to sound in the hallway transformed each and every person in the school. Something shifted for all of us. We all learned something about rising to a challenge, about eclipsing our expectations, and about pushing ourselves to our personal limits, as Clark so often suggested.

Benny returned to his class to a student-led standing ovation. Later that day, the teaching assistant, Willa, overheard a few boys discussing their own desire to become a Junior Announcer. One of them had said to the other, "I was going to try and do it, but now I don't know…I could never do it as well as Benny." When I came to pick Benny and Adam up at the end of the day, my eyes fell first to Adam who was radiant with pride. He had already decided he was going to join Junior Announcers the next year.

There are stages I have passed through over the years as I approach a place from where I can enjoy a richer understanding of inclusion and what it takes to make it work. Third grade took me closer to a place where, for fleeting moments, I was able to peer out and see a spectacular vista. I could see miracles and moments of incredible growth, not only for Benny, but for those around him. I saw it all for a moment, felt it completely at least for an instant, understood finally that we construct the deficits by the way that we analyze and categorize. I saw at last that the labels we choose are subjective, that with freedom and support everyone can excel, that even in the best of situations, the IEP is somewhat meaningless. We must listen carefully to the child and use his or her dreams as the basis for the goals we strive to reach. The old visions I came with of children standing around him helping him function, in part fueled by pity for his difficulties and learning about compassion are fading away. They are being replaced with ones of a dynamic world, a flourishing community of children and adults, learning about each other, respecting one another, giving each other the courage to grow and then inspiring each other in a constant ascending spiral leading to more and more moments of astonishing accomplishments.

***

The theme of this chapter, letting the child be the guide, may sound idealistic to some educators. And yet we see the resourcefulness in children making their own academic games amusing themselves, teaching each other, and reinforcing knowledge while socializing.

In terms of Benny, although it was an unpredictable road, his behaviors, emotions, and actions informed Diane of his general state of mind. This revealed he experienced a great deal of frustration and pain before being given the opportunity to do more by those around him. It was also the first step in giving rise to discussing possibilities with his speech therapist and psychologist of developing new goals.

Despite academic improvement in his school reports, Diane had noted his emotional shifts at home, and "…began to see a sadness take root in Benny… all the time. He was moody and told me several times that he did not want to go to school." Here we can see an example of the emotional toll that school situations and commonplace practices have on some students who struggle in always understanding what's going on, exacerbated by difficulties in expressing themselves. In his pain, Diane notices what could be a pattern observing, "It had been a long time since I had heard him cry like that, maybe not since he was a toddler struggling to imitate a sound. I recognized the sadness as similar to the sadness he felt when there was something he wanted to do but could not." The reports had the opposite effect of pleasing him because Diane notes, "they triggered his feeling that he was not doing all that he wanted to do, all that he felt he could do." Then Benny himself found words, asking his mother the difficult-yet-sensible question, "Why do all my teachers tell me I am doing so well, when I never am able to answer any of the questions?" Benny goes on to inform her why he can never answer the questions explaining, "I know the answers in my head…. but I do not know the words to use." In sum, he has the knowledge, but does not know how to express it.

At first this is a major conundrum for Benny and his teachers, yet it becomes another example of problem solving by professionals and parents collaborating within a specific context. In contemplating the issue, the psychologist, teacher, and speech teacher agreed that Benny's desire to participate was not necessarily just about answering questions in a traditionally expected matter, it was also about the opportunity for sharing of his knowledge with peers. Previously he had been given the chance to present a project to his class, as all of his peers had done. With the provision of time for Benny to research, organize, and display, he had demonstrated his abilities, and Lucy was "prepared to let him do only as much as he could." Based upon his eager yet limited class participation in terms of answering questions, his teacher was surprised when he stood in front of the class "presenting with ease and great pride." What this situation revealed is that "in the moment" sharing of knowledge was extremely difficult (perhaps impossible at that time) for Benny, but "with preparation" he was able to publicly share his knowledge. The speech therapist then used her time to further develop what Benny could currently do, capitalizing upon his strengths and using them to realize his desire for greater participation in class. Likewise, Lucy accepted and encouraged this arrangement, permitting Benny to use a way that worked for him, thereby providing access to his classmates as a sharer of knowledge—just in a different way than they did. The fact that Lucy "would give him a few minutes to share" reveals her flexibility in shifting pedagogy to match the needs and abilities of her students. Having Benny share for two minutes and his classmates benefit from engaging with the knowledge he provides is an example of an organic response to the conundrum originally presented. Its success can be measured by Diane's observation that Benny's "sadness faded fast, his spark intensified, and he dove into these projects with great enthusiasm." Providing an alternative method that permits students to share and contribute what they know and think permits them to be an active—and equal—member of the community. Benny's situation has shown us that holding up hands and providing an on the spot response to teacher directed questions is not for everybody. These are the learnings that we, as educators, come to know from students in the context of our classes. Getting 100% on a presentation about Kenya can only serve to further motivate a child who is trying to figure out himself in relation to the world (including the academic, social, and emotional realms of school) and his place within it.

Having confidence in speaking before others is a skill that even most adults do not posses. For a child who struggles with expressive language, it seems like a contradiction to expect this. Yet it can be argued that Benny expected it of himself when adults around him did not. Diane and the professionals at Boulder came to realize that "...he craved these opportunities. Sitting quietly was no longer enough for him, and even though it was enough for us, we had to listen to his desires; his goals for himself had to be recognized and addressed." It was at this moment when Diane put two-and-two together, noticing Benny's mimicking school announcements and subsequently "feeling him out" about the possibility of being an announcer. His first response was that it would be "very hard and he was not sure." Yet his smile betrayed a desire to rise to the challenge, and as Diane realized, "we had found another part of the solution." This particular situation strikes me as a clear instance of Vygotsky's Zone of Proximal Development (ZPD) (1987). Among many of the theories I have been exposed to, this is one of them that resonates with me the most because it is so simple it seems like commonsense. In sum, Vygotsky noted that in order to have growth in learning knowledge and/or a task, a student's current abilities have to be recognized and then with assistance and encouragement from the teacher, a student could then progress to their next level of growth. Such assistance and encouragement can take many forms, including modeling, providing examples and non-examples, specific dos and don'ts, repeated exposure to the task, along with trying multiple times with a student—gradually transferring the knowledge and skills—before expecting the student to "own" the task. In the case of Benny possibly making an announcement to the school, the timing was right to encourage him in reaching for a greater level of public speaking than previously accomplished. He had the calm demeanor, clear speech, the ability to extensively practice the task expected, the encouragement of his teachers and parents, and the desire to push himself. Who knew Benny would ever want to do this? Diane is surprised, given Benny's struggles with expressive language, a tendency to mumble, and shyness—a child who scored near the lowest point on official tests determining language delays. She understands that, "This was a challenge he was craving, he delighted in... that revealed to us a child with a fire inside, a child who wanted to be heard and seen." Indeed, Benny's self-awareness was growing, including ways in which he could consider possibilities of setting himself challenges and taking the initiative.

When the time came for Benny to make the announcement, we witness an everyday act within most schools, including Boulder, the type that most people take for granted without a second thought. But for Benny, his family, and the team of professionals that have been working with him, making a school announcement is a watershed moment. For this child, it is a major accomplishment, leaving Diane to observe, "Something shifted for all of us." This success impacts Benny's sense of who he is, what he can do, and how his brother, peers, teachers, and parents perceive him. Indeed, Benny is demonstrating to the school community that he can do what some other children are not yet able to. This is something the children observe themselves when they comment, "I could never do it as well as Benny."

In terms of DSE, I see these episodes of Benny's presentations to class and school connected together in ways that touch upon the importance of family and community, and the "inclusion of disabled people in theorizing about disability" (Connor et al. 2008, p. 448). As I have argued earlier, I believe in the importance of family members theorizing about disability, in particular mothers, who come to know their child in so many ways that others do not. In Diane's representation of Benny, we are able to see how he is making sense of the tasks expected in his class, his school, his community, and the world beyond. Since challenged by his teacher in the former grade about the expectations she held for Benny, Diane now has a far greater sense of what Biklen and Burke have termed "presumed competency" (2006, p. 166). This is a very important concept as it invites us to begin our understanding of a person in terms of their competencies, many of which we, as able bodied people—because of our own limitations—have not yet discovered. It goes beyond the value of having a "strength-based approach," as it is a deep disposition toward how we should primarily view everyone in an open ended way.

Although using a strength-based approach with students is important, it is not enough. While IEP formats vary enormously from state to state, and within each state between local education authorities, it can be claimed that most versions could be considered being strengths-based. Yet the technical framing of the concept of "strengths-based" in IEPs leads educators to mechanical understandings of a child's academic skills and social abilities. The point I wish to make here is that the IEP is a guide, required by law. That is all it is, a guide; not something etched in stone akin to a religious text. However, educational systems tend toward rigidity over fluidity. The former is easier to manage, to predict, to control, to budget, to schedule, to revert to when unsure of a situation and seek documented expertise… the latter, in contrast, is far less so. Diane comments, "I saw that those static [IEP] goals were not enough for Benny. He desired something greater, something momentous. He wanted to be heard, to contribute fully and reflectively to his class." In doing so, she calls attention to the limitations of IEPs, and the danger of clinging to them lest they—in their reductive nature—inadvertently contain possibilities for the child. Benny's experiences challenged his own mother into sharing what many educators may find shocking when she writes, "I saw at last that the labels we choose are subjective, that with freedom and support everyone can excel, that even in the best of situations, the IEP is somewhat meaningless." We are witness to Diane's epiphany that the context determines the disability, and if teachers and administrators understood the concept of disability in this manner, then classrooms and schools could become far more inclusive. For educators who ask, "What do you mean by a social model of disability?" this is a prime example.

Unfortunately the field of traditional special education believes the social model of disability to be heretical, challenging the orthodoxy of established scientific knowledge that determines what label a person "is" (Gallagher et al., 2004). The reification of differences into a disability by a constellation of professionals signifies that the disability permanently exists, is concrete, and predictable. As we have seen so far, Benny's dis/abilities are quite fluid, malleable, and highly contextual. This chapter calls to mind ideas found in the work of Skrtic (1991, 1995) who analyzed how educational bureaucracies—including special education—function, with professionals primarily viewing themselves as rational and efficient. He point outs out the limitations of technical approaches to measure "success" within education, and argues against a technocracy in favor of an adhocracy. This is an admittedly highly concentrated version of Skrtic's important idea, but I include it to highlight the difference between approaches to education. What is needed for a child's growth is created as a response to knowing that child within a particular context (making the supports ad hoc) versus what has been prescribed as part of a formalized professional system (making the supports technical). Much of what has come to be known as special education is a dense conglomeration of laws, rules, and regulations, with IEPs serving as a pro-forma document rather than an actual plan developed in part by students to help them grow. Boulder's approach to education is one of thoughtfulness, of making multiple connections with view to people sharing what's best and therefore what's next for Benny. This is not how the majority of the NYC public school system works, with an emphasis on managing over 185,00 students who are identified as disabled. I bring this up as the sheer size of the city poses massive logistical problems in terms of adherence to laws, compliance of regulations, the organization, funding, and provision of services (if you recall, Diane mentioned eight people had been at Benny's IEP meeting), and so on. However, at the same time, I see how many practices employed at Boulder are still possible within city schools, indeed have previously happened, and are currently happening in pockets here and there. In order to better understand inclusive practices, and encourage their growth, I believe it is useful for educators to become familiar with the adhocratic model of education as a way of thinking. For me, this model values teachers as reflective thinkers, collaborators, and allies with parents. It encourages them to study the children they are working with and be professionally invested in being pro-active problem solvers. In contrast, the technocratic system appears to utilize educators as small cogs in a big machine, training them to unthinkingly generate pro-forma often decontextualized goals for students with disabilities and then (maybe) check the box if students approximate them.

If teachers have no real voice in analyzing and making contributions to solving the challenges of inclusive education, then there is even less likelihood that students can be heard. Diane writes, "We must listen carefully to the child, use his or her dreams as the basis for the goals we strive to reach." While some may argue that this is pure idealism, Diane's sentiment is actually very much in line with the intention of special education laws that seek to include children in their educational process, particularly explicit in adolescence when transition plans are developed (Cavendish, 2013). Learning from students about what they think, know, and want, allows teachers to work in ways that are deeply satisfying to both, as possibilities for learning are endless.

References

Biklen, D. & Burke, J. (2006). Presuming competence. *Equity & Excellence in Education*, 39(2), 166–175.

Cavendish, W. M. (2013). Student perceptions of school efforts to facilitate student involvement, school commitment, self-determination, and high school graduation. *School Psychology of Education*, 16(2), 257–275.

Connor, D. J., Gabel, S. L., Gallagher, D. & Morton, M. (2008). Disability studies and inclusive education--Implication for theory, research, and practice: Guest editor's introduction. *International Journal of Inclusive Education*, 12(5–6), 441–457.

Gallagher, D.J., Heshusius, L., Iano, P., & Skrtic, T. M. (2004). *Challenging Orthodoxy in Special Education*. Denver, CO: Love Publishing.

Skrtic, T. M. (1991). The special education paradox: Equity as a way to excellence. *Harvard Educational Review, 61*(2), 148–206.

Skrtic, T. M. (1995) (Ed.), *Disability and democracy*. NY: Teachers College Press.

· 1 0 ·

EXTRAORDINARY EXTRA CURRICULARS

I walk down the block to pick up my boys and am aware of something different in the air. I feel the beat first with my feet and then my ears. I see that the doors to the yard are open wide and can hear children singing and cheering from their classrooms, poking their heads out of the doors and windows. The music is familiar, "Believe it Not," the theme from the TV series The Greatest American Hero, and we hear strains of being able to walk on air. Suddenly, Captain Boulder flies out, arms stretched for balance, cape billowing behind him, tiny tight yellow shorts, glowing skin—a superhero principal from top to bottom.

Clark's face is open and bright until his smile creates strong dark lines which overlap and crisscross like wires connecting his features, the electric current passing from his lips then to his eyes, where it flickers for a moment until it takes off once again and resettles in his cheeks, creating a pattern of lights across his features. He is riding on a cart created, in part, with padding from the gym floor. Fueling his fantasy is three of his male staff, a grade 5 teacher, the gym teacher, and a reading specialist. They flank him on three sides for support as well as to tip him from his perch when mid flight they fear his ego gets too large. He is not afraid to be vulnerable, he is not afraid to be himself. It is an ordinary Tuesday and the Principal of Boulder is simply trying to find his way to the parent teacher softball game.

Boulder offers a delectable menu of extracurricular activities. I had never seen so many options provided to elementary students. At first I was skeptical about the ability of these youngsters to take advantage of so many varied options, but over the years, I saw how integral these programs were to the growth of the students. As I lived through these activities with my children and set down to analyze them, I saw a progression through them, from those that took place entirely within the school day to those requiring time and coordination outside of the school. Some were required parts of the school day, while others had voluntary components. From ballroom dancing, which was a required activity for all grade four and five students, to the annual literacy week that spanned all grades, there were so many entry points for families. Most events are open to all grade levels; thus students are mixed, creating a texture that contributed to building in the acceptance of difference. Students are expected to interact with everyone in the school, which relates directly to the success of the inclusion program. To give a sense of the way these activities unfold and envelop the community I will take you through one typical year, with each month marked by a different activity, each staffed by teachers from the school. In addition, I will "zoom in" on a couple of these activities, allowing for descriptions in greater depth, including the specific impact they had upon my sons.

September: Back to School Barbeque and Dunk Tank

September comes with a back to school barbecue. After school, four to seven families are invited to join their children to play games, eat, and socialize. Teachers from the school staff all of these activities. One of the highlights is the dunk-tank. For a few pennies, children and adults can take a turn tossing a ball that causes a lever to flip making Clark tumble into cold and slimy water, with a smile on his face each time he goes down. Other teachers jump in and take a turn, but no one spends as much time in the water as Clark, and no one is as much fun to dunk.

October: The Halloween Parade

Students and teachers celebrate Halloween at the end of October, complete with costumes. Teachers are most creative, dressing as crayons, carrots, or chickens. A few faculty members take the opportunity to cross-dress, as have some of the students. A blond boy who is a friend of Adam came dressed as their grade four teacher, Sophia, tripping in his mother's high heels all day. He carried a baby as she had recently had her second child. After lunch the entire school parades around the grounds of the school. Each class has a few minutes to create figure eights around the play yard while the rest of the school and many parents cheer on the side. Younger siblings are invited to join in as well.

November: Thanksgiving Feast

The Tuesday before Thanksgiving recess is the Boulder feast. The entire school gathers together in the lunchroom. Each child designs placemats and the grade five students design and create floral settings with decorated clay pots and fake flowers. There is something beautiful about seeing the entire school together, an ocean of orange in their school shirts. Parents volunteer to set up and serve so that the teachers can sit and eat as well. The meal is simple, turkey and corn and potatoes, but the sustenance comes from the atmosphere. We see the kids with disabilities with their peers. Some of the children with more severe impairments need help eating and most often there is a typical child with them. At some point Clark gets on a chair and addresses everyone in a short and simple speech. We see at this event that even a school of 400 can come together and be a family.

December: Mad Hot Ballroom

The cold December air ushers in the Mad Hot Ballroom Show. This is one of the few events only for certain grades. Grades four and five participate in weekly dance lessons with a professional ballroom dance group. At first the grade 4 boys can be squeamish about dancing arm in arm with the girls, but after a few lessons, they embrace it with gusto. The performances, all four that I have had the privilege of attending, have taken my breath away.

January: Pie in the Face

It took me a few years to understand and appreciate Pie in the Face. During mid-winter, teachers and students gather in the gym and toss all sorts of pies in the face of the principal. The event is recorded and linked to the school website for all to enjoy during the year. Footage reveals Clark standing in the line of fire, getting covered in pie, with cream washing down his face. A shower and a change of clothes awaits before he is ready to go on with the daily routine if that ever does exist at Boulder. The event speaks to Clark's ability to take a risk in front of his students. It speaks to his desire to spice up life, to create good memories, and to bring the community together for a short and savory treat.

February: Literacy Week, Family Fun Night

February comes with a district wide Literacy Week. Each day has a different special event. Students in all grades complete one common activity, creating an original work of art, usually with a drawing and caption, related to a theme. Students who cannot yet write dictate their caption to a teacher or another student who writes it for them. The halls are lined with these drawings, with every student's work represented. One year they all drew a self-portrait and wrote one word to describe themselves. Another year they drew a scene from a book they loved and wrote why they chose that book. Yet another year, the theme centered on where they like to read and why. Every February the halls pulsate with these drawings and words. At Boulder, the week includes a visit from a children's author, a whole school art project, and a bagel breakfast in pajamas. When Boulder has pajama day, it is for everyone, teachers, and administrators as well as students.

February also brought family fun night, which went through a few permutations over the years. Family fun night has been a night of dancing, of games, a sports night for boys and their moms, followed by a sweetheart dance for girls and their dads. In any of the above forms, it is a night to come out of the house and frolic with your child as well as the staff of Boulder school. It provides a low-key way for parents to get to know the staff, opening the possibility of conversation that is low risk, enabling each to get to know the other on a level deeper than is customary between parents and teachers.

March: The Circus

The covert circus is a night to remember. It is an auditorium filled with circus music, and the bellowing voice of Mr. D as he calls out the moves. It is swarms of children from different grade levels coming together, balancing plates on sticks, volleying devil sticks, juggling colored scarves and feathers. It is many moments for each child to show off individual skills, and twice as many moments where they cooperate in these tasks. After a free-style on each circus instrument, Mr. D choreographs activities requiring students to balance and toss in pairs, trios and even quartets. He builds partnership and cooperation into every act. The older students work alongside the youngsters, helping, building an appreciation of difference. Mr. D strategically designs the seemingly random performances that consist of color and sound and laughter. The finale of the show is always the stilt-walkers, usually reserved for the oldest children. There is a hush as they walk out, and a swell of cheers as they begin to march across the stage. The grand finale is always the same. Children on stilts step over a line of teachers, often including Clark, lying end to end across the stage. They walk forwards and then backwards, ten or so in all, marching cautiously over their teachers. Here, too, we see an element of the philosophy of Boulder, that of trust, with teachers willing to turn things upside down, to be vulnerable, not insisting on being "on top" all the time. The faculty teaches from a place different than I am used to, we see this over and over again in subtle ways, but on Circus Night it is a bright and bold statement.

April: The Variety Show

Just days after the students return from the holiday break in early January, flyers come home announcing the Annual Variety Show. The yellow flyer brightens the grey icy days when darkness arrives way too early. The first sign of spring here in Boulder comes in on the wings of this 8 ½ by 11-inch sheet of paper. The Annual Variety Show is a performance opportunity open to all of the students, grades K through 5. Students form groups with one designated parent leader. Together they create and rehearse a routine based on the theme of the year. One year the theme was the 1970's, another year the theme was TV shows. Students and parents choreograph original dances to a song consistent with the theme. They can lip sync, sing live, or act out a small segment, performing for up to two minutes. That may sound short, but when you are in charge of ten 2nd graders, it is a challenge to get them to create and perfect a two-minute piece. The groups have about two months to work on their performance and some parents get very involved, creating elaborate costumes for the event. With my two jobs and other responsibilities, this was an event I shied away from as long as I could.

May: Relay for Life

Relay for Life came about through an interested teaching assistant who volunteered some time for this event. It is part of the philanthropic mission of Boulder school, and another opportunity for the entire school to come together, wearing purple, creating luminaries, and recognizing the need to unite and raise awareness and funds to fight cancer. It is always a risk to open discussion with young children about a topic that can be frightening. Boulder does not shy away from these topics, but want students to grow up strong, and be active members of society from the earliest of years. The event is a beautiful day with swarms of children running around the field, dressed in purple.

June: Field Day

June brings a traditional field day, but nothing at Boulder is traditional. At this event, students are paired together in mixed aged groups. For certain activities, younger students are given older buddies, fifth grade is paired with kindergarten students, fourth graders with first graders. It is another moment where children learn to cooperate across developmental levels. The day ends with a massive water balloon fight, where teachers are more drenched than students. The local fire truck drives by as well and sprays down the hot and sweaty students, who dance together under the mist until the final bell for the school day rings.

As can be seen, the full school year is strategically planned to ensure that school faculty and staff, parents and their children, have frequent opportunities to celebrate, showcase existing talents, develop new ones, and simply have fun. At the same time, it encourages the experience of being part of, and contributing to, a community. In the following two examples, I highlight ways in which these events helped shape the overall growth of both Benny and Adam.

Dancing at Family Fun Night

On the first Friday in February it is hard to bounce out of the house, after dinner, into the dark evening air that blankets the ground like thick velvet, and go back to school. The first family fun night was just two days after we moved to the district. We did not attend due to still navigating within the boundaries we were used to, not yet aware that this is a school with few. Nor were we yet aware of the beauty that can take root when boundaries are allowed to be flexible.

We did not attend this annual event until Benny was in grade four and Adam in grade two. Once again it was Adam who insisted we make the trek back to school on one of the coldest and darkest days of the year. I am so grateful for the fact that my boys could attend the same school so that one could influence the other to take advantage of all that the school community had to offer. The event proved to be an evening that showed me a side of Adam that I did not know existed. We arrived at the beginning and Adam found a small group of second graders moving together to the music. He was able seamlessly to join them and together they wiggled to the beat, taking turns lifting their shirts to reveal their still buttery soft bellies.

Adam's friends soon tired but he did not. Once he began to dance he could not stop. Adam's moves developed quickly from silly second grade antics to ones that reflected the mood and rhythm of the music. When his face became red and sweat began to collect under his bangs I tried to entice him to sit down but he would not. He simply could not stop dancing. He danced freestyle to the music; he learned The Electric Slide and The Macarena. He joined a train of kids, dancing under a pole that was lowered progressively until participants had to squat backwards. He seemed to be able to adapt quickly and effortlessly to whatever music the DJ chose.

Benny did a little running and found a spot on top of some mats from which he had a nice view of the dancers. Our neighbors came, danced, and left. Adam kept dancing, his body moving in ways I did not know it could. He used his arms, and his neck. Every possible moving part was in motion, not just his feet, as amateurs often do the very first time they dance.

Many teachers come with their own families, eager to introduce them to their students. This night was no exception and I had the chance to chat with Benny's teacher, Sophia, and meet her family. She was chasing around her two-year old boy, and her students were excited to meet him. Her students took turns holding his hand, while many of the parents just scooped him up into their arms. Toward the close of the evening, the DJ stopped the music to announce the dance contest winners. I was chatting softly with a parent on the side when I heard Adam's name. He had won for the best dancer in the second grade. He did not expect to win, he did not dance to win; he just happened to discover a passion that evening. His friends helped direct him to the front to get his prize and then gathered around him in support and showered him with a great amount of cheer. We did not know that evening that dance would become such a focal part of Adam's life. We did not realize that by grade 5 he would be taking tap, hip-hop, and ballroom classes at a dance school in town. I shudder to think of how our first inkling of the tremendous talent that Adam has might have lain dormant for years if not for the fact that he dragged us out of the house that cold February evening to attend an event that did not quite make sense to either David or myself. I realize now how fortunate we are to have found a school that opens the door to so many possibilities for its students.

We were one of the last families to pick up our coats left behind in the auditorium. Even after the music had stopped and the DJ was on her way, Adam continued to dance. He swirled up and down the hallways, while other children ran by leading their parents to their classrooms eager to show them work they had done. In the middle of it all was a highly animated principal, laughing, joking and hugging the parents of his students. Although on many occasions I have heard Clark speak of the family he wants us all to be, something on this night spoke to me in ways that his words alone had not been able to do. His mission often cuts across priorities he is told to have by bureaucrats in education but it has managed to take root in his school. It is alive in the eyes of his teachers who come out on a Friday night to enjoy their students. It is flourishing in Adam who has always had gifts in the academic areas and is now nurturing new talents. He would have been a good student at any school he happened to attend. Boulder has given him the ability to discover new sides of himself, to let go, and to move in ways he never knew he could. A quick glance around the school on family fun night reveals a small oasis full of teachers, students, parents and a wacky principal dancing among them in spite of an educational system that is increasingly hostile to anything resembling spontaneity and creativity in schools.

Participating in the Annual Variety Show

Benny expressed no interest in the variety show until Adam announced he was going to be in a group when he was in grade two and Benny in grade four. On the night before the forms were due, Benny told us he also wanted to be in the show. In order to perform, students had to find a group and convince one parent to take responsibility for organizing rehearsals and making sure all the paperwork was in on time. The faculty member who organized the show was a stickler for punctuality. Adam was invited into a group early on and had me fill out all of the necessary forms. I was shocked and surprised when Benny told us late in the evening, the night before the forms were due, that he wanted to be in the show. He said he had asked a few friends in school but he was not sure what they said in response. I felt terrible that I did not ask him earlier or listen carefully to him as I was sure he must have said this before, but in my rush to get through the routine of the day, I must have dismissed it.

We were not quite sure how Benny's request would play out. He did not like to go to other homes in general, partly because he was afraid of dogs, and we did not see him as a child who would want to perform on the stage. I called his friend's mother, but she did not call back. I worried that he might not be able to find a group with whom to perform. In any case, his announcement came late and he had not secured a group. When bedtime came he looked up at me with his large brown eyes and told me again he wanted to be in the show. I suggested that he could do an act with Adam. Benny looked up at me and with wisdom and strength and said: "Mom…that is the most ridiculous thing a mother could ever say." He wanted a group of peers with whom to perform. In his eyes was both frustration and forgiveness.

The firm deadline was just 12 hours away and I did not know what to do. He fell asleep with warm wet tears flowing down his cheeks, and I stayed up in a tortured state of despair. I emailed his friends' parents asking if he could join their group. I slept fitfully and when morning came and there were no responses, just minutes to 6AM, I emailed Clark. I was afraid to bother him with what seemed like something that was not part of his job. I asked for an extension and help finding Benny a group to perform with. Inside, I was afraid his friends would not include him. I feared that I had let Benny down. At 6:01AM Clark wrote back: *Absolutely! I would love to see him in the show… Wow, what amazing progress! Sophia and/or Beth, do you have anyone in mind that Benny could perform with?*

By the end of the next school day he came out of the building surrounded by his friends, rallying around him, celebrating his wish to perform. Apparently, even though Benny asked them, he must have done it in a whisper, because they did not seem to realize that he wanted to be in the show, until his teacher mentioned it in class. I realized how complex interactions between people can be.

I walked home and later that night sent a quick email to Clark telling him how the situation was resolved. Once again, with fingers hovering over the send button, I wondered if I should or should not, if it is okay to bother a principal with an item that seemed so small. Inside, I knew that this was far from small and was, in fact, the beginning of a tremendous explosion in social growth not only for Benny but for me and for his friends and for the parents of his friends. Clark replied immediately, his response was one word, and tucked inside this seven-letter bundle was the essence of it all. Despite its brevity, his word choice made it clear that he understood. On my screen, sent from his phone, at a time he must have been almost asleep, was:

Awesome

After months of rehearsals, the show date finally came. Both Benny and Adam excitedly awaited the chance to perform on the stage of the middle school. Benny's act was in the first half; Adam's the second. Benny danced to the theme of "The Monkees," the 1960s television show. Seven boys came out from the wings in bathing trunks and white tees with the name of the group on their shirts. They each carried boogie boards that they placed on the front of the stage. They did a casual dance, swaggering up and around, moving backwards, giving each other high fives and handshakes. They personalized the steps and Benny bounced with a palatable joy. He had one of those smiles that radiated through the entire auditorium, touching all who came. He did not miss a beat. The instability we would see during gym class, and unpredictability within offi-cial evaluations, the balance issues that continued to qualify him for occupa-tional therapy and physical therapy vanished while he was on the stage. We saw only his talent and grace. When the song ended, the seven boys took hands and bowed while their arms swung between themselves. Benny was ecstatic. We see that his disability was, in this instance, contextual.

Adam's skit came soon and he ran out first, soon followed by three of his buddies. They had an enthusiasm that bursts forth and engulfed the audience. The song, "Shout" by the Isley Brothers was a perfect fit for the natural state of second grade boys who are wearing colorful tie dyed shirts and dance with sparkly plastic microphones in their hands. Adam danced with such zeal that even though his leg had been hurting he was able to give his all to the perfor-mance. They began together and then branched out, first in pairs, and then on their own. They rotated on their strong legs and then had a moment when they took turns doing wild jumps before the music got softer, and then fell one by one to the floor, legs in the air. The tempo then picked up and in one last burst of energy, they were rising and running around and around the stage in circles, while the crowd went wild. After the show, Adam received many compliments on his dancing. He turned to me late at night and said: "Well mom, I guess tonight I am professor of the variety show."

For Benny, these yearlong activities provided opportunities for socialization that did not always come naturally to him. For Adam, these activities enabled him to find talents that we never knew he had. While he began elementary school with a reputation for academics and a talent for mathematics, these events showed the community that he had great talent in the arts as well. Sometimes we box kids in early when we identify them as having certain strengths. We do not always expect the most academic kids to shine in the arts. Perhaps we create this by our own assumptions and by the way we limit children early on. While I love math and am excited by Adam's strength there, I felt a sadness when they referred to him as "Professor" originally in grade 1, as if it somehow came with a suggestion that he was somehow acting older than his age. When he turned the word around years later into the phrase "professor of the variety show," it showed that he, too, sensed limits within the way the term was used initially. While being a professor is an honor, it is a term that fits with some rigidity on a six year old. I am grateful that Boulder enabled Adam to find that his strengths and talents extend far beyond the academic realm.

There is so much to learn from the way Boulder uses their monthly activities. They naturally level the playing field, offering stepping-stones for participation. From ballroom dance, which is in school, to the circus, which takes place mainly during school time, to the variety show, which involves extensive interactions outside of the school day, these occasions offer options to participate while continuously building upon on each other. They symbolize that school is not just about academics, but rather offers opportunities for each child to grow and discover his or her interests and talents.

***

The opening of this chapter purposefully describes Clark dressed as Captain Boulder, being supported by members of his staff who Diane describes as "fueling his fantasy." Although the primary implication is that Clark enjoys being in costume and the focus of attention, the phrase also speaks of how the school itself is his vision, and the teachers literally carrying him physically must also carry him—and the school—metaphorically. As Diane notes, "he is not afraid to be himself," and that includes making himself "vulnerable" in some of his choices—reflected in several of the extra curricula activities scheduled throughout the year. Just like his willingness to be dunked in a tank of water, the pie-in-the-face opportunity provides pleasure to children, and reveals "Clark's ability to take a risk in front of his students...his desire to spice up life, to create good memories, and to bring the community together..." In doing so, he deliberately undermines his own authority as a way to model a level of openness that is rare (a topic we take up again in the following chapter). In addition, and importantly, his spirit serves to diminish some inhibitions held by faculty and parents.

Teachers follow his lead in what they are willing to do in terms of interacting with students. For example, at the circus, "Children on stilts step over a line of teachers, often including Clark, lying end to end across the stage. They walk forwards and then backwards, ten or so in all, marching cautiously over their teachers." Again, this literal act symbolizes the metaphorical level of comfort between students and teachers, "with teachers willing to turn things upside down, to be vulnerable, not insisting on being 'on top' all the time." It is an indicator of professional and personal satisfaction when teachers dedicate time to school activities outside of their contractual hours. As recognized, Clark's "...mission often cuts across priorities he is told to have by bureaucrats in education but it has managed to take root in his school." This achievement is secured by an unwavering commitment to a strong sense of community in an era marked by relentless reforms and policy changes than can best be described as challenging. On Family Fun Night, Diane notes that, "A quick glance around the school ... reveals a small oasis full of teachers, students, parents and a wacky principal dancing among them in spite of an educational system that is increasingly hostile to anything resembling spontaneity and creativity in schools." In other words, Clark's steadfast adherence to his own principles provide the anchor to a school that genuinely embraces the concept not only of community, but of actively building and maintaining that community. The continuity of a solid community base is achieved through a cycle of annual activities, providing a strong framework for social opportunities between children, parents, and teachers. Knowing that these are annual events creates expectations and the a sense of looking forward to the upcoming year, with the opportunity of practicing skills in anticipation of events, such as Ballroom Dancing or The Variety Show.

Community involvement in general is highly compatible with principles that undergird inclusive education. Although initially taken aback at first by the number of school-wide events, Diane came to see "how integral these programs were to the growth of the students," because "students are expected to interact with everyone in the school, which relates directly to the success of the inclusion program." At each event, everyone has access to everyone else participating and, month-by-month, connections among participants have the potential to grow exponentially, including friendships between adults and between children. Of course not everyone has to attend every event; that is their option. However, because there are so many different types of events including fairs, games, dancing, sports, arts, literacy, pajama breakfasts, and fund raising activities for social awareness, there are ample opportunities to mingle, participate, and share in an organic manner.

Each of the events is inclusive by its very nature to invite all to attend and participate.

Thanksgiving is noteworthy, among other things, for having parents serve food to both students and teachers, ensuring that "a school of roughly 300 can come together and be a family." The Variety Show permits students to showcase their selected talents be it through singing live, lip synching, or acting. Literacy Week is a prime example of how all students contribute to a communal ritual by sharing a self-selected piece of their work, be it a caption, a dictated statement, a descriptive word, or a sentence. These words are combined with art, enabling other talents to be displayed and deepening conceptual connections about what is being conveyed in writing and visuals. Everyone counts in that there is public recognition when the school walls are "lined with these drawings, with every student's work represented…each year the halls pulsate with these drawings and words." Because of the assumed inclusive nature of these events, the social worlds of Diane's entire family changed. She credits the extracurricular activities as "the beginning of a tremendous explosion in social growth not only for Benny but for me and for his friends and for the parents of his friends."

The theme of the power of socialization is palpable throughout this chapter and brought to mind some connections to what is broadly termed the social model of disability. Generally speaking, there are different versions of this model (see discussions, for example, in Gabel & Peters, 2004; Shakespeare, 2006; Shakespeare & Watson, 2001). However, among different interpretations of the model, one constant is the shift from seeing disability as an inherent problem of the individual and a burden to society to that of society changing toward increasing access to all aspects within it—so that citizens deemed disabled have equal opportunities and the same life choices as their non-disabled peers. One of the main purposes of DSE "…is to provide advocacy for, as well as viable approaches for enacting, meaningful and substantive educational inclusion" (Connor et. al, 2008, p. 447). In the context of this chapter, I assert that the extra curricula activities are educational and inclusive. It can be argued that the school self-advocates, so to speak, for all of its students in regard to these events, and of course, parents such as Diane and David support their sons' desires to be a part of community events. In this way, the calendar of events typify a tenet of DSE in that they "promote social justice, equitable and inclusive educational opportunities, and full and meaningful access to all aspects of society for people labeled with disability/disabled people" (p. 448).

In contemplating the very notion of extra curricula activities I cannot but help associate this concept with "the unofficial curriculum" that we have evoked in a previous chapter, that is, valued knowledge and skills that children come to know in the process of schooling that ostensibly appear outside of the "pure" academic curriculum taught. Through attending and participating in these annual events, they experience the power of community as an actual, tangible phenomenon, not merely empty words and lip service as can be found in so many institutions and organizations. Students in particular benefit enormously as they experience a multitude of social situations in which numerous skills are developed and honed as they variously commit, participate, share, and contribute individually and collectively to an event.

While these events are always described with the prefix "extra," they can carry as much weight—if not more—than the official curriculum. What are some of the strongest personal recollections we all have of our own K-12 schooling? Many memories revolve around competitive sporting events, various competitions, school performances, high school dances, fund raisers, and so on. These tend to overshadow how much we liked one field of study or struggled in another. At these social events we were with friends, likely laughing, and enjoying the experience. We found out things about ourselves, including what we were good at (or not), what we were interested in (or not), and what we wanted to try to see we could do (or not).

Adam's interest in dance was unexpected, as "he just happened to discover a passion that evening." Yet a door became opened to dancing, an activity that allowed him to explore an entirely different side to himself to "The Professor." He has since further excelled in this area, with Diane giving credit to Boulder's community events that allowed Adam to "discover new sides of himself, to let go, and to move in ways he never knew he could." Likewise, Benny would likely not have been spurred to push himself, had not Adam attended the same school. Influenced by his younger brother's excitement and drive to perform publicly, Benny self-advocated to participate in the Variety Show. At first this causes great concern for Diane as the timing is not conducive and she may even possibly have reservations about Benny taking such a risk. At that moment, we see an instance of how worlds are rocked at the micro level, with Benny's tears born from a longing to participate, and Diane's deep personalization of the dilemma, making her stay up throughout the night "in a tortured state of despair." While to many these emotions may seem extreme, even exaggerated, they reflect the reality of those concerned, sharing how the situation actually felt. It also highlights—behind the scenes—how children's and parent's anxious worlds appear to themselves when fearing not being able to have the opportunity participate in these community events. Benny and Diane's respective responses of tears and despair are related to feelings about their identity, hopes, values, relationships to others, in sum, their sense of self. As can be seen, extracurricular activities can exert a great influence over the general well being of children and parents.

In contemplating extra curricula activities, we see the importance of these social opportunities and begin to see how they never should be under-estimated. I recall working at a school in which students in the special education department were oftentimes uninvited to social events such as assemblies or job fairs. Once faculty from the special education department brought it to the attention of administrators, these arrangements—call them oversights or exclusions—were ameliorated. However, the damage was done to students who realized they were not worth counting, and their perception about having unequal status in comparison to their non-disabled peers was confirmed. I still hear such stories from graduate students working in schools, and we discuss ways to challenge these arrangements without jeopardizing the position of the teacher. That said, I am happy to share that these instances of segregation have rightfully lessened over time, although experience has taught me to still be vigilant and not take anything for granted.

In many ways, Boulder's extracurricular agenda exemplifies the broad concept of inclusion in principle, inviting all children and family members to participate. Although not explicitly stated, the annual cycle of events adheres to the tenets of Universal Design that seeks to ensure maximizing access for all potential participants from the very beginning. By consistently providing such diverse communal options as part of their established norms, the school—led by a principal committed to equity—recognizes the value of emphasizing opportunities to socialize, celebrating being together. In turn, these opportunities help create a synergy among children, families, faculty, and staff members, which further galvanizes the schools' mission. In closing, it may be more accurate to say what we have come to see as extracurricular community-based activities are not actually supplements or "add ons," but rather strategic and integral elements to creating and maintaining an exemplary school. At least I am sure that's what Captain Boulder thinks.

References

Connor, D. J., Gabel, S. L., Gallagher, D. & Morton, M. (2008). Disability studies and inclusive education--Implication for theory, research, and practice: Guest editor's introduction. *International Journal of Inclusive Education*, 12(5–6), 441–457.

Gabel, S. L., & Peters, S. (2004). Presage of a paradigm shift? Beyond the social model of disability toward a resistance theory of disability. *Disability and Society* 19(6), 571–596.

Shakespeare, T. (2006). The social model of disability. In L. Davis (Ed.) *The disability studies reader* (pp. 216–221). New York: Routledge.

Shakespeare, T., & Watson, N. (2001). The social model of disability: An outdated ideology? Exploring theories and expanding methodologies: Where we are and where we need to go. *Research in Social Science and Disability*, 2, 9–29.

· 1 1 ·

THE INFORMAL BENDING OF
BOUNDARIES

Shortly after we had moved to our new neighborhood in March 2008, it was clear that Benny was adjusting to kindergarten with some ups and downs. We were about to put him on medication for ADHD, but I did not want to do so. I was worried that he would suffer side effects. I was concerned that he would still display impulsive behavior. I was afraid that if it did not work, the district might suggest another placement.

Clark came up to me after school in the playground. He put his arm around me, squeezing my shoulders. He told me he just broke up with his partner. Clark shared a little more about his relationship. I looked at him with questions in my eyes. I wondered why he was telling me this in the midst of possible chaos with my son. I realized I had not had a personal conversation with a principal, ever. He asked how I liked living in suburbia. I told him I missed my city. I was afraid to bring up Benny, but he did, casually, as if there is nothing noteworthy about a five-year-old who recently kicked his teacher. He pointed to him on the playground equipment running after another child. Clark recognized the growth that had already taken place. He said to me, "See, I told you it would work," as if it was already a done deal and it was working, even though Benny was still a formidable challenge in the classroom. I did not know quite what to make of the principal at my side, becoming my friend. Just two months before I was being

followed through the playground by a principal who threatened me with legal action if I failed to accept a most restrictive placement from my home district and remove Benny from her school.

First Names

Each year, we began the exchange of emails with the teachers and therapists the traditional way. I would address them with their last name and they would address me with my last name. Each year, by November emails and notes would transition into a less formal exchange, as the staff would begin to sign their notes with their first name only. They continued to address me as Mrs. Berman, creating a subtle invitation to connect in a less formal manner. I would do the same in return; address them with the traditional formality, but sign my own first name, suggesting that I was also open to being less formal, but still reigned in by tradition. It took many years and until Benny graduated that I could no longer pretend that the relationships built together were strictly professional. The Boulder staff felt like family and finally I was able to address them by their first name and they returned the sentiment by addressing me with my first name. It seems like a small change but in reality it reflects a big transition to a place where we had come to the table as equals with different roles, rather than different places of power.

Sunday Morning Music

Even though Benny graduated Boulder over two years ago, Miriam, his former music teacher, continues to teach him piano each week on Sunday morning. Her relationship with him is one of the most beautiful teacher-student relationships I have ever seen. They sit together at the grand piano nestled in a bay window of her home, overlooking a serene section of the garden. Miriam has way of bringing out Benny's most musical voice, and even though he has little time to practice, there is growth each week, between her sessions and within each one. She continually refuses to accept payment for her services.

Her time with him has a restorative richness for me as I sit near to the alcove in which they play. Benny, who can become frustrated easily, does not in his time with her. Instead he relaxes into the new challenges she creates for him, his profile developing a maturity not seen yet in other moments. His hands seem to grow longer and leaner in their hour together as they move across the keyboard. Though separated by decades and almost every aspect of their lives, Benny moves with Miriam as if they are one, when they focus intently together on bringing out the music from the manuscript paper which sits atop the piano, releasing the little black dots from the page, and sending them into the universe with an intense and refreshing passion. It seems like everything has come together in that moment, and I can't help but feel that birds in the garden gather together and sing along, while the trees sway as if dancing to the tunes. I sit beside and write, catch up on emails, while listening each week with interest and excitement.

Miriam's ability to teach Benny has opened up many doors to him in school. When he began to study with her he did not know how to read music, even though he had played several instruments by ear throughout elementary school. Since learning to read and write was a struggle for him, we did not require him to learn the technicalities of reading music and never imagined he could learn to read two clefs simultaneously. Benny's ability to play by ear made him feel that learning to read printed notes was superfluous, and we decided not to push. Miriam knew, though, that without reading music he would be at a disadvantage throughout middle school and high school. Today in grade eight, Benny is a part of a performance choir in middle school. He had to audition and one of the requirements was the ability to sight-read. Without the ability to read music, this opportunity would not have been possible.

Miriam first suggested to me that Benny learn to read music upon his graduation from elementary school. She offered to give him a few ten-minute lessons to see if he could be engaged. She refused payment for such a short lesson, suggesting that ultimately if he wanted to continue we could discuss it then. One ten-minute lesson led to many more, and slowly the amount of time she could engage with him increased. Benny started to practice and he began to decode the written page. Miriam built on his abilities by giving him opportunities to improvise, teaching him chord progressions and inviting him to fill in notes by ear from pieces he knew well, like Dvorak's 9th, *Theme from the New World Symphony*, and other pieces he loved. By the end of summer Benny was playing with her for 30 minutes but she still refused to be paid in money. Miriam repeatedly told me she would not teach him if she did not love working with him. She is a sought-after teacher, with students back-to-back most weekend days. Each week I bring her a gift, a small token, a bag of apples, boxes of tomatoes, an occasional cake. Each week she tells me it is not nec-essary. Over the years, we have become friends. I am an amateur clarinetist. We began to play clarinet and piano music together. Often we talk as much as we play, finding friendship in the midst of music. It is a most delightful way to begin my Sunday. In between movements of various sonatas, she attends to a late breakfast which first cooks and then cools in the kitchen. Benny bounces on his yoga ball while we play in the living room.

We were not always this close. In fact, when we first had occasion to speak, I was upset with her and she would have been entitled to be annoyed at me. Our history provides an excellent example of the kind of frustrations that can happen surrounding inclusion. Our story suggests that we can overcome these misunderstandings, these oversights, and develop rich, real relationships when we listen and work hard at understanding the perspective we each bring to the table.

Early in our relationship we noticed that Benny has a lovely singing voice. In grade three, he learned to play the recorder, which he did largely by ear, resisting the instruction to read music. Nevertheless his peers told me daily that he was one of the best players in the grade. He could even play two recorders at the same time, harmonizing with himself. His penchant for doing most activities backwards as well as forwards enabled him to play right or left handed recorder.

Early in Benny's grade 4 year, another parent (the parent of the lovely red haired girl who had helped Benny with his potholder two years before) told me that Miriam was leading an extra curricular recorder group. Typically the children have recorder class in grade three and choose band and orchestra instruments by grade 4. Benny was playing trumpet in band, but still enjoyed playing recorder from time to time. The recorder group consisted of fourth graders who met early before school to rehearse. The ultimate goal was for them to represent the school in an all county recorder festival. This parent wondered why Benny was not in the group. I assumed that the group was by invitation and that Benny was not invited. I was disappointed and also a little upset with Miriam. I caught her one morning after I dropped off the boys and confronted her in the hallway. I asked her why he had not been invited. She explained that she had offered the opportunity to the entire grade and only a handful expressed interest. I tried to explain to her that Benny's disability made it difficult for him to focus on whole group announcements. She looked sympathetic and at the same time somewhat perplexed. In retrospect I realize that as a music teacher for the district she did not know the details of his disability. She had signed off on an abbreviated IEP summary sheet, and did not know that he was in the decimal percentiles for most language scales. I realize now that it would have been better for me to have arranged a meeting with her to discuss this issue, rather than confront her in the hallway before the start of a busy day.

She agreed to allow him in on a trial basis. If he could perform the required pieces, by ear, if not by reading, he could stay. I knew he could learn them by ear and I was overjoyed that he could be a part of the group. A few weeks later we found that she had changed the rehearsal schedule by making an announcement over the loudspeaker that Benny had not been able to process. Consequently, he missed these two rehearsals. Miriam warned me that if he missed too many he might not be able to learn his part. I asked her to send me a note via email. I got angry. I told her again that his ADHD and processing issues made it impossible for him to follow changes presented over the loudspeaker, and that she had a legal requirement to accommodate his disability. She was quiet and suggested that with 400+ students she simply could not give each of us a personal message. I felt the mix of defeat and anger, the acceptance of consequences born from Benny's disability and I felt powerless to change the circumstances. She how-ever, was not powerless and she had an idea. Later she called me and told me that she had asked another student, incidentally the same red haired girl who wanted Benny in the group, to keep Benny informed and call him the evening before each rehearsal. I was relieved but never for a moment anticipated the kind of relationship that ultimately formed between Benny, Miriam and me.

Benny learned the pieces by ear and since he came to know them that way he owned them in a manner that those of us who rely on music never do. In late spring the group represented the district at a recorder festival that drew hundreds of players. Each district learned a certain part of a piece that they would perform with all of the other recorder players from other districts. Each district learned a different line, some on recorders of different sizes. There were alto recorders and tenor recorders. Some of the students were thrown off a little by hearing all the other harmonies. Benny was intrigued with the new sounds and listened with an openness and excitement that set him apart from many of the other players. He knew his part so well that he did not have to think about the notes but played them with accuracy and confidence while he listened to all the new melodies. His friends watched his fingers for support. Benny's peers kept their eyes glued to his fingers at the final show. He was elated. I was so glad that he could have this feeling. Music is an area of strength for him, coming to him with ease, but there were so many boundaries there that potentially stood in his way of performing with his peers. After years of lagging behind academically, he had found a place where he had expertise and mastery. Miriam had come right to my side during the performance, and together we watched his fingers fly. Without words we forgave each other and, in retrospect, our friendship began within the silence where we stood that day.

It is interesting that a friendship was able to form where initially there was friction. The situation calls to mind the kind of continual negotiations we must take part in to find what works when we break down boundaries. By including a child with significant delays we open the door to reconfiguring our expectations. While I was initially upset with the way the door seemed closed to Benny, I learned that I had the power as his advocate to open that door, to push back, challenge a boundary. Miriam was accepting and by the time Benny was ready to graduate she had decided to do something about the fact that he did not read music yet, aware that without this skill he would be kept out of performance opportunities in the future. She literally opened her home to him.

Like many others, this situation that reflects Benny's interests and abilities in music is in stark contrast to our previous experiences. In NYC, I remember Benny's IEP meeting as he transitioned into Kindergarten. He had already been singing in a choir on the weekends with typical peers but when I requested that he attend music with the general education students, I was told that would not happen. We insisted it be written on his IEP but in fact the school refused to implement it, citing his disruptive behavior in his self-contained classroom as the reason.

When I think of boundaries I often would wonder how it is that the group of teachers at Boulder breaks these down so often and with such abandon, in such seemingly disparate ways? Upon closer reflection I see that the boundaries fall as teachers and students do not see Boulder school as separate from their real lives. Sometimes we create boundaries between work, school, and home because we need to protect ourselves from the stress of our daily responsibilities. Boulder has become such an oasis for the entire community, that there is a degree of comfort in forging past traditional boundaries. I grew up in an educational system ripe with strict boundaries. Teachers did not become friendly with parents, and administrators kept their distance from both families and teachers. Even as a teacher, I learned to keep my personal life separate from my work, and keeping a safe space between myself and most of my supervisors. In my mind I am convinced that this is best. In contrast, I look over the relationships formed at Boulder between teachers, administrators, therapists, students, and parents and find myself continually surprised by the depth of the friendships formed between members of the Boulder community. As a teacher I am envious because I have not worked in an environment with this level of trust and honesty between supervisor and faculty. As a parent, it took me years to relax enough to enjoy the depth of the connections possible, and to allow friendships to form in these places where I was taught friendship was inappropriate. It was not until Benny was in grade four that I had ever hugged a principal.

I often wonder to what extent the atmosphere created at Boulder, the way the school has become for many an extension of family, adds to the ease with which the school is so inclusive of difference. I know that it is an integral part of the reasons why inclusion is so successful here, but the reasons are complex and spread far and wide, defying the vocabulary we expect to draw upon when discussing educational issues. Do we need to let down the boundaries to achieve such success, and if so, will this be a "deal breaker" for many schools? A few of the reasons why this idea is so integral to inclusion follow.

Communication between school and home is essential for many types of success in school, but is crucial when the student is one who has some differences in the way that she or he learns and or behaves. When teachers see school is an extension of family, they give more freely of their time and energy. We speak of the need for schools to create connection with families. This is important for all students but perhaps especially vital for families of children with disabilities. These families tend to be less vocal and (we) need some help and encouragement connecting with other families. I certainly did, even with my white-middle class, educated background. There is something silencing about being told your child is behind the others, or in need of so much more support. The invitation to connect at Boulder came so frequently and in different forms it eventually caught us and drew us into the web of activity and connection. The process was neither easy nor immediate. We were tired and busy and it was too easy to push aside an outstretched hand from our child's school, especially when that hand reached out late in the evening after a long day of work. However, Boulder reached out again and again, both formally as discussed in chapter 10 and informally as discussed here, in ways that became so fervent and tempting, we had no choice but to step into the relationship.

***

At the heart of this chapter lies the desire to examine what can be achieved when assumed "professional" boundaries between parents, teachers, and children give way to more meaningful relationships. What is the relationship between inclusive education and boundaries? Is it paradoxical in that inclusion means the opening up of, reconfiguration, and even perhaps the eventual removal of existing boundaries? Is it more useful to think of inclusive education as the constant negotiation of existing boundaries—the push against the pull toward the nebulous state of "normalcy" that appears largely set even though it is always in flux? What boundaries can we speak of—physical, academic, emotional, social, other? Each one merits a separate look, yet all are bound together in the daily operations of schools, including teaching and learning within classrooms.

Negotiating professional and personal boundaries with parents and students make for pithy, oft-debated topics within teacher educational programs (Lawson, 2003). They are also ripe with contradictions about teaching, helping, supporting, respecting children and their parents on one hand, while on the other hand not becoming too involved and overly invested. It is generally recognized that lines have to be drawn to ensure space, with real and imagined legal implications hovering overhead like buzzards at all times. Yet it is not always a neat and tidy process for educators to divorce the personal from the professional, if it can be done at all. For many, the personal becomes the professional, and the professional becomes the personal. Effective teachers are aware that they have to know their students well if they are to teach them well (Collison, 1996). Likewise, for teachers to have parents as allies can greatly benefit the child they both have in common (Lord Nelson, Summers, & Turnbull, 2004).

And yet, to some degree, there is a perpetual tension between parent and teacher relationships in many schools. In terms of inclusive education, parents of children with disabilities have sometimes characterized general educator resistance as indifference, over-extendedness, hostility, lack of understanding, and so on (Soodak, Podell, & Lehman, 1998; Valle, 2009). In turn, teachers have sometimes characterized parents of students with disabilities in inclusive classrooms as entitled, unrealistic, and unwilling to face the truth of their child's limitations (Valle & Aponte, 2002; Vaughn, 1994). Among other things, this chapter allows us to reflect upon what have been our own educational experiences in regard to boundaries, whether it is from our viewpoint of student, teacher, principal, or parent. In addition, the chapter reveals ways in which all stakeholders can consider their current assumptions about personal and professional boundaries—and how these can impact the success or failure of inclusive experiences in general.

I recognize the importance of the concept of professionalism for teachers, including how it legitimizes the profession, providing recognition, guidance, support, and the security of a union (although not in all states). At the same time, I seek to highlight some of the drawbacks of professionalism. The general discourse of professionalism contributes to the notion of objectivity, of having borders, of being decontextualized through a professional positionality associated with power that is removed from children and parents served (Hilfery, 2007). Such notions of professionalism permit teachers the option of stepping back from the students they teach, akin to researchers working with their subjects. To get too close to students potentially muddies the waters for teachers, hence striving for a division between the personal and the professional is desirable for many. In this respect, it could be argued that the broad notion of professionalism, for many people, is primarily associated with the execution of a required skill set within an area of expertise acquired through an academic degree, usually reinforcing all kinds of unquestioned norms (Skrtic, 1991; Dudley-Marling & Gurn, 2010). Teachers with this type of professionalized disposition usually do not seek to primarily understand the context of the student, family, and their school experiences, as they are more concerned with adhering to the official script that already exists and getting their job done (Brantlinger, 2004).

The strong pull of professional discourse also comes within a hierarchy of expected knowledge, a sense of "knowing better" than someone who does not have the same training, including parents (Harry & Klingner, 2006). Such dispositions of professionalism reflect belief systems that traditionally distance parents from schools and teachers (Valle & Gabel, 2010). In this particular chapter, Diane illuminates the dilemmas of teachers who do not know alternatives to professionalism that distances them from the very people they seek to help. At the same time, as a teacher herself, she conveys how it is difficult to being more open. Diane's experience of professionalism had been quite reserved until actively challenged by the principal and faculty at Boulder, yet she knows their approach is an integral element of the school's success in inclusive education. Clark is uncharacteristically open for a principal, sharing his domestic situation, a separation from his partner. It was then that Diane realized she "… had not had a personal conversation with a principal, ever," as if they were a different species without the ability to relate to one another.

It is clear that the principal's comfort level in sharing aspects of his own life influences staff members in how they approach engaging with children and families. Diane notes, "I see that the boundaries fall as teachers and students do not see Boulder school as separate from their real lives." Simultaneously, she acknowledges that, "Sometimes we create boundaries between work, school, and home because we need to protect ourselves from the stress of our daily responsibilities." While we both believe each person can and should decide the degree to which they "mix" their professional and personal lives, it is clear that the staff at Boulder veer toward an openness that seeks to dissolve boundaries if they are understood to be preventing a child's academic, social, or emotional growth.

As can be seen in the exchange between Miriam and Benny, I think it is safe to say that student and teacher relationships can often be life transforming (I suspect that most people reading this book have had at least one teacher who took a particular interest, and helped develop a specific talent). There is a definite symbiosis at play in the growth evidenced within, and continuation of, piano lessons. Yet, this deep and mutually satisfying relationship could never have been imagined at one point. In fact, the beauty of this narrative lies in how a well-respected and accomplished teacher is challenged by inclusive practices. When Miriam's initial response to Diane was that she would not individualize communication for one student because she had over four hundred others, we see an example of the proverbial last straw that we have all experienced at one time or another ("Given all that I do already, I can't do one more thing"). As a former teacher and current college professor, I can understand this. At any given moment, an educator feels they simply cannot do any more or change anything else as we frequently run on automatic, managing the often overwhelming nature of the job. However, I also know that upon reflection, with time to think, most teachers are agreeable to a solution if it helps the student and does not take the teacher too far away from the core of what and how they are teaching. Miriam's initial "lukewarm" response to include Benny soon gave way to simple, practical solutions. If he proved that he could play the music, even without reading it, Benny was "in." After a bump in the road concerning the sharing of information over the loudspeaker, if Miriam changed rehearsal times, another student would inform Benny via telephone.

This episode is an authentic instance of negotiating inclusion, complete with the reality of competing ideas about what is right for a child and what is possible for a teacher to facilitate. The push-and-pull experienced is a characteristic of a desire to change the status quo. What becomes rendered here is the example of a strong and understanding teacher, appropriately challenged by an assertive parent, both of whom try to provide a child with access to music, peers, and public performance. Is it a gamble? Yes. Is it a risk? Somewhat. Could the whole attempt have backfired? Possibly. Would we ever know if Benny could rise to the occasion, and excel, if he had not been provided with this opportunity? No. The fact that Benny "was elated," and a friendship born between teacher and parent, speaks to rethinking the boundaries that educators can consciously or inadvertently impose upon students. In this instance, Benny became a leader, a knower, someone who showed his peers how to participate within the expectations of the performance. Once again, it behooves us to invoke his previous school experience in a self-contained class where he was prohibited from having access to Choir—something he liked, could participate in, and do well. In the initial placement in a self-contained classroom, Benny's containment bound him, stunted his musical and social growth, and punished him for his behavior in an inappropriate setting wherein the family had no choice. Worse still, unlike Miriam and her colleagues at Boulder, his teachers and school did not even let Benny try.

In reflecting upon the episodes within this chapter and connections to DSE, I see how the story "contextualize(s) disability within political and social spheres" (Connor et. al, 2008, p. 448) in that Diane believed it to be Benny's right to participate in recorder practice, and also potentially perform at the music festival. Her actions provide and example of how "the education of students labeled with disabilities in non-segregated settings [are] from a civil rights stance" (p. 448). Likewise, albeit reluctantly at first, Miriam did "assume competence and reject deficit models of disability" (p. 448) when she allowed Benny to participate in the music group. Importantly, I also see this as an example of recognizing the "…embodied/aesthetic experiences of people whose lives/selves are made meaningful as disabled" (p. 448), as how Benny learns, processes, internalizes information—in brief, "functions"—turns out to be an asset in the challenging performance required by the festival. Additionally, as embodied in the relationship between Miriam and Benny, and manifest in their Sunday lessons, we see how "Disability is primarily recognized and valued as a natural part of human diversity" (p. 449).

This chapter triggered several trains of thought for me. The first one was how schooling practices contribute to students being humanized or dehumanized, broadly reflected in Benny's contrasting experiences in Boulder and his self-contained placement. What contributes to these practices is the willingness of educators to be open and have informed, sensible responses to the needs of a child in a specific situation, or a strict and unquestioning adherence to institutionally imposed boundaries that often strike me as not in the best interests of the children they claim to serve. In terms of metaphors, the environments can be broadly described as open-endedness versus containment. Each place brings its challenges in terms of management, and I'd argue that it is generally viewed as more predictable, tidy, and easily organized to have students contained versus trying and seeing what is the best context for them.

I stand in agreement with Diane when she asks, "How unfair it is that we limit children in all areas when often there are areas of great strength existing right alongside those areas in which we struggle? How better to develop a child's sense of self than to allow him to find those areas?" In the relentless pursuit of academic excellence for students who struggle in those areas, so much else of the curriculum usually becomes lost—arts, music, theater, sports—leaving students see themselves as complete and perpetual failures, without talent or skills, unable to do anything worthwhile (Cunningham, 2001; Mooney & Cole, 2000; Pelkey, 2001; Raymond & Raymond, 2011).

Another train of thought I had involved thinking about times in everyone's career when the existing boundaries in professional educational practices are transgressed because it feels like the right thing to do. For example, I once watched a principal approach a very angry young woman who had physically and verbally lashed out at everyone despite their genuine attempts to connect with her, and simply say, "Let's go outside for a smoke and a walk around the block." They did. It worked. She was able to calm down and shared the particulars of her very stressful life situation. In turn, the principal was then able to seek the supports she needed immediately.

Likewise, in my own career I sometimes sat with a high school student and said, "Forget I am your teacher for a moment. I need to speak with you as one human being to another." In doing so, traditional boundaries are no longer important, they are pushed into the background in the quest to communicate with a young woman who once attempted to take her life and felt suicidal again, or a young man who has discovered the availability of same sex anonymous encounters. I wanted her to know why life is worth living. I wanted him to know why he had to be very careful. I wanted them both to enjoy the future and know they could exert considerable control over their destinies. As Diane has mentioned, there's a sense of dread and professional risk in conversing honestly, be it with a parent or a student, in case something backfires and "goes wrong." Yet in most of these situations things have already gone wrong for the parent or student, and a direct conversation is needed with view to finding an agreed upon solution that usually spans the worlds of both inside and outside of school.

Diane asked the provocative question: "Do we need to let down the boundaries to achieve such success [with inclusion], and if so, will this be a 'deal breaker' for many schools?" I suspect that the answer will be yes for some schools based on a variety of reasons, including the strong sense of a professional and personal divide. However, as interesting and influential as

Descartes' (1999) idea of the separation of the human body and mind has been, the idea is only that, an idea. Just as a body cannot be separated from a mind, and a mind cannot be separated from a body, I argue that for a genuine educator, the personal cannot be separate from the professional, and vice versa. It may be more useful to think in terms of, to what degree are these artificially binaric discourses both evoked in responding to any given inclusive situation? As educators, how are we reinforcing or opening up boundaries? Who erected them? And in the spirit of Gramsci (1999), who benefits most from the boundaries? Who does not? Most importantly, what can we do to contribute to further removing some of the boundaries imposed upon children and encourage their growth? Although admittedly not easy, I am cautiously optimistic that questioning and renegotiating boundaries is not a deal breaker for many schools while they continue to develop and hone their inclusive practices. As revealed in this chapter, rethinking existing boundaries that uphold the status quo, and recreating new ways of dissolving those boundaries, is within our collective reach.

References

Brantlinger, E. (2004). Confounding the needs and confronting the norms: An extension of Reid and Valle's essay. *Journal of Learning Disabilities, 37*(6), 490–499.

Collison, V. (1996). *Reaching students: Teachers' ways of knowing.* Thousand Oaks, CA: Corwin.

Connor, D. J., Gabel, S. L., Gallagher, D. & Morton, M. (2008). Disability studies and inclusive education—Implication for theory, research, and practice: Guest editor's introduction. *International Journal of Inclusive Education, 12*(5–6), 441–457.

Cunningham, V. (2001). Lovelvet. In P. Rodis, S. Garrod & M. L. Boscardin (Eds.), *Learning disabilities & life stories* (pp. 82–96). Needham Heights, MA: Allyn & Bacon.

Dudley-Marling, C., & Gurn, A. (Eds.). (2010). *The myth of the normal curve.* New York, NY: Lang

Gramsci, A. (1999). *Selections from the prison notebooks.* New York: International.

Harry, B. & Klingner, J. (2006). *Why are so many minority students in special education?* New York: Teachers College.

Hilferty, F. (2007). Theorising teacher professionalism as an enacted discourse of power. *British Journal of Sociology of Education, 29*(2), 161–173.

Lawson, M. (2003). School-family relations in context: parent and teacher perceptions of parent involvement. *Urban Education, 3*(38), 77–133.

Lord Nelson, L. G., Summers, J. A., &Turnbull, A. (2004). Boundaries in family-professional relationships: Implications for special education. *Remedial and Special Education, 25*(3), 153–165.

Pelkey, L. (2001). In the LD bubble. In P. Rodis, S. Garrod & M. L. Boscardin (Eds.), *Learning disabilities and life stories* (pp. 17–28). Needham Heights: Allyn & Bacon.

Raymond, A., & Raymond, S. (Producer and Director). (2011). *Journey into dyslexia*. [Motion Picture]. USA: HBO.

Skrtic, T. M. (1991). The special education paradox: Equity as a way to excellence. *Harvard Educational Review, 61*(2), 148–206.

Soodak, L., Podell, D. M., & Lehman, L. (1998). Teacher, student, and school attributes as predictors of teachers responses to inclusion. *The Journal of Special Education, 31*(4), 480–497.

Valle, J. W. (2009). *What mothers say about special education: From the 1960s to the present.* London: Palgrave McMillan.

Valle, J. W., & Aponte, E. (2002). IDEA and collaboration: A Bakhtinian perspective on parent and professional discourse. *Journal of Learning Disabilities, 35*, 469–479.

Valle, J. W., & Gabel, S. L. (2010). The sirens of normative mythology: Mother narratives of engagement and resistance. In C. Dudley-Marling and A. Gurn (Eds). *The myth of the normal curve* (pp. 187–204) . New York: Peter Lang.

Vaughn, S. (1994). Teachers' views of inclusion: "I'd rather pump gas." Paper presented at the Annual Meeting of the American Educational Research Association (New Orleans, LA, April 4–8, 1994).

· 1 2 ·

GRADE 5 IN THE PENTHOUSE

It is easy to conceptualize how inclusion works in an elementary school classroom, where the goals can so easily be modified. It is harder to understand how an upper level classroom can work. Grade 5 at Boulder gives us a window into this process due to it serving as a bridge year to middle school, when academics begin to take precedence over other activities in the classroom. Benny entered grade 5 still rather far below the level of his peers in math and reading. He tested roughly two years behind his age group. I wondered how he would be prepared for middle school, where I knew already, academics would not be modified for him. I was interested to learn from Tom, both as a parent with some anxiety, and an educator eager to share his secrets for success. I had heard that virtually all of his students went on to do well in the rigorous middle school that did not use ability tracking, offering a high level curriculum for all. Students in grade 8 take a program comparable to what an honors student takes at my own school. Tom presents with a remarkable sense of calm, a person who is hopeful and kind. His classroom never feels rushed or pressured despite the tremendous academic demands upon today's fifth graders.

I asked him first how he manages to meet the disparate goals of all the students in his class. He is often given the children with the more severe disabilities, no doubt because of the supportive, indeed quite beautiful, atmosphere he is

able to create. I think of the academic goals that stretch far and wide, especially in today's world of Common Core. I consider my own two boys, Benny who performs in some areas two grade levels below what is expected, and Adam who performs in some areas two years above. Tom's response to my musings is simple and elegant. "My goals," he says, "are not academic. They are social." He speaks of his desire to create a community in his classroom, describing the need for his students to be "helpful, respectful, and caring." Tom mentions how he tries to teach them how to get along, reach out to help others, and to ask for help. It makes such complete sense and yet sentiments like that are few and far between in education today. By choosing meaningful goals and ones that are realizable within a diverse student body, Tom makes it possible to teach with success.

Teachers need to feel like they are able to reach their goals. When they choose goals that are not feasible, they fail and burn out. We need to realize that our goals are completely within our control. Tom searched his soul and found goals he believed in with a passionate intensity. Suddenly it all makes sense: the beautiful atmosphere in his class comes from one of his simple goals.

December 2012: A Peek into Tom's Classroom

I quickly checked my phone between teaching my classes and saw that there was a message from Boulder's school nurse. I asked a colleague to take my next class and I returned the call. She told me that Benny had been hit in the face with a ball at recess and that his nose had been bleeding for 15 minutes. It was not stopping, and she asked me to pick him up. Although I was used to Benny's nose, which is prone to bleeds, I was slightly panicked. The variable was the ball, this was not a simple winter bleed, but an injury and we did not know the extent. Luckily by the time I got to the school, Benny was back in his class, attending a holiday party to which parents had been invited. His class sat around a fire burning on the smart board and each student had a chance to recount the clues from the secret snowflake game (a play on secret Santa) and make two guesses as to whose theirs was. It has been a long while since I had seen Benny in class and the sight of him sitting content amongst his peers was delightful. Since I had returned to full time work, I had missed many of these in-school events, so couldn't take my eyes off him, and his obvious happiness. The joy extended much further than a simple cerebral pleasure—it was a feeling that permeated every cell in my body. This class was a community, a full and complete world, and Benny was an integral part. He was sitting amongst a group of 10 year olds on the way to middle school the following fall, and he had found himself. I noticed that he laughed so easily with his peers; he listened so well to all that they said.

Somewhere inside of me I still live in those days when he could not even sit in a circle, when he was drawn to corners of the room, and closets, and when even in a class of students identified as disabled, he could not seem to function. To sit there and feel the connections flying by between each and every student and teacher was incredibly satisfying. Although teachers told me just days before at conference time, of his abilities and his warmth, I could not quite register the information without seeing it myself. The children exchanged gifts with their secret snowflakes, and Benny was given a harmonica that he immediately began to play. Beautiful melodies streamed out from this blue shimmery sliver of metal, and the kids in the class flocked all around him to listen. Two girls danced in circles around Benny beaming up at him as he played, each wanting to be close to him and connect to be part of the circle of song he was weaving so effortlessly. They looked up to him for this gift, and I saw again the way he enriches their world as much as evenly and symmetrically as his peers enrich his. Then he asked to visit Adam and we walked down the hall, continuing to play. Teachers and students poked their heads out of classroom to see from where the music came. No one was surprised to find that Benny was the musician. As I walked down the hallway of Boulder with my bright-eyed boy, I was joined once again by the ghosts of whom Benny might have become had we stayed in NYC. They are tall and thin, like Benny, and handsome, but they are not smiling, they do not radiate a confidence in every step. They are not dancing down a hallway in a school that fostered tremendous growth. They are scared and frustrated, hollow. They remain far below grade level. They join me now and then, suggesting to me of what could have been, reminding me to accept and to celebrate differences, compelling me to teach my teachers to be strong, and to embrace every child who walks through their door. These phantom children, I expect, will live with me for life, faces of what might have been, crystallized by stories I have heard, from parents I have met along the way. I carry them along with a certain appreciation as they keep me centered, focused, and grateful. When we walked home later I asked him about his nose and the ball that got in his way. I expected that he was on the bench or standing around when a ball unrelated to him came smashing down. I knew recess had been a time when he vacillates between playing with others and being alone. He seemed okay spending time alone. In fact, I finally accepted that he enjoys it, but part of me still yearns for indications that he does also enjoy time with his peers. That day, though, he told me it was not a ball after all, but that he and three boys were horsing around in a hula hoop together, when they tumbled down and by accident he got hit by an elbow. When I saw Benny horsing around in my mind's eye, swoons of pleasure began to swell up from my knees to my chest, making me almost seasick with delight. My Benny was playing with the boys horsing around he tells me, together in a hula hoop with his friends, not standing alone on the side. I felt so grateful for the nosebleed and the call from the nurse, and the job nearby, and the holiday party that I almost missed, and the harmonica, and the children who love him, and most of all, for the boy who could finally tell me with sunshine in his eyes about how he horses around.

One Week Later

It was just days later and we had turned the thermostat low to keep the dry heat from the Benny's delicate nose. It was 58 degrees in the house and Adam climbed into our bed at 3:50 AM to get warm. We snuggled and cuddled and fell back to sleep—a delicious warm reminder of the days when he would nurse on and off all night, sleeping with a delicate satisfied smile, his tiny feet tucked into my belly, just like when he was inside. Suddenly it was 6:50 AM and Adam was stiff, pale, and wheezing in a horrifying labored way. I screamed, still hoping I was just in a bad dream, but then David joined me and his voice told me this is really happening. I ran and called 911 while David tried to breathe into him, telling me that Adam seemed to be breathing on his own. I heard the sirens and Adam reached toward me, and pulled me in, a sign that he was somewhat aware although he did not answer to his name and his eyes remained unfocused with more white than brown pupils showing. The volunteer from Emergency Medical Services (EMS) who lives across the street came first. He said that Adam was having a seizure.

The word somehow relaxed me. It was defined, it had an ending, and it was not a death sentence. More people arrived into my bedroom and began to mull around. They placed an oxygen mask on Adam, which he removed, showing he has some spunk, and clung to me as they tried to lay him on the stretcher. Subsequently, they told me to lie on the stretcher and then placed Adam in my arms. Benny was pale and frightened. He stayed in bed, head under his pillow, peering out of the door, watching them carry his brother. The look in his eye was one of profound devastation. It was then I realized that Adam was the most important person in Benny's life. I told Benny that Adam would be okay. But he did not hear my words; they meant nothing in view of Adam's limp body. In the ambulance EMS personnel asked Adam questions and he nodded and mumbled, but no words came. What if he would recover but had some damage to his mind, his wonderful brilliant mind? I held my son and know that so long as he would live, I would love him and I tried not to ask for more. First I felt strained to think these thoughts, but suddenly I was in a new place altogether, a place of pure love, for his body, for the smell of his sweat, the vanilla scent he has had since birth, for the gentle turn of his ear. I could concentrate only on the rise and fall of his chest. I was in an inexplicable state of bliss, being in the ambulance with him on me breathing was all I needed to function. To ask for more was to water down the most important thing and that was that he should live, that he was alive in my arms, and that we loved each other. At first I was making bargains with the universe, but soon I found myself at peace. I realized that responsive or not he was here and I did not need words to connect with him. By the time they attached the intravenous line he was asking questions, and I was elated. Every word he uttered was a gift, a priceless jewel, something I would never take for granted again, but I knew I would never forget the moments we shared when all of this was in question and somehow that was okay, too. Those moments of silence bonded us in a new way, a way we were long ago when he grew within me.

Adam passed all the tests and they sent us home with a temporary diagnosis of seizure disorder. We had appointments to come with our neurologist to follow up, to look for clues, to try to predict the future, to decide what precautions to take. The word epilepsy did not scare me, though a few years ago it would have. If this is what he has, I was ready to accept this as part of who he was. The perspective I had come to own helped me embrace this as part of Adam. I understood now that we all come with a complex array of neurological connections. These differences, these apparent glitches also give us our individuality. To rail against the glitches is to argue against our unique makeup. Our job became to make sure that he is safe, that we adapt the environment to fit his needs, and that he never felt like there was anything he couldn't accomplish.

The next few days I slept beside him, at the request of the doctors. It was a cozy feeling to lie next to him and feel as though I could keep him safe. We met with the neurologist and he had an electroencephalogram (EEG). I could see from the technician's face that he had some abnormality--another word I detest. We left with a diagnosis of Benign Focal Epilepsy of Childhood along with a handful of prescriptions. It was treatable, limited, and he would grow out of it I was told. Still, I was shaking inside. As soon as we reached home, I ran over to Boulder. Stepping into that school felt like a warm bath after a very hard day. There was an immediate and profound sense of comfort, knowing how well these teachers know Adam, and how eager they were to support him and me. Clark greeted me in the office with a hug, I had already told them of the events and of our pending appointment by email the night before. Many faculty and staff had already expressed their support. They felt like family to me. Lucy came into the office and she put her arms around me. Would I be able to send Adam back into the hands of anyone else? The nurse came by and we spoke for a while. This situation was not new to them, and their experiences relieved some of my anxiety, making me feel calmer. Benny's teachers came by as well, wanting to be a part of this too, offering their expertise, empathy, and interest. Clark told me that school staff turns down the fire alarm lights in one room before drills because the flashing lights affect a student. That does not seem to be a trigger for Adam, I explained, but I am relieved to hear the questions, to hear their willingness to adapt, so that Adam can be safe. Lucy told me that when Adam comes back to school I could call her throughout the day. She told the office to put me right through to her classroom enabling her to tell me that Adam was okay, understanding how hard this has been for all of us.

What have faculty and staff at Boulder done to amass this expertise aside from experiencing this issue with other students? When we ask ourselves what teachers need in order to prepare to embrace children designated as having special needs, is there anything more than experience that they require? How lovely to know that this is not new to them, how beautiful that while I shudder and shake, they can be calm and consoling. How wonderful to know that they will make sure Adam is safe without treating him like a stranger. How quickly a "typical" child can become one with special needs, how vulnerable we all are to our bodies, and how whole we can feel if these changes and challenges can be absorbed into the routine with love and with laughter.

Is it unreasonable to suggest that all schools should be a haven for parents as well as children? In this time of social instability isn't there a role for schools to play in the emotional lives of the families they serve? How can we call attention to the possibility of a school support team as a balm for aching and weary souls? Can we create well-rounded, emotionally stable citizens if we fail to harness the power of the most accessible and universal community?

Two years later, Adam had the privilege of being in Tom's class. Adam had continued through grades 3 and 4 to do exemplary work. By grade 5 he was involved in many clubs, the newspaper club, the gardening club, math olympiads, orchestra and band, and took advantage of every possible moment to shine in the Circus and the Variety Show. In class he developed a side of himself that was quite entertaining. Tom had the greatest way of channeling Adam's behavior. First he allowed himself to appreciate Adam's humor and talent. Adam somehow developed the nickname "Berminator" in grade 5, and Tom allowed him to go by that name. He confessed to me that he found Adam so entertaining he often had to squelch his own laughter for the good of the order and also because, as his teacher, it was his duty to make sure that Adam did not cross the line or take too much of the attention away from the lesson. It was interesting to me that Adam developed this side of himself since the rest of the family was usually so quiet and preferred to go unnoticed if given an option. Adam had an incredible year as he honed his humor and discovered that he loved the limelight. Tom and Adam had a special bond that I do not think was rivaled by any other bond that Adam formed in school. Tom was the first teacher Adam felt comfortable enough to turn to for advice on many matters. It was in grade 5 that Adam solidified his friendship with his best friend He also discovered girls and became friends with a few, taking great joy in his ability to make them laugh. Though he still suffered occasional seizures, which sapped his energy, grade 5 was an exceptionally wonderful year for Adam. He developed sides of himself I did not know he had. Most interesting is that Tom and the other teachers at Boulder consider it their responsibility to oversee the emergence of personality as much if not more so than the academic development of their students. Tom's class was an inclusion class, and there were many children in Adam's year that received special education supports. In no way did they impede Adam's progress in grade 5. In fact, they created a culture of differentiation that was beneficial for all of the students. There were three children from the self-contained program in Adam's class. He had asked on occasion why these kids do not spend the whole day with his class, wondering why they only spent half a day with him and their other peers. I was always interested in listening to his thoughts about this. Adam made many suggestions, never once alluding to their disability, although he knew they had Down syndrome. To him, it was just a label, and he never associated this label with any sort of justification for the fact that they left to go to another classroom midway through the day. Adam adored Grace, Shira, and Tim. He suggested many possible reasons for the fact that they went to another classroom in the afternoon, but disregarded most of them because they did not fit with what he perceived. In the end Adam reasoned that they were allergic to cheese and had to leave before lunch because some kids in his classroom ate cheese. It is interesting to me how most (of not all) schools, even Boulder, do have some boundary between who can be included and how extensively. The children in the self-contained program still got more time in general education than in most schools in the region, but they only get to spend half a day with their typical peers. I wonder how the day would be for them if they would be fully integrated in the general education classroom? It seems widely accepted here that half a day is best. No one seems to question that, except for the children, like Adam and his friends, who miss them when they are taken back to their self contained classroom.

One of Adam's best friends, Todd, goes to visit the self-contained classrooms as much as possible. He has been praised over and over for this "act of kindness," but he just does it because they are his friends and he misses them when they are not in his classroom. One of my graduate students at Hunter pointed out that regardless of how far inclusion spreads, in the end, it is still the "typical" folks who decide when and how to include those with disabilities in society. We, the "normal" still broker the arrangements and regardless of how far we move towards the social model, it seems tragically inevitable that this will continue to be the case unless we develop a significantly different understanding of disability.

At the grade 5 ballroom dance show, emotions ran high as this was the last event of its kind for students at Boulder. Adam wore his best suit and tie. He asked for a rose to be fit within the lapel of his jacket. On his face he wore a smile full with sunshine. When the show began, students from grade 5 came in the auditorium, boys escorting their partners. Adam came in with a noticeable presence. He had two children he was escorting. Each of his arms was intertwined with one of the students from the self-contained program. Grace was on one side and Tim on the other. I felt a surge of pride that my son was chosen to escort two of the children from the Core class, but quickly questioned this emotion. Adam was overjoyed to be paired with them because they were his friends. My pride was a remnant of my past, a part of me that still thinks we do a favor to society by accepting difference. It is hard but not impossible to escape our upbringing. He was delighted to be paired with Grace as he and a few other boys vied constantly for her attention. When she laughed her whole face sparkled and they would try to outdo each other and make her laugh first. The chance to escort Grace gave Adam some extra time to try to make her laugh with his homegrown jokes. There was not a hint of sympathy or even empathy in the love these children have for each other. The power of inclusion lies in the way children accept each other. It is we, the adults, who have to unlearn so much of what we have internalized over the years, including the messages we are bombarded with daily. I have my Hunter College students keep a weekly journal, and once they open their eyes to the issues surrounding disability in society, they see instances of inequity all over. The purest form of acceptance (I do not even like that word) lies in the hearts of our children. When we can harness that power, we have successful classroom communities.

***

Tom is the central force in this chapter that weaves together many issues. He is a teacher that serves as an anchor in the elementary school of Boulder, preparing students for the bridge to middle school. Diane's narrative of Tom calls to mind the perennially posed question: What makes an effective inclusive educator? Of course it is tempting to construct and ideal, a composite picture based upon all things that we know. However, a truthful response lies closest in studying successful teachers of all children, in their particular contexts, to observe and take note of "what works" in those contexts. Bearing this point in mind, what we do come to know about Tom and his context at Boulder are the following: he is child-centered; committed to character education; holds strong community values; believes in everyone helping and supporting one another; utilizes heterogeneous group work, peer, and self-learning during his classes. When Adam is in Tom's class, we come to know his teacher's other characteristics that include being good-natured, patient, humorous, understanding, and tolerant—as well as being focused, thoughtful, and well-organized.

When asked by Diane to explain his philosophy and general disposition, Tom's response of "My goals...are not academic...they are social," are described by her as, "simple and elegant." However, they can also be viewed as educational heresy within the current orthodoxy of the state's priorities for mandated testing. Tom speaks of his desire to create a community in his classroom, describing the need for his students to be "helpful, respectful, and caring." He also mentions his efforts to teach them how to get along, reach out to help others, and to ask for help themselves. This desire of Tom, also reflected in the other teachers at Boulder, reveals how they consider "their responsibility to oversee the emergence of personality as much if not more so than the academic development of their students." Tom's disposition toward teaching is essentially humanist, concerned with the dignity and welfare of everyone. He is therefore a teacher who understands the principles of inclusive education. As Diane writes, "...there were many children in Adam's year who received special education supports. They in no way impeded Adam's progress in grade 5. In fact, they created a culture of differentiation that was beneficial for all of the students." Tom not only understands the principles, he practices them in what appears to be an effortless manner. He is able to achieve this success by discerning, with the help of his colleagues, "...meaningful goals and ones that are realizable within a diverse student body," thereby making it "possible to teach such a body with success."

Both Benny and Adam benefit enormously from having Tom as a teacher. In Adam's case, he developed a bond that was unrivaled with any other faculty member, as "Tom was the first teacher Adam felt comfortable enough to turn to for advice on many matters." Recounting the discovery of Adam's epilepsy reminds us about the fragility of an existence that we usually take for granted. It also ground us in the reality of schools' responding to medical needs of students. Although Diane, David, and Benny are traumatized by Adam's then-unknown condition, it becomes clear what are sometimes the fears and nightmares of families are actually everyday issues that are manageable in schools. In brief, Adam's condition was something the school would be aware of and respond to when needed, thus, "normalizing" the situation. Of course, this is the essence of inclusive education, recognition that disabilities are actually absolutely normal. Diane reflects, "How wonderful to know that they [Boulder staff] will make sure Adam is safe without treating him like a stranger."

Her family's experience with Adams' epilepsy also gives her pause to ask, "What have faculty and staff at Boulder done to amass this expertise aside from experiencing this issue with other students? When we ask ourselves what teachers need in order to prepare to embrace children designated as having special needs, is there anything more than experience that they require?" This point raises the forever-present important issue of experience. Throughout my career, I have heard objections against inclusive education along the lines of, "I don't have the experience," "I don't have that expertise," "That's what special educators are for," and so on. I understand the universal fear of the unknown, but at the same time, as educators (and as human beings in general), we know that we learn through experience. More importantly, put another way: we must have experiences in order to learn. Many years ago I recall listening to one pro-inclusion speaker address an audience of largely unreceptive administrators, who could not see beyond the fact of existing teachers having a of lack of experience with students who have disabilities, thus making inclusion impossible. The speaker's response was simple, and went along the lines of, "A mother who has a child with a disability—say, for example—Down Syndrome, does not have any experience of people with Down Syndrome… she learns to take care of, nurture, and educate by understanding her child. There's no magic. The experience teaches her." This exchange stuck with me as it encapsulated some of the core issues of inclusive education. Without wishing to oversimplify, on one side we have educators who may say, "We can't, because we don't know how…" and on the other we have families who say, "Try, like we did, and you'll learn along the way…" In the influential documentary Including Samuel (Habib, 2007), Douglas Biklen, then Dean of Syracuse's School of Education was asked, "Does real inclusion exist anywhere?" His response, paraphrased, was "Absolutely… in families… they do it all the time." Families are the experts of inclusion, not because they went to college and studied it, but because they had to figure it out as they went along. I emphasize this point as I believe that we learn how to teach students with disabilities—indeed all students—by teaching them. At the same time, as an educator, I do recognize that a teacher cannot stand alone and know everything about the human race. It is actual experience coupled by support of the teacher that makes for a successful inclusive classroom. This support can take the shape of inclusion specialists, special educators, speech therapists, occupational therapists, paraprofessionals, school aides, accessing knowledge of former teachers, and of course, families. Teacher education programs featuring many different ways that students can be taught skills and knowledge, should have a foundational understanding of disability as a natural part of human diversity, and recognition that educators will be lifelong learners throughout the course of their careers by virtue of teaching all types of children.

Adam's epilepsy also illustrates how quickly a "typical" child can become one with a disability. A phrase once employed widely by the disability community when describing non-disabled people is Temporarily Able Bodied (TAB). In one respect, the phrase highlighted the vulnerability of everybody. In another respect, it sounded ominous. (I recall Disability Studies scholar Simi Linton expressing her dislike of the term as it suggested the sentiment, "We're gonna get you next!"). That said, this chapter reminds us that anyone in our families, anyone we teach can, and even ourselves, can become a person with a disability at any moment in time. Diane's response to her youngest son's condition conveys how we can understand differences among us. She shares, "The perspective I had come to own helped me embrace this as part of Adam.

I understood now that we all come with a complex array of neurological connections. These differences, these apparent glitches also give us our individuality. To rail against the glitches is to argue against our unique makeup." In other words, our differences play an integral part in making us who we are.

The same sentiment is evoked in this chapter when considering Benny. Although Diane is thrilled that Benny's nosebleed is a result of horsing around with friends, providing evidence of "typicality" and authentic social integration, she is also keenly aware of his exceptionality. I am wary of using this word—exceptionality—as it has been co-opted by the special education community, providing a euphemism that deflects from their reality as people disabled by society. However, there are instances wherein Benny's abilities are unique, such as his recorder playing. Diane notes how his friends, "…look[ed] up to him for this gift, and I saw again the way he enriches their world as much as evenly and symmetrically as his peers enrich his."

DSE often challenges the concept of exceptionality as those who evoke it never render the mythical normal against which the exceptionality is measured against (Baglieri, Bejoian, Broderick, Connor, & Valle, 2011). Elements of DSE in this chapter suggests ways in which "Disabled students are supported in the development of a positive disability identity" (Connor et. al., 2008, p. 449). For example, Adam's epilepsy does not interfere with who he is or what he does in school and at home. As Diane conveys, it becomes an integral part of who he is and how he comes to understand differences within himself that deepen his understanding of differences in others. The chapter also "Contrasts medical, scientific, psychological understandings with social and experiential understandings of disability" (p. 448). While it is interesting to know the medical name for Adam's condition is Benign Focal Epilepsy of Childhood, and the implications for the term, the episode's emphasis on the family's understanding of this disability, along with the social implications within school, portray an authentic picture of disability as a manageable phenomenon rather than simply a tragic form of sickness that often serves as the master narrative.

Tom's class, in which both Benny and Adam flourish, is a strong exemplar of what exists at Boulder, is an environment that "promote[s] social justice, equitable and inclusive educational opportunities, and full and meaningful access to all aspects of society for people labeled with disability/disabled people" (p. 448). It is also a place in which students are being prepared—academically, socially, emotionally—for middle school. In contemplating this "bridge" year, I also thought of students, in time, transitioning from middle to high school. These bridge years sometimes serve to make or break the success of students with disabilities in inclusive classrooms, as the gap between grade-level expectations and student academic performance becomes widened. Teachers face very real challenges and pressures of standardizing test scores, making some believe inclusive classrooms are not the place for some students with disabilities (Avramidis & Norwich, 2002). Pedagogical approaches and materials have been developed to help teachers plan units, lessons, organizational devices, and so on. See, for example, the Strategic Instruction Model developed by Don Deschler and his colleagues, illustrated with examples (Deshler, Schumaker, Harris, & Graham, 1999). While helpful in a practical way, these approaches represent largely technical responses to inclusive education—and are not sufficient in and of themselves to support the social, emotional, and philosophical components. Successful accounts of middle and high school inclusive education document a healthy balance between philosophical groundings of teachers, creative pedagogy, and acknowledgement that standardized expectations serve as a guide that are modified when needed, with "success" being defined and gauged in multiple ways (Danforth, 2014; Hehir & Katzman, 2012).

What is considered successful inclusion at all school levels is complicated by the notion of "partial inclusion," a topic Diane raises. She notes, "It is interesting to me how most (if not all) schools, even Boulder, do have some boundary between who can be included and how extensively." This issue is highlighted by children with Down syndrome who are included for approximately half of their school day, raising the question of how to view the situation: is the glass half full or half empty? Arguably, if ironically, it can be both. On one hand, children with Down syndrome are included more than they are in almost all other schools across the nation. On the other hand, if it were partial integration of any other group of children—be they females, African Americans, Jewish, those with speech and language challenges, and so on—there would be an uproar. My initial response is that, like everywhere else, Boulder is a work-in-progress, and this direction toward inclusion is something they are learning about, and learning from. That said, at least within this narrative, it seems like the included children question the situation more than the adults. Adam is puzzled by the disappearance of his friends Grace, Shira, and Tim halfway through the day, eventually putting it down to their allergies to cheese.

The vestiges of how we, largely able-bodied people, view who should be included, why, when, where, and how, are present in considering students in the Center program. It seems like children with Down syndrome still fall through the net of being fully included, because their perceived needs merit a different environment. Diane notes how, "One of Adam's best friends, Todd, goes to visit the self-contained classrooms as much as possible. He has been praised over and over for this 'act of kindness,' but he just does it because they are his friends and he misses them when they are not in his classroom." Here we see the differences in perception of children with Down syndrome by adults and peers. It is also an example of "… the way children accept each other. It is us, the adults who have to unlearn so much of what we have internalized over the years." The situation of partial inclusion is far from perfect, yet it is a form of progress that rightly yields a level of ambivalence through discomfort. Likewise, in thinking about her initial reaction of pride in seeing Adam escorting two children from the Center class to the school-wide Ballroom Dancing event, Diane observes, "My pride was a remnant of my past, a part of me that still thinks we do a favor to society by accepting difference," reminding us all that we, too, are always a work in progress, and that "It is hard but not impossible to escape our upbringing."

Finally, this chapter again alludes to Diane's constant wonderings of "what if?" in regard to Benny. She cannot escape thinking about how Benny's life would have been had he stayed in NYC's more restrictive environments. Such thoughts are inescapable and disturbing. They conjure specters in the form of children who are "scared and frustrated, hollow …remain[ing] far below grade level," having lost opportunities to learn, socialize, and develop in general. They join legions of disabled people who have been historically segregated, exemplified by Willowbrook, the notorious asylum on Staten Island (Goode, Hill, Reiss, & Bronson, 2013), and similar places around New York State as documented in Burton Blatt's Christmas in Purgatory (1965). While not as extreme as these institutions, a more restrictive environment in schools still contains—even restrains—students, denying opportunities, stunting growth, and maintaining a parallel word, a legacy of unfulfilled potential based upon how we have arranged society. Parents who advocate for their children not to be in a restrictive environment opt for what the poet Robert Frost called The Road Not Taken (1993) or at least "one less travelled" (p. 1). On reaching the fork in the road, and asking, "Where is the best place for my child to learn and be part of society?" they reject a system that has placed children on a parallel track to their peers. In choosing the lesser-known road, parents and children are in often in unfamiliar terrain, with far fewer signposts along the journey's way, sometimes not even sure of the eventual destination. In some ways, they can be viewed as pioneers.

As part of the road less travelled within the story of Diane's family, Tom's classroom exemplifies the possibilities of what can be done to teach and help all children to develop in academic, social, and emotional realms. Given what we know can be done, some lingering question include: How can we make sure that at the fork in the road, parents are better educated about existing options and supported in choosing more inclusive settings? In addition, how can we continue to learn from the successes of teachers who do this as their daily work? As we have mentioned already, it is by doing inclusion responsibly and in good faith that we know what works for whom and in what context.

References

Avramidis, E. & Norwich, B. (2002). Teachers' attitudes toward integration/inclusion: A review of the literature. *European Journal of Special Needs Education*, *17*(2), 129–147.

Baglieri, S., Bejoian, L, Broderick, A., Connor, D. J., & Valle, J. (2011). [Re]claiming "Inclusive Education" toward cohesion in educational reform: Disability studies unravels the myth of the typical child. *Teachers College Record*, *113*(10), 2122–2154.

Blatt, B. (1965). *Christmas in purgatory: A photographic essay on mental retardation*. Syracuse, NY: Human Policy Press.

Connor, D. J., Gabel, S. L., Gallagher, D. & Morton, M. (2008). Disability studies and inclusive education—Implication for theory, research, and practice: Guest editor's introduction. *International Journal of Inclusive Education*, *12*(5–6), 441–457.

Danforth, S. (Ed.) (2014). *Becoming a great inclusive educator*. New York: Peter Lang.

Deshler, D. D., Schumaker, J., Harris, K. R., & Graham, S. (Eds.). (1999). *Teaching every adolescent every day*. Cambridge, MA: Brookeline.

Frost, R. (1993). *The road not taken and other poems*. Mineola, NY: Dover Publications.

Goode, D., Hill, D. B., Reiss, J., & Bronson, W. (2013). *History and sociology of the Willowbrook state school*. Washington, DC: American Association on Intellectual and Developmental Disabilities.

Habib, D. (Producer and Director). (2007). *Including Samuel*. [DVD]. Available from http://www.includingsamuel.com/home.aspx

Hehir, T. & Katzman, L. I. (2012). *Effective inclusive schools: Designing successful school-wide programs*. San Francisco, CA: Jossey Bass.

TEACHING IN MY CITY

In preparing to teach my first class to a mix of pre-service and in-service teachers at Hunter College on the inclusion of students with disabilities in general education I read many articles and watched many videos. I began to analyze both my own experiences as a parent of a child with serious disabilities who was included successfully in a general education classroom, as well as my experiences as a teacher in an inclusive school. As I prepared, I was witness to a marriage of my personal and professional lives. I would go as far as to say that this book was born from the opportunity to teach classes of current and future teachers. It was their excitement at hearing the real life stories that gave me the motivation to write and it was their questions that prompted much of this text.

One of the most thought provoking works I came across was a video of the Axis Dance Company. It is a 4-minute dance performed by two dancers, one of whom is in a wheelchair. In this short work the able-bodied dancer moves her body in ways designed to duplicate the smoothness, the roundness of the wheelchair. Her body twists in new ways as she is the one to bend to her partner. He moves with a grace unthinkable and together they create an art form above and beyond what any able bodied dancer might be able to do. This video expressed better than anything else what happened for Benny at Boulder. It shows how much more than mere "acceptance" is at play, that inclusion at its highest form

is a kind of interpretation that changes every person's expectations, that allows new forms of expression to take root. Inclusion is not about making it possible for a person with a disability to join or participate; it is about changing the entire nature of the community to one where expectations change for all, where new forms of expression are born, the quality of transformation is one of art as much as it is of science or academia. When we entered Boulder, I hoped that Benny would function. I never in my wildest dreams expected him to flourish, to teach his peers about the subway system, to play trumpet by ear in the band, to dance onstage, to become a role model by making announcements over the PA system. The entire community of Boulder allowed itself to change when Benny entered, to grow with, in, and around him, to learn from him in real and substantial ways. And because of the way Clark and the staff wrap their arms around us parents and pull us in with the intensity of overbearing relatives, I, too, have been able to change. I am still not quite where I was at age six, that summer, surrounded by sand and sunshine, but I am closer than I ever thought I would be. I am open to change and able to adapt to those I am with, my children, my students, and strangers I meet on the bus. I am growing every day and life is now filled with a complexity of color, an ever expanding palette of human possibility, and that makes every day a new adventure. It is hard to explain how having a child with 8 diagnoses including Pervasive Developmental Delays can open new vistas and how having a student with autism can recharge a teaching career, but it is true. We are not stagnant individuals. We need to move and grow and to experience the multitude of perspectives possible. Those people that are wired differently from the majority bring these possibilities to life. While so many of us learn early to strive for commonality, those that are different bring diversity into our lives.

Early on I expressed my desire to share Boulder as much as possible in spirit and in practice with my students. I arranged meetings and interviews with teachers from Boulder and within one of these meetings came the offer from Lucy, that one or two of the staff might join me for an actual class at Hunter College. This idea grew into a tradition, a connection that enables my relationship with the staff to grow years after my children have moved on to Middle School. It became an opportunity for friendship to deepen between myself and the staff, and ultimately, these experiences provided answers to critical questions raised by my teachers, and addressed here in this book. Moreover it is the transformational effect these talks have had on my college and graduate students that fuels my desire to write this book and widen the circle of influence.

The suggestion came first when I spoke with Lucy but within just a few days, Lucy approached me and apologetically told me that Marina and Cara expressed an interest in joining us as well. Soon I had a list of seven professionals who wanted to be part of my class, eagerly hopeful about sharing their experiences with inclusion. Shortly after, Clark approached me before school, looking shockingly serious. He mentioned the fact that so many of his teachers were to be speaking to my class, and in a surprisingly sheepish manner (Clark is least like a sheep as anyone I have ever met) asked why it was that I did not ask him, as if I intentionally left him out. Truth is I felt (awkward) already as if I were taking advantage of 7 teachers. To ask the Principal seemed truly over the top. Inside, though, I was jumping for joy that he wanted to be there because I knew no one could speak for him. No one could better convey the essence of his spirit, his open mindedness, and his ability to be on level with everyone, while holding a title that has the power to elevate and separate. This is part of the secret, the essence of inclusion at Boulder, that Clark does not see the world in levels and layers. He strives to connect, to live fully, to share his talents, and to be open to others. He views these opportunities as chances for him to learn from his staff, from me, and from my students.

And so it was that a now eight-semester tradition was born. Over the years students in my classes at Hunter College have participated in both in person question and answer sessions as well as online videoconferences with members of Boulder School. Of all the elements of my course, it is this one which seems to have the greatest power of transformation for my students and myself. Each conference leaves me energized and open to new ideas. In these talks they independently and collectively speak about so much that makes inclusion flourish within their school. The main topics that come up repeatedly relate to the general questions I outline in the balance of this chapter.

They are concerned about how to effectively implement differentiation: "How long does it take to differentiate instruction well for a class of 30?"

To this the responses vary but all suggest that differentiation is a way of thinking that becomes more natural over time. Barbara creates individual goals for each child and conferences with them in order to discuss their individual goals. Barbara and Tom speak about the importance of giving the students scaffolds in varying degrees of intensity. This can come in the form of a template or a graphic organizer. Some students may use blank ones while others might receive templates with some information filled in already. Lucy speaks of the varied projects she does with her students. She has them create picture books, for example, a task which differentiates naturally. The activity takes place over many weeks as she carefully guides all of the students through the creation of the story to the finished product, which involves a bound book. She conferences with them and they can choose the theme of the book. Benny's class developed memoirs and he wrote about a visit to his grandparents' house, while Adam class created myths and he wrote his own, explaining how a frog got the ability to hop. Here the kids have opportunities to choose a topic, draw pictures, and then physically assemble a book. Lucy brings in cardboard and wallpaper which she has them use to create a hard cover. There are many talents and skills coming into play and numerous options for success. We can see how from the beginning to end of the project there is simple and natural differentiation.

Lucy also frequently creates heterogeneous groups and has them research and present on a topic from the grade three curriculum. She had them research countries and also animals in this way. This kind of group work leading to a presentation opens up many possibilities for student contributions. Those that might struggle with research and writing often excel at the design of the poster board, or the presentation itself. Children begin to see that they each come with a myriad of strengths, alongside their weaknesses or less developed areas. By strategically monitoring the way the students divide tasks, she can insure that the strengths of one group member are utilized while simultaneously building upon an area of need for another. Barbara speaks a lot about how we teach to strengths but remunerate weaknesses. Heterogeneous group work provides a golden opportunity to do this as children work alongside each other, contributing through their strengths but learning and observing how other students work. They all agree differentiation seems a daunting prospect, but once comfortable with the perspective, it becomes natural. Tom also utilizes group work to create opportunities for all of his students to shine, such as working together on science experiments to share results through keynote presentations. His room is set up with several areas in which to work. During a recent visit there were three different groups of students working in different ways. The largest group was involved with a whole group lesson, a smaller group was working on the side with the assistant teacher, and then a handful of kids were clustered around a teacher's aid.

They want to know about extremes:
"The most successful cases, and the least.
They search for boundaries: When is a student too
disabled to be included? What are the limits to
inclusion? When has it failed to work?"

This is a question whose answer has changed over the years. For the first few years Boulder faculty members were able to happily report that they have never counseled out a student. Benny was by far the most challenging student they had at the time he entered, but when they saw how well he did, they opened their doors to several children with even more challenging behaviors. Benny was a game changer for them, his success opened possibilities for other children, and in most cases they were successful in educating those who came with even more differences. However, they were not successful with them all.

In the past year there have been several instances of children who were sent out of the building for programs that would be more intensively aligned to their needs. In all three cases, Clark and Marina stress that this move out of general education is temporary. In one case a child had severe emotional disturbance and the parents were not consistent about following through with medical intervention. The hope is that with an intensive program at a residential facility, the child could come back to Boulder. Another case involved a child whose parent felt that he needed more intensive support as he was entering third grade and was still non-verbal. Pressed by my students to verbalize a boundary between those included and those asked to learn in a separate school, the staff of Boulder suggests that those children who are not verbal have a hard time in general education past the very early grades. Parental support is also a huge factor for children requiring intensive support requiring psychiatric consultation. While Boulder has successfully supported some children with violent tendencies and frequent outbursts, Carrie cites the frequency of outburst as a predictor of success in inclusion. A child who has violent outbursts several times a day for several months is a child who has become a danger to the school. They have worked well, though, with students whose daily outbursts can be reduced to weekly ones, even if those outbursts require the child to be removed from the classroom for the duration of the outburst. They like to see some progress over time. My students wonder if children are ever moved into the self contained classrooms at Boulder? The self-contained classrooms at Boulder are primarily for out of district children who could not be served by their own district. They classes are called the Center classes. There are two, one for grades k-2 and one for grades 3–5. Many, but not all have Down syndrome. There is no clear objective criterion, but they often the children in the Center classes have intellectual disabilities. Many children ride buses from far away to be part of the Center program. Part of the appeal for this program is that these children are included up to half of the day in the general education classrooms.

It is interesting to reflect on the fact that even in the three instances described, the staff is hopeful that these children will return within the next few years. There is also recognizable sadness in their voices as they describe the few times when they were not able to keep the child in the school. It should be noted that the decisions to move a child out of the school were made after 1–2 full years of failed attempts at reshaping behavior.

They ask about strategies for severe behavioral challenges: "What strategies do you use when a child is not cooperating? Are there special tricks?"

All of the team presents with astonishing clarity and consensus on this question. They share their own strategies for keeping behavioral challenges limited and for shaping behavior using positive supports. Marina, one of the inclusion specialists, speaks beautifully about the importance of making the child part of the solution. She works to empower the child to change his or her problematic behavior. She helps the child make good decisions. At each age level, Marina discusses the expectations with the child, giving them their own tools to stem negative behaviors. She calls it a "tool box" and in it are personalized techniques, like taking deep breaths, asking for a break, and other ways a child can cool down when riled up. Marina stresses the fact that there is no one magic solution. Teachers must remain flexible with both their rewards and consequences. She and Barbara reiterate over and over the importance of keeping the direction clear and positive. If we say, "Do not run in the hall," the child hears "run." It is therefore more effective to say, "Walk, please." Barbara recounts a favorite mentor who told her that there is nothing really in it for a child who misbehaves, that most children want to behave, but some cannot. Often they can not sit still, in which case, we must be flexible, let them walk a bit, stand at their seat, fit in a break where they can go to the Occupational Therapist's room and bounce a bit.

Barbara also reminds us that some kids are unfamiliar with what it means to "behave." We, as their teachers, must unpack that term for them. Sometimes, a child does well with a reminder card on their desk with specific directives for certain time of the day. My own son, Adam, has some difficulties with attention. When he was in Barbara's class in second grade, he did not pay attention at first, not knowing what paying attention meant. She conferenced with the team and me, and we came up with an idea that Adam would be the note taker for the class. This process enabled him to see what it meant to "pay attention" because now he was charged with writing down the important points from a lesson, at least once a day. After a few weeks, he understood what paying attention meant and he no longer needed to "take notes" to do it. In sum, we devised a way for him to learn the meaning of the words. Barbara reminds us that it is important to stay positive and phrase everything in terms of what you do expect, and to keep those expectations high.

Cara, our Occupational Therapist, tells us about students with sensory issues who need certain accommodations to function. These can be breaks to jump on a trampoline, or special cushions that have some "bounce" in them. Some kids attend better when chewing gum or when sipping cold water through a straw. Cara works hard with her students and teachers to find what works for the students. She asks that teachers be flexible and open minded in implementing these supports. Cara knows which students need breaks and often suggests that teachers send certain kids on "fake" errands just to give them a chance to leave the classroom. The request to carry a heavy book across the school is a chance to give a child with sensory needs some proprioceptive input. This often makes it easier for them to participate in the classroom activities. The important thing to realize is that not all kids can participate all the time, and the type of participation we expect has to vary.

Wendy, the inclusion specialist for the older grades, describes intricate systems of positive support for children with Behavior Intervention Plans (BIPs). She and Bella remind us that these support plans follow a child all over the building so that behavioral expectations are constant. Wendy stresses the importance of a continual chance to improve. Wendy offers short and long-term rewards for some children. If they miss a short-term opportunity for a reward, there must be another chance on the horizon, or else there will be no incentive to behave.

Bella who teaches one of the two self-contained classrooms in this school, notices that kids who have BIP'S, often do not even need them when in the general education portion of the day. The consistent modeling of appropriate behavior is a powerful tool for these children. Yet Wendy tells us a story of a child who had been having a violent outburst a few times a week through grade 3 but showed progress each year in his ability to control himself. She designed and implemented a behavior plan that included a weekly meal from Burger King, as a long-term reward. This child graduated Boulder and went on to be a productive student in middle school, despite a complex and not always completely supportive family life. Perhaps part of the success of inclusion at Boulder is that we have no easy alternative. If a child cannot be served in an inclusive classroom, they must transfer to the special education district.

They are curious about how to implement Common Core with a diverse student body. "Can inclusion and Common Core always be compatible?"

The challenges of implementing common core are real and intimidating. My students want to know how they can possibly do this with children of such diverse abilities. Bella, who teaches the less academically adept of all of the students shares a story of how three of her third graders were an integral part of a common core lesson. The lesson was on map skills and while most children had a blank template, some had symbols filled in. By using a graphic organizer for all the students, we can give some more supports easily by filling in selected key points or giving some a word bank, for example. Another frequently asked question is: What do you do if a child is years below grade level? Barbara suggests we must figure out why the child is so far behind, and then fill the gaps. If a child has severe dyslexia for example, then we can work to teach him to read with that in mind, but at the same time we can make the grade level content available in accessible ways. These days with technology it is easier than ever to make any content available in a myriad of ways, from video to interactive text. There must be a blend between remediating underdeveloped areas and keeping the student involved with the current class topics. This district's policy does not leave students behind, recognizing the importance of the peer group. Instead they find ways to creatively offer extra support while differentiating the grade level curriculum. The teachers who come to my class remind us that not all parents are capable of navigating the system. They see their role as coach to the parents, searching out therapies that might be useful, helping the parents advocate for what the child needs.

They accept that for some children they will have to work harder and longer because there is no support at home. Some parents do not have the time to do homework alongside a student. They offer after school and before school help for these children.

They want to know the basics of 'How to': "What are the most important ingredients for inclusion?"

Tom stresses the importance of creating a safe place for kids to learn. He deals with the tensions of competing demands by focusing on one overarching goal of his classroom, and that is for all to come together and create/become a community. Most responses from Boulder faculty ultimately point to attitude. Many faculty members credit Clark for being open minded and spreading that philosophy. Carrie points out that Clark does not expect either kids or teachers to fit a mold. Lucy expresses her joy in the freedom she has day-to-day as she constructs her lessons. Her own son, in a nearby district is in a class where the teacher does not have the same freedom. One time Lucy suggested a movie to her son's teacher and she said she would have to convince her principal first. Barbara had developed a tradition where she would allow each child to bake with a partner in class for their birthday. Through this activity the children would see fractions in action and learn hands on about customary units of measure. When Lucy returned from a maternity leave, she was placed in another school run by a controlling principal. She was no longer allowed to bake for birthdays. When Clark tried to woo her to come back to Boulder, when an opening arose, he made her all sorts of promises. When she asked if she could bake, he said "of course." The deal was sealed with that promise. By giving teachers freedom in the way they meet state standards, Clark allows them to meet the varied needs of their students. He also enables his teachers to teach from their heart and to bring their passions into the classroom. Lucy brings her love of travel, Barbara brings her passion for real world experiences, and Tom brings his talent for highlighting good citizenship. Dr. Ruby our school psychologist consumed with all things colored pink is aware that Boulder allows her to be open about her obsession. When students see adults with a diversity of interests they are more open to finding their own interests and respecting difference in others. Clark allows and celebrates different teaching styles and by doing so opens the doors to differentiation on a global scale. He says he wants the kids to see happy adults. He loves to be outside, meeting and greeting his staff, students, and parents. Clark wants his teachers to laugh together, to become friends with each other and with the parents. He even vacations with his staff and with some parents, deliberately blurring the boundaries most of us have grown up with in educational circles. Ultimately, Clark leads from a position of responsibility, not power, treating his teachers with respect, recognizing each of them personally, while understanding them as human beings that embody their own sense of professionalism. What comes across from the staff as they present is the tremendous positive energy emanating from the overarching belief that inclusive education will work.

As I get to know the staff at Boulder on more and more levels, I appreciate the way that they allow relationships to form between themselves and parents. The openness I see between them and parents is mirrored in the way I am able to share my own story with my classes of college/graduate students. I assumed somehow the closeness that would ensue would lessen my authority, but instead it has brought something much more dynamic. It has taken my classes to a level of community where we feel comfortable enough to relate the issues we discuss to our own experiences. It took a few semesters to find my footing—to stay steady and focused while processing the new depth of discussion within my classes, making me aware that when we open ourselves to connection that we can really adapt our classrooms to suit our learners. It is through these connections that we can really come know our students, and ourselves.

As Barbara always reminds us, in the end: "We teach people, not curriculum."

✳✳✳

Teaching about inclusion within teacher education programs has proven to be a deeply satisfying experience for Diane. In preparing to teach the "who, what, when, where, why, how" of inclusive education, she describes herself being "…witness to a marriage of my personal and professional lives." Having developed and taught the same course, I am well aware of the opportunity it presents to purposefully question the predominantly medicalized knowledge of disability—largely gained through traditional special education classes—that students bring (Connor, 2015). The inclusion class is grounded within a DSE framework, and the bulk of the course content is on the practical considerations of inclusive education, such as collaborative teaching, building classroom community, using universal design for learning, developing differentiated instruction, and being flexible in lesson and unit planning.

The questioning of knowing and "owning" why inclusion is desirable must come before the all-important "bread and butter" of how we teach. There have been different interpretations of inclusive education, that often characterize it as an "add on" to general education (Baker & Zigmond, 1995) or an appendage to special education (Kauffman, 1999), a reworking of special education (Kavale, 2002), a revised sorting mechanism for those who approximate normalcy (Fuchs & Fuchs, 1998), and so on. However, in Diane's screening of the Axis Dance Company segment, the class focuses on the exchange of movements between a wheelchair user and a non-wheelchair user, conveying the meaning of inclusive education. It lies far above the mundane platitudes of tolerance and acceptance that undergird many educators' initial associations with inclusion. The video she purposefully chose invites students to reconsider their perceptions of inclusive education. She explains the possibilities, "...at its highest form [inclusion] is a kind of interpretation that changes every person's expectations, that allows new forms of expression to take root. Inclusion is not about making it possible for a person with a disability to join or participate; it is about changing the entire nature of the community to one where expectations change for all, where new forms of expression are born, the quality of transformation is one of art as much as it is of science or academia." The dance is a metaphor for what can be achieved. It is new. It is different. It is typical dynamics reimagined, and born from the interactions of the people involved. It is also equally akin to the humanities as well as the sciences. In some way inclusive education poses grave dilemmas for traditional educators as the predictability associated with science cannot be solely relied upon. It is just as likely that a student's progress will be made through unpredictable pedagogical creativity necessitated by the situation. This open ended thinking within a problem-solving disposition is what we seek to create within inclusive educators.

In many ways, Boulder's faculty is committed to teaching a diverse student body, sharing dispositions that encompass the creativity and flexibility in their daily work. Their generosity in traveling (uncompensated) for a significant distance from the suburbs into Manhattan exemplifies a commitment to inclusive education, and never ceases to make a strong impression on Hunter College's graduate students. Diane has structured this chapter around some of the broad questions students ask of Boulder faculty. This format mirrors the actual classes as each question is responded to by anyone on the Boulder panel, with most participants sharing their thoughts. The two the main areas of interest are usually instruction and classroom management. Given the course content's emphasis on differentiated instruction as developed by Tomlinson (1999; 2001), and expectations that students will utilize this approach by documenting evidence in unit and lesson plans, students are eager to know more, asking: What does it look like in your classes? When do you do it?

By Lucy sharing her objectives, outlining day-to-day routines, and describing options within her ongoing use of project-based learning, Diane notes, "There are many talents and skills coming into play and numerous options for success. We can see how from the beginning to end of the project there is simple and natural differentiation." Likewise, Barbara's responses range from simple and straightforward (reminder card on the student's desk), to more sophisticated ideas such as having Adam become the class note-taker so he could learn what it means to pay attention. In addition to being practical, Barbara's wisdom is evident in the simple but effective advice of, "...stay positive and phrase everything in terms of what you do expect, and to keep those expectations high." Tom, too, shares ways in which he scaffolds information for students, using blank or partly completed graphic organizers. In this way, differentiated instruction is demystified, becoming not only credible—but preferable—maximizing student engagement with everybody's reach.

The frequently asked question, "What do you do if a child is years below grade level?" will remain with us as long as schools exist. The very nature of how schools are configured actually creates instances of "at," "above," and "below" level (Brantlinger, 2004). Barbara's response is quite simple: know the student's learning profile, the student's strengths and weaknesses, and "figure out why the child is so far behind, and then fill the gaps." She provides the example of a child with severe dyslexia, stating, "We can work to teach him to read with that in mind, but at the same time we can make the grade level content available in accessible ways"—that could include audio versions, appropriate book levels, and specific activities within direct instruction.

Classroom management is always of major interest to both in-service and pre-service teachers. In cases where small modifications can be made for hyperactive children, Cara the Occupational Therapist suggests "doable" ideas such as allowing students to jump or bounce a little, chew gum, sip cold water, or go on manufactured errands. All of these have the opportunity to work in terms of helping a child be successful in focusing on the work at hand. For children with more significant behavioral challenges, Behavior Intervention Plans (BIPs) are developed and implemented with view to providing "a toolbox" of strategies to help students self-manage. Interestingly, Lisa, one of the teachers of the two self-contained classrooms at Boulder, "...notices that kids who have BIP's, often do not even need them when in the general education portion of the day." This is quite telling, as it suggests students can self-monitor and behave in different contexts, in this case a less restrictive environment. While BIPs can formally assist students who struggle with managing behaviors, they can also come to dominate a students program, subsuming all other aspects of it. It is refreshing to see them used with flexibility here, and similar to Diane's charge in an earlier chapter that IEPs can actually be "meaningless" if the context, goals, and desires of the child and parents are not factored in to help make the plan malleable, similarly the BIP can be lip-service to support unless used otherwise.

The faculty at Boulder is also willing to share what their "failures" in terms of including children. Diane describes "a recognizable notable sadness in their voices as they describe the few times when they were not able to keep the child in the school." It seems as if their mission did not work for a handful of students, and "the decisions to move a child out of the school were made after 1–2 full years of failed attempts at reshaping behavior," with view to having an open door policy for the possible return of the student. The issue of students with chronic behavioral problems and violent tendencies is very real, and as Dawn notes, "Parental support is also a huge factor for those children requiring intensive support and psychiatric consultation." She also states that "Boulder has successfully supported some children with violent tendencies and frequent outbursts," yet recognizes that if the frequency of violent outbursts does not abate, even with ongoing support, then it is deemed that the child be changed to a different setting. While few working within DSE support segregated settings, they are merited, on occasion, if they are able to provide the degree of support unable in general education, for example, as can be see in the case of the young woman with psychiatric difficulties featured in Including Samuel (Habib, 2007). Of course, the ultimate goal is to re-integrate this small number of children when they are ready.

In terms of this chapter's connections to DSE, the faculty of Boulder agree with "disability and inclusive education" (Connor et. al, 2008, p. 449), and "assume competence and reject deficit models of disability" (p. 448) in the children they teach. Instead of viewing children with IEPs as additional work, these faculty members understand that "Disability is primarily recognized and valued as a natural part of human diversity" (p. 449). They also have the disposition of "supporting the education of students labeled with disabilities in non-segregated settings from a civil rights stance" p. (448). At the same time, with a genuine sense of knowing the limitations what Boulder can offer to a small number of students, they acknowledge the need for an alternative environment, only as a last resort and, as previously mentioned, with view to having children return.

In reading this chapter I was reminded of times in which I'd presented as part of a panel in classes or at conferences, or invited people to be on a panel in my inclusion class. The first that came to mind dates back to the late 1980s when I was a classroom teacher working in a high school that has been selected as a pilot model to increase youth with disabilities into general education classes. As teachers, we had not been given much direction by administration other than to "do your best" and "make it work." I recall one day, without much notice, I was informed that I would be part of a meeting about this initiative coordinated by the Department of Education. The eight teachers involved, four general and four special, were picked by a mini-bus and shuttled across town to another large school. We were then paraded on stage and told to sit and face an audience of teachers from other schools who would be beginning similar inclusive work next year. There had been no information shared, no preparation, no prompts, and I recall feeling very anxious having to speak off the cuff to a large audience of indifferent-looking teachers in the presence of high-ranking educational officials. Although we did our best to explain to our colleagues how we co-taught, planned, dealt with pedagogy and discipline issues, the event seemed hastily thrown together, amateurish, and a lost opportunity to genuinely engage with—and build—urban inclusive classrooms.

I contrast that panel with others I have brought into my own inclusion classes. Without a doubt, those that have the most impact upon students are panels composed of high school students identified as disabled or parents of students with disabilities. Having a panel of three high school students who are "experts" in attending school and the challenges it places upon them provides the option to share their expertise with in-service and pre-service teachers. These occasions have always proven very insightful as what students know, think, understand, and manage, can be quite different from what teachers imagine. For example, students share how they secretly like teachers "to be on top of them," regardless of how they themselves act, as it is a form of care. Interestingly, it is also worthwhile to host a panel of adults with disabilities, for example those LD and/or ADD. When I have arranged such a panel, and adults are able to share their strengths, areas of need, and ways in which the LD label has impacted their sense of identity, graduate students develop a greater awareness of the "social and experiential understandings of disability," (ibid., p. 448), as this form of sharing "privileges the interests, agendas, and voices of people labeled with disability/disabled people" (p. 448). Finally, I think the panels of parents make a very strong impression. In informal feedback at the end of the course, students identify the parent panel as impacting their thinking the most—hearing parental expertise, thoughts about disability, challenges with school systems, and their overall journey in coming to know and advocate for their child.

The panel from Boulder clearly has a similar impact upon graduate students. Diane always alerts me to the class in which they come, and I do my best to attend. Having seen them several times now, I have a strong sense of their commitment and, dare I say it, how "laid back," they strike me in terms of all things inclusion. Clark has an engaging, effusive style that can, at times, inadvertently overshadow his faculty members. However, it speaks to his genuine excitement about his job in supporting faculty who, in turn, support children. Boulder teachers do get a chance to share their experiences, too, and are both candid and sincere in their responses. The panel is not "to sell" inclusion per se, but rather share how one school has committed to the principle and reveal ways in they manage their day-to-day business of teaching and learning for all students.

References

Baker, J. M. & Zigmond, N. (1995). The meaning and practice of inclusion for students with learning disabilities: Themes and implications from five classes. *Journal of Special Education*, 29(2), 163–180.

Brantlinger, E. (2004). Confounding the needs and confronting the norms: An extension of Reid and Valle's essay. *Journal of Learning Disabilities*, 37(6), 490–499.

Connor, D. J. (2015). Practicing what we teach: The benefits of using disability studies in an inclusion course. In D. J. Connor, J. W. Valle, & C. Hale (Eds.). *Practicing disability studies in education, acting toward social change* (pp. 123–140). Peter Lang: New York.

Connor, D. J., Gabel, S. L., Gallagher, D. & Morton, M. (2008). Disability studies and inclusive education—Implication for theory, research, and practice: Guest editor's introduction. *International Journal of Inclusive Education*, 12(5–6), 441–457.

Fuchs, D., & Fuchs, L.S. (1998). Competing visions for educating students with disabilities: Inclusion versus full inclusion. *Childhood Education*, 74(5), 309–16.

Habib, D. (Producer and Director). (2007). *Including Samuel*. [DVD]. Available from http://www.includingsamuel.com/home.aspx

Kauffman, J. M. (1999). Commentary: Today's special education and its messages for tomorrow. *Journal of Special Education*, 32(4), 244–254.

Kavale, K. (2002). Mainstreaming to full inclusion: From orthogenesis to pathogenesis of an idea. *International Journal of Disability, Development and Education, 49*(2), 201–214.

Tomlinson, C. A. (1999). *The differentiated classroom: Responding to the needs of all learners.* Alexandria, VA: ASCD.

Tomlinson, C. A. (2001). *How to differentiate instruction in mixed ability classrooms* (2nd ed.). Alexandria, VA: ACSD.

· 1 4 ·

BROTHERS

I grew up as an only child, in a family that seemed to me a simple and sometimes lonely trio. My parents were the deeper voices, providing the structure and the beat. I was the melody, singing my song at each family dinner, on every family car ride and every evening as bedtime neared. I was also often alone, creating worlds of pretend friends and siblings. My closest friends were and still are other only children. We find each other and become sibling replacements but we never have to vie for attention, time and money. We provide each other with pure companionship and understanding.

I was totally new to the dynamics between brothers. I worried about having two children. I was unsure how as a parent I could divide my attention and my love. As soon as Adam was born, I understood that love needed not be divided because, as Cantor explains, sets of infinite size are equivalent and equally vast. I loved Adam and Benny each with an equally infinite expanse of emotion. My attention, though, is finite and I struggled daily with that divide, a divide made more challenging because of the time and energy Benny required.

By the time Adam was rolling over, Benny had been labeled many times over and his own frustration level was rising rapidly. Adam was an incredibly easy to soothe baby. He woke up with a smile and was content in almost every situation. I would strap Adam to my chest and vacuum, chase Benny around the

playground or peal him off the sidewalk during meltdowns, then make dinner. Sometimes I first really looked right at Adam after his bath when we would steal away for an end of day nursing session before he settled down for the night.

As Adam grew, his incandescence enveloped everything he touched. One time an old friend came and commented on Adam's radiance. My sudden look of sadness puzzled this wise older friend. She questioned my reaction and it was then that I realized my gripping fear that in the light of Adam's radiance, Benny might not be visible. I knew from the moment Benny was born, that he possessed great light and had a soul of pure goodness, but I knew also that to truly see Benny one had to look hard and listen in ways we do not all know how to do. I knew it was hard for others to see through the meltdowns and the tantrums. I considered it a gift that I could see his beauty so clearly, but all too easily accepted that others were not able to see him fully.

It was hard for me initially to see them together. My mind was trained for years on the fine art of comparison. As first a student and now an educator in a world where we separate more than we unite, Adam's strengths seemed a direct contrast to Benny's weaknesses. It was hard to keep them both in mind simultaneously, without Benny coming up on the short end of the stick over and over again. Adam, despite the garden variety ADHD many boys display, not only passed the early milestones on time, but was counting by the age of one and stringing together addition sentences by the age of 18 months on the floor with a set of magnetic plastic numbers. It seemed at times that after gazing at Adam's light, it was impossible then to see Benny clearly. I thought back to Plato's allegory where he describes a group of prisoners who lived their lives in a dark cave. Once they were able to come to the surface and adjust to the light, they had trouble going back into darkness. Adam seemed to be our light and after interacting with him it was painfully hard to appreciate Benny's attributes, often clouded in some sort of shadowy darkness. What would it take for my eyes adjust back to Benny? To see his strengths for what they were?

We both knew families that struggled with similar issues, but most celebrated the successes of the more able child, often to the detriment of the child with the more pronounced issues. Some even expressed outright frustration, embarrassment and sometimes anger toward the child with the disability. We did not make a conscious decision to avoid those behaviors because we did not have to. We were without a doubt Benny's biggest fans and adored him, quirks and all. Also we did not understand how a child was to grow in any other than a positive environment. Still, we saw all too clearly the way his unusual behavior was perceived in the world, making trips to the bookstore and local bus rides difficult if not impossible. While this made us angry at society, in the comfort of our family we delighted in Benny, somehow unconsciously grappling with the DSE approach into our own home, before we even knew the term.

My husband and I never wanted Benny to feel that he was any less than any other person and so we minimized his struggles while we celebrated his successes. We had heard so many times about his limitations, we were told so often about all that we should not expect to see that when he surprised us all, we were bowled over by his accomplishments. His first steps at the age of 2, his first words at the age of 3 and his clumsy sentences at the age of 6 shook us to our core. These milestones set off cascades of joy which made David and I both giddy with happiness. In the background was Adam pushing a plastic yellow table across the living room when he was ten months old, wobbling courageously on his small plump legs, pronouncing complex words like "helicopter," at 14 months, discovering addition facts before the age of 2, and socializing naturally before he was even steady on his feet. We would notice these things with a mix of relief and awe, but were both careful not to look too hard or long, as if his accomplishments somehow made Benny's delays all the more striking. It was a torturous time, trying to support them both through these early years when their strengths and weaknesses made comparisons so stark. So while we were partly there at that time, we were not fully there. We could accept Benny and celebrate Benny but could not yet negotiate the simultaneous appreciation of our children.

Over the years, I began also to see that different is not deficient. By navigating into the hands of therapists and educators who embraced a positive social model I began to adopt the perspective as well, and one day it became truly my own. It did not happen overnight, it is a continuum through which we journey. Benny has not become "normal," but we have all learned to see his differences as his own personal gifts, as valuable as Adam's more traditional accomplishments. It was both a shift in what the world around us accepted as well as my own acceptance of Benny's disabilities as beautiful and powerful. While Benny has learned to engage with the world, he does it in his own way in his own time, and that has become something we all admire. This shift enabled us to appreciate and celebrate both our children in ways that are now equitable and equally exciting. I can watch them perform in the same play, Adam taking a lead role with finesse and charm and Benny sharing his voice, softer, dancing with his own particular, at times, unusual moves and know that they are both amazing and shining in their own way. I can now look over both of their grades and celebrate Benny's ability to pass Regents Algebra with an

80 while Adam sports an average over 95 in almost every class. It has taken so long but I do not see one as better. I see them as both equally worth celebration. The boys have learned to accept each other as well and have found peace with their accomplishments.

It was not until Adam entered Boulder that the divide began to close and that Adam's exuberance and excitement for everything became fuel for Benny's development rather than anything else. When Benny entered Boulder and Clark spoke of the talents he was going to nurture in all of his students, I was far from understanding how that would be possible for Benny, but it was. Benny found he could sing, and he had an incredible ear for music. As his behavior settled and he began to feel pride in his successes, he began to shine out as well, and suddenly he was on stage beside his brother, the two of them illuminating the auditorium. It was also Adam who brought Benny into the limelight, encouraging him to participate in the annual circus, variety show and family fun nights. By enabling my boys to attend the same school, we took advantage of the natural support of siblings. Benny and Adam were able to strengthen their relationship while harnessing the power of their bond to encourage Benny to partake in all of the wonderful activities. We saw that attending the very same neighborhood school impacted the family in real and profound ways. The impact spread like ripples, shaping not only their relationship as brothers, but also my relationship with Adam as well, today and for years to come.

I have spoken to many well-off parents in neighboring districts who feel such shame with respect to their child with a disability that they embrace the opportunity to send them far away to school, traveling for hours. In some cases, these children are housed in residential centers. These parents worry that the issues of one child will stigmatize their other children. This shame is put there by society, reinforced by the books and articles parents are bombarded with as soon as we hear that our child has a label. Then the school system augments the shame. It breaks my heart to see these families split in esteem for their children, but I know exactly how it develops. I also see that we struggled with a related problem. In our efforts to celebrate Benny, we turned away at times from the tremendous accomplishments of Adam. It is not simply that Benny learned how to succeed it is that I went through a transformation that enables me now to celebrate success in other terms than I had been able to before. This no longer seems paradoxical to me. We define success not in absolute percentiles but in the way it reflects a personal journey. It might sound trivial but it is not a simple shift in perspective. It involves unlearning much of what we internalize in education. Similarly as a teacher,

I have to reeducate my peers. There is no such thing as an "honors" type, or a child who belongs in a particular track. All children deserve access to a highly rigorous curriculum and all teachers deserve support in its implementation. In this way inclusion goes far beyond the opportunity to learn grade level curriculum. It transcends the classroom and enables families to flourish and all children to grow together.

In the class I teach at Hunter, I ask my students to join me on a personal journey, to be open to transformation. I am with them on this journey. Together we move closer toward a place where everyone can learn and grow together. I admit that I am not all the way there.

When Benny was 2 ½ and Adam just 1, a speech therapist told me as if she was delivering good news, that one day soon Adam would overtake Benny. She went on to tell me how lucky I was that Adam was typical and would be able to take care of Benny one day when my husband and I were both dead. That was one of the last days I allowed her to work with Benny, but her words stayed with me and still evoke a pain that to this day makes me short of breath. When I watch how other children, with similar disabilities to Benny, develop through years of education in self contained classrooms, and often through a continual downward spiral from less restrictive to more restrictive settings, I see how we create this reality by restricting access to a general education curriculum and to genuine opportunities for meaningful interaction and independence that can come naturally through the school system. I hear the words of top doctors telling me that Benny would not make it past third grade, that an academic program would be frustrating and ultimately impossible for him. I could go on to detail how far he has come, but would rather show this by sharing an essay Benny wrote in grade 7 English class. The essay is about his brother, who as I mentioned has been recently diagnosed with epilepsy. Despite profound language delays that persist, both expressive and receptive, Benny writes fluently and with beauty. He still tests below the 10th percentile on many measures of intellectual growth and receptive and expressive language, but as we can see here, there is no problem with the thoughts in his head. Rather than Benny needing care for his life, he and his brother already look after each other in a reciprocal though not completely symmetrical way. This is an essay Benny wrote about the first time Adam had an epileptic seizure. The directions were to highlight certain sorts of phrases, similes, metaphors and so on. I leave the essay exactly as Benny wrote it for this assignment. We see that we can cross the line from non-disabled to disabled in the course of a few hours, and we see that these brothers will be there for each other.

12/3/14

How the Seizure Happened

What would you do if you woke up and your brother was in an ambulance? That is what had happened to me.

It was December 29, 2012. There was no snow on the ground, but _it was cold inside as ice._ Even though I had a lot of blankets, including my Lightning McQueen, I was still very cold. **I felt myself shivering as if I were getting buried in snow. I heard a siren, sounding like a huge fire alarm which could wake up the planet,** and I was curious from where it was coming from. _I was crazy nervous._ Then I got out of bed and my mom and my brother were not home. Normally my brother goes into my parents bed on cold days. I felt scared.

I looked out the window and there was an ambulance. It was 7:00 am. I was thinking that Adam, my brother, had to go to the hospital and I did not know why. _I saw my Dad, and he looked worried, as a person going to jail._ I asked my Dad what was going on.

My Dad said that Adam was in the hospital and I was worried. I was thinking that maybe he would not be okay. I wanted to call him on the phone but I could not do it. My dad told me that Adam had a seizure. I was curious. _I kept firing questions at my dad like a machine gun firing bullets._ And I asked "What is a seizure? What did Adam look like during the seizure? Was he breathing? Is he going to get more seizures?" **I imagined that Adam would look like someone wearing a scary mask during his seizure.**

My Dad still looked worried. _My Dad was quiet like a cloud._ He said that Adam was very sleepy when he left the house but he was breathing fine. Adam even tried to grab his blanket as the ambulance was taking him on a stretcher to the hospital. He did not know if Adam would get more seizures. _The phone was a quiet as a mouse,_ since my Mom did not call from the hospital. **I was freaked out by the quiet in the house.**

But Adam would be okay,

Eventually My Dad did call the hospital's phone number. My Mom could not call home because you are not allowed to use cell phones in the hospital room. He turned to me and said, "They will get Mommy out of the room to talk to us."

Dad looked scared on the phone. As he was talking to Mommy, _his expression turned bright like a rainbow._ At this point, I knew that things were going to be better. Mommy said that Adam was talking and eating breakfast. I felt happy that Adam was okay, happy like a little kid getting their favorite doll for their birthday.

Finally my Dad and I drove to the hospital. It was still as cold as ice outside. It seemed like we were moving as slow as a baby as we were driving. The roads were as empty as a deserted house. Finally, we made it there.

We finally made it to the hospital. I was moving as fast as a jogger. I really wanted to see if Adam was really okay. Finally I saw Adam and we were very happy.

Since then, Adam has had a few seizures. They have not been as bad as the first seizure. Luckily, he has not any in a long time. He takes pills twice a day which help him stop getting seizures at night. Also, we all try to go to bed early. Sometimes I do not sleep so good. I am restless like a rat, since I worry about him having another seizure at night. However, I am happy that he is okay and I love him.

What are the chances that Benny would have been able to write this at the age of 12 after years in a classroom for the severely and multiply disabled? Where would we be had he stayed in a classroom without an academic program? Where would Adam be without a brother who could express his love and care in this way? What kind of frustrations would Benny feel, with his thoughts trapped in a body that continues to struggle with speech, had he not learned to read and write? What would his behavior be like? Why do we assume that if a child has difficulty with spoken language that they lack the ability to communicate? Why do we give up so easily on these children and fail to give them an appropriate education?

***

The Individuals with Disabilities Education Improvement Act (2004) states that the assumed placement for students with disabilities should be in general education, until that placement has proven to be unsuccessful. The assurance reads:

> Students with disabilities and students without disabilities must be placed in the same setting, to the maximum extent appropriate to the education needs of the students with disabilities. A recipient of ED [(Federal) Education Department] funds must place a person with a disability in the regular education environment, unless it is demonstrated by the recipient that the student's needs cannot be met satisfactorily with the use of supplementary aids and services. Students with disabilities must participate with nondisabled students in both academic and nonacademic services, including meals, recess, and physical education, to the maximum extent appropriate to their individual needs.

As necessary, specific related aids and services must be provided for students with disabilities to ensure an appropriate education setting. Supplementary aids may include
interpreters for students who are deaf, readers for students who are blind, and door-to-
door transportation for students with mobility impairments.

A recipient of ED funds that places an individual with disabilities in another school is
responsible for taking into account the proximity of the other school to the student's
home. If a recipient operates a facility for persons with disabilities, the facility and
associated activities must be comparable to other facilities, services, and activities of
the recipient.
Source: http://www2.ed.gov/about/offices/list/ocr/docs/edlite-FAPE504.html

Although well intended, the interpretation of the law by local education authorities, especially the type and degree of supplementary aids and
services, is complicated by placement options, some of which may be located
at the other end of a state. In discussing the implications of this legislation,
it is common for college instructors to point out that a disabled child has
the same right to attend the school of his or her non-disabled siblings. The
premise of this law had always been a major consideration for Diane and
David, as they sought a school that would be a good fit for Benny. In coming
to Boulder, the family experienced the benefits of having their children go
to the same school, noting, "attending the very same neighborhood school
impacted the family in real and profound ways... spread[ing] like ripples,
shaping not only their relationship as brothers, but my [Diane's] relationship
with Adam as well, not only today, but for years to come." As this chapter
attests, the relationship between the brothers was able to grow organically
in the context of sharing their home and their school. Both know the same
teachers, each other's friends, and move through the same familiar spaces—
opening the possibilities of having many experiences in common. Yet it was
only after several years of struggle that attending the same school became a
valid option.

Diane takes this opportunity, when discussing the close relationship
between brothers, of discussing the alternatives with which families in her
situation are faced. For those who are well heeled and/or well informed,
non-local residential settings for children with disabilities can be obtained
through a legal process, usually with the help of lawyers. She notes how many
parents feel such a degree of shame that they utilize the opportunity to send
their disabled child to a place at considerable distance. This, of course, is akin
to boarding school existence and impacts a family's ability to regularly see
their child and vice versa. Such children do not become an integral part of

their home community. In her conversations, Diane observes how parents in this position sometimes experience "outright frustration, embarrassment and sometimes anger toward the child with the disability." Furthermore, she has observed that "these parents worry that the issues of one child will stigmatize the other," and remove the disabled child from the picture. Family dynamics are deeply personal, and many informative parent and disabled child relationships have been chronicled in depth via personal narratives (Ginsburg, 2003; Osmond, 1993; Park, 2001) as well as disabled and non-disabled siblings (Bisceglia & Thornton, 2012; Rice, 2009; Simon, 2012). The point here is not to blame parents but illustrate how they often respond to shame that "…is put there by society, reinforced by the books and articles parents are bombarded with as soon as we hear that our child has a label." Unless the unlearning of shame can occur, then segregated placements will continue to the detriment of those placed within them. As Diane notes, "When I watch how other children, with similar disabilities to Benny, develop through years of education in self contained classrooms, and often through a continual downward spiral from less restrictive to more restrictive settings, I see how we create this reality by restricting access to a general education curriculum and to genuine opportunities for meaningful interaction and for independence that can come naturally through the school system." It becomes clear to see ways in which how schools structures that contain only students with disabilities contributes to the underbelly of special education with its outcomes of stigmatization, marginalization, low academic achievement, low graduation rates, underemployment and unemployment of graduates, a school-to-prison pipeline, and so on.

What is important here, is our ability to re-think existing structures and restricted options so we can move away from limited views of disability that in turn trigger limited visions and limited outcomes for people with disabilities. Rethinking these interrelated issues is what occurred intuitively for Diane after having a child who was not easily understood and subsequently categorized in many ways. She explains, "I went through a transformation that enables me now to celebrate success in other terms than I had been able to before. This no longer seems paradoxical to me. We define success not in absolute percentiles but in the way it reflects a personal journey. It might sound trivial but it is not a simple shift in perspective. It involves unlearning much of what we internalize in education." This unlearning referred to is at the core of DSE as the discipline recognizes and challenges the limited, misleading, and often damaging conceptualizations of disability and differences as abnormalities that emerge from the field of special education (Baker, 2002; Brantlinger,

1997, 2004; Heshusius, 1989). Diane and David recognized that Benny's unusual behaviors were not understood or accepted in their community, even within special education. She notes, "While this made us angry at society, in the comfort of our family we delighted in Benny, somehow unconsciously grappling with the DSE approach into our own home, before we even knew the term." Here we see her family's rejection of the master narrative of disability in favor of their own knowledge. In other words, their personal experiences superseded the limited scripts available.

Benny's birth and growth opened the door for Diane's re-thinking of much she had been taught to date about human differences, including within teacher education programs. A basic tenet of DSE is that it questions the reification of, and therefore legitimacy of, "normalcy," seeking to unpack it as a phenomenon that only exists contingent upon culturally determined standards that shift over time (Dudley-Marling & Gurn, 2010). She shares, "Benny has not become 'normal,' but we have all learned to see his differences as his own personal gifts, as valuable as Adam's more traditional accomplishments." This "learned to see" occurred over a period of time in which many of the fundamental teachings of human differences within the field of special education, constructed in medicine, science, and psychology, are shed in favor of understanding Benny in his actual context, including the social dynamics within a particular school culture. Likewise, as a teacher, Diane believes she has to re-educate her peers in terms of the limitations of traditional education when it creates hierarchies of children wherein those labeled gifted are valued the most and those disabled, the least. In her view, "There is no such thing as an 'honors' type, or a child who belongs in a particular track. All children deserve access to a highly rigorous curriculum and all teachers deserve support in its implementation." This way of thinking has historically been objected to in a rigorous manner by many traditional special educators (see, for example, Kauffman, 1999; Kauffman & Hallahan, 1995; Fuchs & Fuchs, 1995; Kavale, 2002), and still continues to be disparaged and considered dangerous (Anastasiou & Kaufmann, 2011, 2012, 2013.). There is an understandable feeling in DSE of being the underdog, reflecting the biblical tale David versus Goliath in which a small upstart stands up to a domineering giant bully. Diane's words in this chapter convey an idealism and a vulnerability that are, I believe, an integral part of a person's understanding of inclusive education. She explains, "In the class I teach at Hunter, I ask my students to join me on a personal journey, to be open to transformation. I am with them on this journey. Together we move closer toward a place where everyone can learn and grow together.

I admit that I am not all the way there." At the risk of sounding repetitive, I invoke the mantra of to be an inclusive educator means to always be "in progress." It can never completely done because it is continuous journey based upon whom we are teaching, what we are teaching, and how we are teaching.

For me, perhaps more than any other chapter the narrative about two brothers in a family attending a school within their local community galvanized so many tenets of DSE (Connor et al., 2008). It is, in essence, a story of "disability and inclusive education." Diane's family "assume[d] competence and reject deficit models of disability" (p. 448); Benny and Adam's experiences "contrasts medical, scientific, psychological understandings with social and experiential understandings of disability" (p. 448); members within the family "Predominantly focus[es] upon political, social, cultural, historical, and individual understandings of disability" (p. 448); Diane and David "support[s] the education of students labeled with disabilities in non-segregated settings from a civil rights stance"(p. 448). Diane's thinking is an example of work that "… discerns the oppressive nature of essentialized/categorical/medicalized naming of disability in schools, policy, institutions, and the law while simultaneously recognizing the political power that may be found in collective and individual activism and pride through group-specific claims to disabled identities and positions" (p. 448). The narratives of Benny and Adam "recognize[s] the embodies/aesthetic experiences of people whose lives/selves are made meaningful as disabled, as well as troubles the school and societal discourses that position such experiences as 'othered' to an assumed normate" (p. 448). Instead, "Disability is primarily recognized and valued as a natural part of human diversity" (p. 449). The brothers' tale "recognizes and privileges the knowledge derived from the lived experience of people with disabilities," including "disabled people in theorizing about disability," and both are "disabled students…supported in the development of a positive disability identity" (p. 448). Each of these tenets is woven like threads throughout this story, albeit many times in unconscious ways, illustrating how the values of DSE exist—regardless of whether people know an attempt has been made to formally state them within academia. These DSE values become transformed into thoughts and actions designed to improve people's lives, including where and how we best educate everybody about human differences.

In many ways Benny's essay about his brother Adam symbolizes Boulder's successful work in inclusive education. As Diane points out, "Despite profound language delays that persist, both expressive and receptive, Benny writes fluently and with beauty." The actual essay serves as a micro-narrative nested within the overall story, an insightful tale privileging Benny's voice by revealing his perceptions, fears, and feelings about Adam. In it, among the bountiful similes and metaphors (for which I am sure he received a high grade), we see a complex human being who has grown enormously since his move to Boulder, a place where he had the opportunity to share every aspect of his life—educational and otherwise—with his brother. If we re-read the words of IDEIA at the beginning of this commentary, this is exactly as things should be.

References

Anastasiou, D., & Kauffman, J. K. (2011). A social constructionist approach to disability: Implications for special education. *Exceptional Children, 77*(5), 367–384.

Anastasiou, D., & Kauffman, J. M. (2012). Disability as cultural difference: Implications for special education. *Remedial and Special Education, 32*(5). Retrieved on September 15 from: rse.sagepub.com/content/early/2010/09/21/0741932510383163.full.pdf

Anastasiou, D., & Kauffman, J. M. (2013). The social model of disability: Dichotomy between impairment and disability. *Journal of Medicine and Philosophy, 38*(4), 441–459.

Baker, B. (2002). The hunt for disability: The new eugenics and the normalization of school children. *Teachers College Record, 104*(4), 663–703.

Bisceglia, M. F. & Thornton, E. T. (2012) *To walk with my brother: A story of courage, humor and love*. Portsmouth, NH: Peter E. Randall.

Brantlinger, E. (1997). Using ideologies: Cases of non-recognition of the politics of research and practice in special education. *Review of Educational Research, 67*(4), 425–459.

Connor, D. J., Gabel, S. L., Gallagher, D. & Morton, M. (2008). Disability studies and inclusive education—Implication for theory, research, and practice: Guest editor's introduction. *International Journal of Inclusive Education, 12*(5–6), 441–457.

Dudley-Marling, C., & Gurn, A. (Eds.). (2010). *The myth of the normal curve*. New York: Peter Lang.

Fuchs, D., & Fuchs, L.S. (1995). Inclusive schools movement and the radicalization of special education reform. In J. M. Kauffman & D. P. Hallahan (Eds.) *The illusion of full inclusion* (pp. 213–243). Austin, TX: ProEd.

Ginsberg, D. (2003). *Raising Blaze: Bringing up an extraordinary son in an ordinary world*. New York: Harper Collins.

Heshusius, L. (1989). The Newtonian mechanistic paradigm, special education, and the contours of alternatives: An overview. *Journal of Learning Disabilities, 22*(7), 402–415.

Individuals with Disabilities Education Improvement Act (2004), U.S.C. 1400 *et seq*.

Kauffman, J. M. (1999). Commentary: Today's special education and its messages for tomorrow. *Journal of Special Education, 32*(4), 244–254.

Kauffman, J. M., & Hallahan, D. P. (1995). *The illusion of full inclusion*. Austin, Texas: Pro-Ed.

Kavale, K. (2002). Mainstreaming to full inclusion: From orthogenesis to pathogenesis of an idea. International *Journal of Disability, Development and Education, 49*(2), 201–214.

Osmond, J. (1993). *The reality of dyslexia.* London: Cassell.

Park, C. C. (2001). *Exiting nirvana: A daughter's life with autism.* New York: Little, Brown, & Company.

Rice, C. (2009). *Always Liza to me: A memoir for my silent sister.* Crow's Nest, Australia: Allen & Unwin.

Simon, R. (2002). *Riding the bus with my sister.* New York: Plume.

· 1 5 ·

GRADUATING BOULDER

Today we walk from the train station back to school after an orthodontist appointment. Benny does not want to go back to school. He says to me, "Nobody, and I mean nobody comes back to school after leaving early." I ignore his words and we walk on. "Oops, I was just bitten by a dog he says with a smile." "I do not even see a dog," I say. He looks up and tells me "I was actually bitten by a ghost." Then we pass a small dog. Benny looks up and adds, "And now that dog bit me." Then he coughs and tells me he is sick, very sick. I finally give in and tell him he can stay home the rest of the day. We can walk the long way home and have a leisurely snack before picking up Adam. Then he tenses up, "No, I have to go to school, what would we tell my teacher if I stayed out the whole day?" I say to him we could tell his teacher that two dogs and a ghost bit him. Benny starts to cry, "No, no then he might think I am lying." Tears form and he looks up at me and tells me that he was in fact lying, is that terrible? "No, Benny not terrible at all." He has become such a fascinating blend. A few minutes later he asks me to pretend that he has no mouth; he tells me he will not speak for a while or eat. We walk in silence. Then he motions to me to go into my pocket and signs to me that in my pocket I have a mouth. I reach into my pocket and pull out a pretend mouth. Benny takes my hand to his face and pretends to sew it on, then drops his hands and instructs me to continue. I do for a few more minutes until

he gets a huge smile on his face and says that now he has a mouth and is able to talk. So many times I have wondered what this journey feels like to him, and now he has told me. It is simple. He was a boy without a mouth and now he has a mouth. I remembered his very early days of life, when swallowing was difficult. On his very first day when he could not take down even breast milk, the doctors took him for some tests. They thread long tubes down his throat to check for blockages. They found all that all was normal anatomically. Days later when he still was not eating, we took him back to the hospital. He had lost weight and they kept him overnight, feeding him for us. When we left they told us to pour the milk into his mouth while tickling his toes. It took him weeks to learn to eat, but he did. In retrospect that was the beginning, the first glimpse of his difficulties, controlling the muscles of his mouth. When therapists told me later he did not want to talk, I wondered if they would have said he did not want to eat. Benny could not swallow, he could not speak, at first, but all of this he has learned. I tell him every day now that he can do anything he wants to, but it will take more time and effort for him than it will take his peers.

I remember the hours I spent sitting beside him by day and lying beside him by night trying everything I could think of to help him speak. Even after he had words, it was years before he could converse and David and I would lie awake at night and wonder if ever he would be able to speak freely, to tell jokes, to engage in a full conversation. I know that without the chance to learn beside his peers, this day would not be here. Last evening I heard a segment on the news about a group called SNAP (Special Needs Athletic Programs) in New Jersey. They are described as a group of typical teens meets weekly with a group of special needs children many "on the spectrum," to share recreational activities. The typical teens are called volunteers and they learn compassion. I feel sick to my stomach as I hear these words because here at Boulder we call everyone students. Then parents come on the radio show and speak of the great strides their child with special needs has made since the inception of this program. Yes, this program is great. Yes, we all agree kids do very well when they are integrated. But I shudder at the thought that parents so easily accept that this is enough. Imagine how much growth could occur if everyday every hour or every school day, your child was integrated? Then one mom says that it is nice for her daughter to have a place to go when other kids have their sports activities over the weekend. These kids, she says, cannot do those other activities as their social skills are so lacking. Again, imagine if your children were educated alongside these other kids who come out on the weekend to volunteer? I look at the children from Boulder; I look at Benny who participates in band, who attends a musical theatre group, who swims alongside his peers. Why does this seem such a stretch for to others? If it can be done at Boulder, it can be done all over.

And if a child is told from the start that they are so different, so disabled, that they cannot be educated alongside their typical peers, what are they to think about their future? How are students going to grow up if they are asked to volunteer their time to help a person with a disability, the implication being that having a friendship with a person who is different is something that is noble, and not just something natural? How will they feel when it is time to hire a disabled peer or work alongside a disabled peer? Or do we assume that these children with special needs will grow up and sit by while everyone else gets jobs? Or will those with disabilities be destined to take a "low level" minimum-paid job at best?

Benny's Graduation Day, 2013

While I anticipated Benny's elementary school graduation day for months and expected it to come in heavy and hard, it did not. Instead it came as a soft summer day for which we prepared with an ease of spirit and lightness that I found unexpectedly delightful. While David and I held seats for our parents and waited for the processional to begin we made easy conversation with our friends. I remembered well Benny's last graduation, from preschool, over six years ago, when we sat shaking in our seats knowing that he was leaving a safe haven and heading towards uncertainty. Adam came out first along with the entire third grade. The entire grade lined the stage behind the rafters and began to play Beethoven's Ninth Symphony on recorder, while the graduating class began their processional. This was just one more delicious reminder of our luck in finding a school where our boys could attend together. The fact that Beethoven's Ninth has always been Benny's favorite composition was just another small sign that we had made the right choice.

Benny was on the top rafter, standing tall and proud with such a confidence radiating out from his broad smile it was impossible to feel any sadness. Clark spoke briefly then they handed out awards. Every child got at least one. While at neighboring elementary schools each child walks up to receive a diploma, at Boulder another tradition has evolved. Each child comes to the microphone and shares with the audience and each other, their favorite Boulder memory. This is not a top down, hierarchical administration where

Clark needs to confer his handshake on each student. Instead each child has a chance to shape the day just as they shape every other. So, one by one, each child steps up to the microphone and quickly shares a memory of their time here. When it was Benny's turn, I know his voice will be clear and full. In a voice thick and rich as warm melted chocolate, he said, "My favorite Boulder memory is playing at recess with all my friends." Then and only then did I fall back for a moment to the days he spent beneath the playground equipment counting the bolts, when it seemed he would lead an isolated life. A few moments later another boy shared his memory and it was about Benny. He remembered a game of dodge ball in which Benny caught a ball in his knees, three years ago. He laughed as he told the story and I felt dizzy with joy.

Then Clark did something remarkable. He "graduated" certain families, calling the names of those families who are graduating their last child from Boulder. He is so fully aware that his quest to become a partner with his families means that, for some, this partnership is ending and that demands recognition. Then as the families who were graduating Boulder stood we saw tears begin to fall. I was glad I still had two more years there with Adam, I was grateful Benny would have a reason to visit and that for a time I was still part of this place.

The graduates danced in the aisles and out the doors to "Moving on Up" from the Jefferson's of the 70's. Jackson and James danced beside me and I snapped photo after photo of these children bouncing to this beat I adore. They were moving so fast that all the photos are blurry. Benny was way down the aisle. When he passed we each reached out to grab his hands. He walked by, waving, but we did not touch as he moved with the swagger of a movie star.

We came home only to return for a 4-hour dance. Benny danced the night away, sporting neon bracelets and hula-hoops. I could not be sad for him any longer. I had shed too many tears for him over the years; it was time to dance and cheer.

Adam's Graduation Day, 2015

When it came time for Adam to graduate I was filled with a different kind of admiration for Boulder. Through Adam I saw the extent of what was possible for a child who excelled at so many aspects of his schooling. I wonder if I would have chosen an integrated setting for him had I not chosen it for Benny? I wonder if I could have shed my own educational experiences which

instilled in me the belief that separate was better? I recall my own elementary
school career where my friends and I were constantly grouped and ranked for
purposes of education, leveling us in ways that still make me feel inferior to
some, despite the fact that we were all in the highest of classes. Even within
the honors track, we were grouped by numbers 1, 2 and 3 and then within
each subject by letters, "A" being of course the best. It was a complex matrix
of leveling but we all understood what our coordinates meant. I was in A1 for
English and Social Studies, but B1 for Science, suggesting that I was not as
strong in my all time favorite subject. Friends of mine who were in 2 for each
subject seemed suddenly inferior, regardless of being in the honors program.
One has to ask what the benefit is of such complicated sorting for students
who already scored in the top 3 percent of the country? The three honors
classes almost never mixed with the 9 classes that were not honors. I know we
missed out on friendships with interesting students.

   At Adam's graduation I sat in a different space than the one I sat in two
years before. Adam had become a vibrant member of the graduating class. He
had amassed a following of students for whom he wrote jokes and who lined
up for play money he created with his face upon the bill. He became an enter-
tainer, a singer/songwriter, and also a proficient student. He began to work on
a screenplay and wrote a book with 1000 prime factorizations. He learned to
create opportunities and challenges for himself. Adam was sad about leaving
Boulder but excited for what was to come. His graduation was one of complete
celebration, with no worries for the future.

   When he got up to share his memory, he lit up the auditorium with the
brightness of his voice and smile. His favorite memory was becoming known as
"The Berminator." Clark forgot to graduate the families that year and for that
I was glad. I did not want to graduate Boulder. Adam's graduation party had a
beach theme. The PTA had decorated the gym and lobby so that it appeared
covered in sand and water. Fake boardwalks led the children from the street
to the gym where they danced for hours on end. I volunteered for this event
and feared I would get weary by the second hour, but the joy, the energy, and
the teamwork kept me on my toes. Having worked with middle school kids for
26 years, I anticipated some arguments, some difficulties, but they were few
and far between. Those kids knew how to cooperate and how to get along. At
one point I saw one girl crying heavily. Her face was red, wet, and hot. She ran
to her mother who was also there to help, and sobbed into her arms. I noticed
that one other girl ran after her to offer comfort. It happened to be one of the
girls with Down syndrome who followed her with words of support. I marveled

at how seamlessly the children interact. I saw how they play off each other's strengths so well. While I expected the parent and teacher volunteers to be more involved in guiding the evening, in keeping peace, as I often must do at my own job during unstructured play, there was little for us to do. The children handled things beautifully on their own.

The next morning, still dazed from the night, I went to the final assembly at Boulder. There, in my last few moment as a Boulder parent, I listened to Clark speak briefly about his hope that we all come back to visit, and that Boulder will always be our home. He played a slide show for us all, as scenes flashed from the past few years, to the music of "Shut up and Dance." We see our fifth graders as kindergarten students at the Mother's Day Tea, Clark in a dunk tank, teachers and students dressed up for Halloween. We revisit the variety show, ballroom dance and, of course, the circus. We see teachers and students playing sports, we see older students reading to their buddies from the lower grades. Teachers and students began to cry.

In the midst of this trip down Boulder memory lane, I flash back to my own graduation from elementary school. I went to a school that continuously has ranked within the top 10 of all NYC elementary schools for the past 40 years. I recall mostly the anticipation of freedom, as within my school I felt constrained and bored. At graduation from elementary school I sang a song from my seat. Some students were able to go on stage but I did not sing well enough for that. Instead, I recall my eyes fixed on the thick and vibrating underarm skin of my teacher who conducted with her back toward me, and her face toward those on stage. She moved her arms always in three even when the song was in four. I watched with mild amusement and disgust. During this last assembly I focused on the slip of light that came through the side of the thick velvet curtains covering the large floor to ceiling windows. I wanted nothing more than to be out of that school forever. I knew once out, I would never return. My principal spoke, long droning sentences, rife with platitudes. He never knew my name. He rarely left his office, a big dark, dank place with a smell I will never forget. We all tried to stay as far away as possible, but somehow we all knew the smell, which made its way into the hallway right outside the main office. My career in education has not done much to dispel that image of a principal tucked behind a desk, there to deal with problem students and problem teachers.

Back at Boulder, I snapped back to the present as Clark released a dozen beach balls left over from the night before. Kids began to scream as they were grabbing and cheering. In a flash Clark waved his hands and silently regained full command. There was an instinctive connection between Clark and his students. Like a conductor in tune with his orchestra, he led them from forte to pianissimo in a heartbeat. They were quiet, once again listening attentively to a few last words from his lips. He told them that they would always be family, that he couldn't wait to hear about their accomplishments, and that he would always love them. Later he was be dancing in his office, a weekly Friday ritual that he began that year.

The next day the students went in for one last hour. When they came out many were crying. Adam came out huddled with a few boys. Their faces were streaked with tears. They gathered together, arms around each other in front of the sign that holds the name of the school along with an inspirational message about the philosophy. We stood around feeling proud and also sad. We all know there is not another place quite like Boulder. We know given the choice these kids would even give up summer for more days in their elementary school.

Middle School, September 2015

There are places we only truly can know with the perspective of time and distance. Boulder is one of those places. I have appreciated Boulder for nearly eight years as a parent, but understand it only today from inside out, from a place inside that knows what it means to love and be loved. Adam graduated in June and today was his first day of middle school. The middle school is excellent and has taken Benny far both socially and academically. They have been cordial and kind to me, attending to my every question and concern with care. They have supported Benny beautifully, but they are not Boulder as any Boulder graduate will tell you.

I came home from work after both boys had let themselves in and had a few snacks. When Adam saw me drive up he opened the door and ran down the walkway, slipping and scraping his fair skin on the concrete. He rose quickly, paid no mind to his scratches and continued to run. "To Boulder!" he cried as he took off down the block. I locked our front door and followed, worried about the one big street he had to cross to get to the school he could not wait to visit. As I ran I tried to ask him how his day had been, but he did not answer, wanting to hold on to his exuberance, his first impressions of middle school to be shared first and foremost with his elementary school teachers.

At the corner, he paused for the light, I caught up to him and saw many more 6th graders, running down the street towards the corner, running to pay a visit to Boulder. They ran from all four directions, and converged on the corner, girls with long legs and hair streaming behind them, boys with huge smiles and knobby knees. They did not stop even to greet each other but continued to run with a focus and determination that was striking. Together they crossed the street and ran through the first grade parents waiting for their children. They gracefully were able to weave between the first graders standing just inside the door waiting for dismissal and they ran right into the arms of Clark. He was smiling broadly but with no surprise. I tried to slow them down, told them to wait until the elementary school children had been safely dismissed, but they paid no attention. Clark hugged me and told me it was fine, they can come right in as Boulder would always and forever be their home. They paused for a moment and then dispersed to see all of their former teachers. I waited outside and watched in awe as more and more 6th graders descended upon the school. As little children poured out, bigger children ran in, and I waited outside until the door was about to close for the day. Then I went in, fearing I would feel foolish (if not like a trespasser) hovering in the lobby of my son's former elementary school. To the contrary, I was embraced, and I mean literally as only Boulder staff can embrace. And the love I felt from the staff was intense, a richer deeper love than I had felt before, as I stood in the lobby waiting close to an hour to see my son, and finally hear from him about his first day of middle school.

When Benny graduated I reflected on Boulder for all the support and guidance they were able to provide for him. I was grateful for the academic support and the patience they had for us both. I gave them credit and appreciation for opening the door to academics for Benny in ways no other school had been able to do. As Adam completed his journey through elementary school I saw Boulder in a new light. I saw the passion for school that they were able to ignite in Adam. I began to appreciate the diversity of experiences he was able to have while in elementary school, while still open to trying anything. Today I got a glimpse of the deep love these students have for their teachers, demonstrated in the run so many made right into their arms, moments after stepping off their middle school buses. I have never seen this kind of devotion, not in forty years in education, twenty-eight of which have been as a teacher myself.

I am beginning to see that the magic Boulder created for each of my children is simply two sides of the very same coin. My Hunter students ask all the time how to make inclusion work, they relay to me stories of inclusion gone wrong, and then wonder why they have seen primarily such terrible examples. For each bad example, I ask them to think about how the school works for typical children: Is the school a vibrant happy place for children and teachers of typical abilities? Almost always the answer is no. When we create a school that works on every level, it will work for those with disabilities. When we plan from the head down, a rich diverse differentiated curriculum and give our teachers and students room to grow and find their very own voices, then we will have created a school in which all ability levels can flourish.

***

Graduations, it seems to me, are always a curious mix of endings and beginnings. They serve as a moment in time to take stock of the past, to reflect on the present, and look toward the future. In other words, they make us aware of life connections over the passage of time. This chapter begins with an episode of Benny and Diane walking back to school after a dental appointment. Here we see Benny's imagination and creativity at play, along with his moral dilemma about potentially misrepresenting the truth. Benny's loquaciousness, playfulness, inventiveness, and sense of what is right and wrong, provide Diane with great pleasure as she recalls the difficulty of his journey to speak. She recalls, "Even after he had words, it was years before he could converse and David and I would lie awake at night and wonder if ever he would be able to speak freely, to tell jokes, to engage in a full conversation." And now, here she is, conversing with her son who is speaking freely, humorously, and not only engaging in the dance of conversation, but leading the way. Fast forward to Benny's graduation, where she sat and "reflected on Boulder for all the support and guidance they were able to provide for Benny... for opening the door to academics for Benny in ways no other school had been able to do."

The graduation ceremony itself centered upon the memories of children who were graduating school. In the stories mentioned, Benny's own favorite is of playing during recess, and a friend's is about Benny's catching the ball between his legs. Here we are reminded that for students, schools are primarily experienced and understood as social spaces, with academic knowledge and skills firmly in the background. For the naysayers of inclusive education who claim socialization is the prime objective (Anastasiou & Kauffman, 2011; Fuchs & Fuchs, 1998), they are not entirely wrong—but nor are they right to assume that, for some children, the primary emphasis on socialization is a bad thing. In Benny's case, his socialization at Boulder (that did not occur within segregated settings) played a major role in his peer group's understanding of him, and their ability to help when needed, as in the case of the girl who explained how to make a potholder. With the passage of time, Benny's abilities in music became a model for his peers. While all this was happening, his academic success increased, as did his understanding and empathy of others, witnessed in his essay about Adam. The social arrangements within a community provide a context in which the importance of academics is taught, and children's abilities can subsequently grow.

That the principal graduates families, those whose children have all now been educated at Boulder, speaks to his uncanny abilities to create wonderful social spaces in which everyone is recognized and feels a part of. The slideshow that encompass the year highlights all of the fun extracurricular events, sporting activities, and selected academic projects. After the slideshow screening, "Teachers and students began to cry." Crying in public is very much a social taboo, particularly for males, yet it appears commonplace in this situation because both teachers and students feel unequivocally emotional due to the collective swell of happiness they cannot control. Clark's leadership style, the willingness and openness of faculty, and the commitment to their work are reflected in the graduation ceremonies. Diane cannot help but call to mind the memory of her own graduation from elementary school that likely resonates with many readers. In comparison to Boulder, it is stark and bleak, wishing she be out of the school forever, elaborating, "I knew once out, I would never return. My principal spoke, long droning sentences, rife with platitudes. He never knew my name. He rarely left his office, a big dark, dank place with a smell I will never forget." Leadership is crucial in creating and maintaining an atmosphere that can either make students want to attend or not, welcome or repel parents, make faculty feel appreciated and happy to be there or not. The qualities of successful inclusive principal have been described before, and their profound influence upon shaping all who are in their school (Guzman, 1997; Hehir & Katzman, 2012; Riehl, 2000). The same children who Clark fetes on graduation day return to see him on the first day of their fall semester at middle school. Diane notes this unusual phenomenon, describing the situation: "They were quiet, once again listening attentively to a few last words from his lips. He told them that they will always be family, that he couldn't wait to hear about their accomplishments, and that he would always love them." In a nutshell: family, attention, expectations, love, elements that make all of us feel part of something bigger than ourselves—connected, appreciated, respected, and cared about.

These values have been imbued throughout many levels of Boulder and are reflected in all chapters of this book. Such values gives rise to Diane's thought about parents of non-disabled children proactively seeking placements in inclusive classrooms. She ponders about Adam, "I wonder if I would have chosen an integrated setting for him had I not chosen it for Benny? I wonder if I could have shed my own educational experiences which instilled in me the belief that separate was better?" In turn I am also left wondering, what are the obligations of parents and families of non-disabled children to proactively seek placement in schools that specialize in inclusive approached to education? We often hear the converse, of parents not wanting their children in inclusive classes, fueled by stereotypic fears of lowered academic standards and challenging behaviors (deBurgh Thomas, 2001; McQuillan, 2003). However, it is interesting to consider it from the other side, and there are instances of excellent inclusive schools—such as the Bill Henderson Elementary School in Boston (Hehir & Katzman, 2012) who claim long waiting lists of typical students whose parents wish them to enter. I also have a colleague who recently requested this at her local school in New Jersey. On the pro side, she likes that there are multiple adults in the classroom. On the neutral side, a lot of cooperative learning is used, but not in an organized manner as it should be. On the cons side, her daughters get used a lot as "helpers." Although not perfect, she said she would do it again, and recognizes that the teachers involved are stretched thin, with the special education teacher also serving as the reading intervention teacher. To me, it seems to be another case of what is being called inclusive education not being done properly. Given levels of parental anxiety about the need for academic excellence in their children, I suspect many would opt for not choosing inclusive classrooms as preferable, although those who respect the value of human diversity would be more inclined to do so. In actuality, it should not be a case of either/or, as these issues are often portrayed, but rather both.

The graduation ceremonies of Boulder, embodying the values of the school in general, are compatible with several DSE tenets. They are an event, symbolizing a school that "promote[s] social justice, equitable and inclusive educational opportunities, and full and meaningful access to all aspects of society for people labeled with disability/disabled people" (Connor et al., 2008, p. 448). The school faculty have dispositions reflecting that "Disability is primarily recognized and valued as a natural part of human diversity" (p. 449) thus allowing an environment in which "Disabled students are supported in the development of a positive disability identity" (p. 449). Both Benny and Adam benefitted enormously from their experiences at Boulder, with each having different needs as well as overlapping areas. Diane explains, "I am beginning to see that the magic Boulder created for each of my children is simply two sides of the very same coin," referring to the care and quality of education available within the school.

In addition to the celebrations of graduation, this chapter also raises some serious questions about inclusive practices. The SNAP group in New Jersey is well intentioned but does not seem equally weighted in terms of receiving benefits. Of course social interactions between disabled and nondisabled youngsters are desirable, yet having them in a formal group rather than in naturally occurring situations can be a double-edged sword. Yes, an organization can provide access to non-disabled peers and vice versa, and people with disabilities become demystified. However, these situations can also reinforce stereotypes of where people with disabilities belong. We must grow organizations that promote the integration of everyone yet, at the same time, be mindful of what overt and covert messages are being sent. Jerry Lewis' telethons were famous for raising awareness and money for children with disabilities but they also reinforced stereotypes of pity, tragedy, dependency, and charity. In sum, able-bodied people became glorified as they called attention to perceived negative attributes of people with disabilities (Haller, 2010). Charlton's disability mantra, "Nothing about us without us," (1998, p. 1) is important to invoke in these situations, making sure that people with disabilities are fully or partly in charge of, or at least consulted about, these kinds of projects. Some of the bigger questions were raised by Diane when she asks, for example, "...if a child is told from the start that they are so different, so disabled, that they cannot be educated alongside their typical peers, what are they to think about their future?" It is sobering to think this is the actual situation of every child in a self-contained class. In another instance, she asks, "How are students going to grow up if they are asked to volunteer their time to help a person with a disability, the implication being that having a friendship with a person who is different is something that is noble, and not just something natural?" Here we see the assumption that people with disabilities do not have the same expectations or opportunities for friendships. These thoughts impact non-disabled people's perceptions, causing Diane to ask, "How will they feel when it is time to hire a disabled peer or work alongside a disabled peer?" They would have far less concerns if they had their education in an inclusive school, where differences that we label disabilities are understood as part of natural human variation.

When graduate students bring "stories of inclusion gone wrong" (and they are plentiful), we realize there have been exposed to few and far good examples, of committed principals and teachers, and of systems to support teachers and students. When pre-service and in-service teachers describe schools that do not function well for typical students, this cannot be used as an excuse—as it so often is—to not commit to inclusive education. Instead, it is further reason to change schools for all children, including those identified as disabled. We have to look seriously at the flaws that exist within education, and work toward developing better systems and structures, shaping committed principals and teachers, and provide the supports needed by students, teachers, and principals.

We know what makes inclusion work. There has been a significant body of research developed over the past quarter-century, complete with practical suggestions within reach of educators (see, for example, Baglieri, 2012; Danforth, 2014; Friend & Bursuck, 2002; Lawrence Brown & Sapon Shevin, 2014; Salend, 2007; Udvari-Solner & Kulth, 2008; Valle & Connor, 2010). As Diane notes, "If it can be done at Boulder, it can be done all over." And while I agree, I am also cognizant of the many challenges faced by different communities all across the U.S. and around the world that can impact the degree of success in supporting inclusive education. Boulder is not meant to be a template or a prototype for all, but rather a one example of "what works" in one public school—from which others can recognize possibilities for their own situations.

Given that we have reached the happy ending of graduation, we need to pause and take stock of this story about a child, a family, a school, and a community. In the next and final chapter we have a conversation that includes looking back over this story, and what we hope the book has achieved. By doing so, we recognize its scope, promise, and limitations, as well as having the opportunity to include some outstanding items, issues, and concerns we would like to continue encouraging the educational community to discuss.

References

Anastasiou, D., & Kauffman, J. K. (2011). A social constructionist approach to disability: Implications for special education. *Exceptional Children, 77*(5), 367–384.

Baglieri, S. (2012). *Disability studies and the inclusive classroom: Critical practices for creating least restrictive attitudes*. New York: Routledge.

Connor, D. J., Gabel, S. L., Gallagher, D. & Morton, M. (2008). Disability studies and inclusive education—Implication for theory, research, and practice: Guest editor's introduction. *International Journal of Inclusive Education, 12*(5–6), 441–457.

Danforth, S. (Ed.) (2014). *Becoming a great inclusive educator*. New York: Peter Lang.

deBurgh Thomas, E. (2001, August 5). An everyday tale of hell in an inner-city school. *The Sunday Times* [London].

Friend, M., & Bursuck, W. D. (2002). *Including students with special needs: A practical guide for classroom teachers*. Boston, MA: Allyn & Bacon.

Fuchs, D., & Fuchs, L.S. (1998). Competing visions for educating students with disabilities: Inclusion versus full inclusion. *Childhood Education, 74*(5), 309–16.

Guzman, N. (1997). Leadership for successful inclusive schools: A study of principal behaviors. *Journal of Educational Administration, 35*(5), 439–450.

Hehir, T. & Katzman, L. I. (2012). *Effective inclusive schools: Designing successful school-wide programs*. San Francisco, CA: Jossey Bass.

Lawrence-Brown, D., & Sapon-Shevin, M. (Eds.) (2014). *Condition critical: Key principles for equitable and inclusive education*. New York: Teachers College Press.

McQuillan, R. (2003, June 3). Classrooms under siege; "Discipline gets out of control so quickly you feel on edge all the time." A typical comment from a teacher as our schools are disrupted by unruly pupils. Is a policy of social inclusion backfiring? *The Glasgow Herald*, p. 12.

Riehl, C. J. (2000). The principal's role in creating inclusive schools for diverse students: A review of normative, empirical, and critical literature on the practice of educational administration. *Review of Educational Research, 70*(1), 55–81.

Salend, S. (2007). *Creating inclusive classrooms: Effective and reflective practices for all students* (6th ed.). Upper Saddle River, NJ: Pearson.

Udvari-Solner, A., & Kluth, P. (2008). *Joyful learning: Active and collaborative learning in inclusive classrooms*. Thousand Oaks, CA: Corwin Press.

Valle, J. W., & Connor, D. J. (2010). *Rethinking disability: A disability studies guide to inclusive practices*. New York: McGraw-Hill.

ONGOING QUESTIONS: DIALOGUE

Given the dialogic nature of this book, we pondered how best to "wind down," so to speak, and thought a conversation about our own lingering questions would be apt. We hope our questions, related observations, and open-ended wonderings will serve to help continue the dialogue about inclusive education and the many issues it relates to. As we have noted in this book, authentic inclusion cannot be packaged, it is an ongoing process that needs to be negotiated within a context. For this reason, it may appear to be a challenge, so some educational institutions continue to resist. Our position is that rising and responding to the challenge is what we seek to cultivate within those who are both entering the profession and those who have been working within it for a time.

David: Diane, now that we're finishing the book, what are you thinking about at this time?

Diane: What goals should I have for Benny now? How do I teach him to become an advocate for himself...how do I help him understand his disability, when I do not even understand it myself? How do I prepare him to explain himself to the world? How do I make sure he keeps holding himself accountable to the highest of standards even in the face of tremendous struggles? How do I prepare him for adulthood?

I know how to help him understand his disability without resorting to labels and other manifestations of the medical model, but how do I prepare him to advocate for himself in a world that uses labels?

David: These are such good questions. Of course I know they are somewhat rhetorical in nature, yet also reveal a yearning to know the way, understand more, to be more sure of things. In some ways, you've been doing this all along. In other ways, because Benny is growing and maturing, his self-awareness is coming more to the fore. If he can manage without using any labels, that's fine. If he needs to use them in order to help himself, so be it. As we've noted, labels are a double-edged sword and if they can't be dispensed with altogether, I encourage "disabled" people to use them for their own advantage, being able to calculate how, when, and why to use them for leverage—be it to seek legal accommodations or to explain to another human what they need to be successful in a particular context and why.

Diane: Recently, Benny's school psychologist called to warn me that his IQ score came out in the Cognitively Impaired category, which I assume is the new term for MR or the "borderline" area as they call it? Then he reported that his achievement scores are within average and, of course, he is passing all his classes, including two regent level HS classes, though he is only in grade 8. When I asked how he explains the discrepancy, he said, "Well he has excellent compensatory skills." I have to ask: Since when are "compensatory skills" independent from Intelligence? Isn't intelligence to a large degree how we compensate? Why are we still forced to subject our students to hours of testing that means little in the real world?

David: It never ceases to amaze me how psychologists seem so uncritical of, and invested in, intelligence testing. It's like they can't let go of it as a source of their expertise used to fortify their decisions as legitimate. "Compensation" is one of those catchall phrases that gloss over "discrepancies" between school expectations and assessed ability of performance. Psychology's use in schools could be so more progressive than it is if it allowed itself to be free of the type of assessments it specializes in that you rightly note are not connected to real world people and circumstances.

Diane: More importantly, do I ever need to share the information from the psychologist with Benny? And if I do what do I say? How would I feel if I found out I was cognitively impaired but being asked to do honors level work? Would I be grateful or would I be angry? Can I tell him this is nonsense, just a test so he can keep his supports? How do I make sure he understands the entire history of segregation and abuse that is tied in with these labels, so he understands the fact that we push him so he can have opportunity?

David: These questions get to the heart of the dilemma of talking with children and youth about the structures and practices within schools, including how intelligence is conceptualized. While we cannot predict Benny's response, it is likely that thinking through being caught in the crossfire of schooling, disability, and a history of segregation, will be tough to make sense of—in particular, the messages of inferiority that are pervasive throughout multiple discourses. At the same time, he is aware of many inequalities, and can begin to see how important it is to critique messages from mainstream culture that largely misunderstands and devalues certain types of differences. If something is wrong, it's okay to name it as such—even though the majority of institutional knowledge claims otherwise.

Diane: How do I respond to parents with same age children who have been segregated? How do I gently nudge them towards inclusion when inclusion may not be a possibility where they live, or if it is, knowing how much more difficult it is as kids grow. Is it appropriate to be gentle or do I come in heavy handed like an old friend did for me when she told me I was wrong to allow Benny attend a self-contained kindergarten?

David: I think the more parents are fully informed about the options, the more they can make a decision that is right for their child and themselves. It's high stakes. I would not want to tell anyone what they MUST do, but I think presenting pros and cons of inclusive education, and engaging with parents about actualities and possibilities—sometimes based upon their wishes—is desirable. Part of inclusive education is working together to create meaningful structures that are not necessarily there yet.

Diane: I also wonder how does inclusion look for a post high school student who has never been included? How can a family begin to move in this direction at this point?

David: It's much harder, but still doable. That's another argument why to do inclusive education earlier and so transitioning back to a general education setting would be a moot point. If kids have been segregated in middle school, and are now entering an inclusive high school—a situation that happens every year, by the way—schools must help them prepare. This can be done with orientations, active transition plans, teacher support, and so on.

Diane: When Boulder staff come to present to my classes at Hunter, I realize again how fortunate we were to have found this district. What can schools within the city learn from this example, despite the fact that conditions in the city are not nearly as favorable? What can an individual teacher do within the classroom to create a positive atmosphere?

David: It's my hope that readers will be able to see possible ways of rethinking limited notions of inclusive education. It's important for each school culture to always have inclusive education at the center of their value system. City schools do face particular challenges that we actually highlighted in a 'compare and contrast' within a chapter. It's true that New York City and other large metropolises need to revisit how they do business. At the same time, I believe individual teachers, or better yet, individual teachers working together, can do many different things to ensure that their classroom has a safe and supportive environment and that the curriculum is accessible, so that all kids have the opportunity to succeed—academically, socially, and emotionally, albeit in different ways at times.

Diane: For many years I have been trying to uncover the "secret" to how Boulder managed to include Benny so effortlessly. As you mentioned they have no blueprint, no policies for including kids with multiple disabilities and yet they found their way. To what extent is attitude, along with available and flexible supports the answer? It seems almost too simple, and impossible to test with traditional instruments. The very nature of the flexibility needed to accommodate Benny and others like him defy the procedures we hear about in education. How can we encourage others to share? How can we gather more stories?

David: This is exactly why we wrote the book! In some ways, inclusive education has become overly complicated, and unnecessarily so. It's about problem solving so schools and classrooms work for all kids. I agree that available supports and a flexible disposition are vital ingredients. At the same time, the right attitude is the number one ingredient—absolutely crucial. Scot Danforth's book on *Becoming a Great Inclusive Educator* is full of great stories, actual accounts from teachers who do this work. They convey far more authenticity than much of the formalized research. I'd love to see a growth in success stories, big, medium, and small. These should be collected in our pre and in-service classes, too—to help students be better grounded in what's going on, what works, in what context, and why.

Diane: What can we do to ensure that students like Benny are held to high standards but are assessed through truly differentiated means? I know more than one HS student who had to take various Regents Exams 3–4 times before passing. At what cost do we keep pushing? How do we begin advocating for alternative assessment that counts the same as the more typical assessments?

David: The system has torturous aspects to it. I have seen high school students with IEPs take BOTH sets of exams (Regents and local), essentially doubling their work—two exams, two formats, two things to practice for. In other words, the most academically challenged kids must do twice the work. Who does that make sense to in New York State? States need to listen to local education authorities, kids, and parents, so all students have an opportunity to graduate. The one-size-fits all policies enforce normalcy and that sorts out those who can be counted as "approved" and those who fail to meet the grade and are "disapproved" for a societal stamp. States go back and forth on this, the pendulum swinging... we all agree that high standards are good, but that means different things for different individuals, too.

Diane: I feel grateful to be in a school district that supports Benny in his desire to get a quality education, but I do wish he could do so without daily blows to his self-confidence. I know he can master much of the material. He could display his understanding better more differentiated ways. As a teacher for 26 years, I feel more and more constrained to teach to the multiple assessments myself, and as I do so, I loose my most divergent and innovative thinkers.

David: I think we agree that this era in education is very stifling and over regulated. There has to be a better balance than no guidelines and overwrought requirements. I know those of us in teacher education feel the same kind of pressure to answer to many bureaucratic masters and that squeezes the life out of many good courses as we continue to incorporate and center upon so many things. We have to keep maintaining the good things we know that work and will help students.

Diane: Norm Kunc, the keynote speaker at the DSE conference in 2016, stated that he would not give up his disability if offered the chance. This prompted me to ask the boys about whether, given the opportunity, they'd give up their disabilities? I was surprised to hear Adam say he would not be so quick to give away his epilepsy while Benny seemed to imply he would give away his disabilities in a heartbeat. What would have to change in the world to enable Benny to feel proud and successful going through this world with the disabilities that do shape him and make him who he is?

David: I love to discuss Norm Kunc's ideas in classes as nondisabled people in general usually are shocked at his claim of not wanting to change. That said, they begin to see his logic—although it has never been presented to them in this way before. It's an intriguing idea and I can see why folks with various disabilities don't want to change who they are. I am not sure that Benny quite understands the idea in the fullest sense yet, as his identity is still forming and his feelings about being a person with a disability is just beginning to be addressed. It always strikes me as a deeply personal decision that is not clean cut, particularly if physical pain is involved. At the same time, I do understand challenging majority group assumptions that minority group members would change if given the opportunity. This brings me to wondering about teacher ed. programs in general. How often do they stress a disabled person's point of view? How often family points of view? How do these points of view often differ from "clinical" portrayals of disability and are grounded in complex realities that can be more helpful that much of the information found in traditional special education texts.

Diane: I know and I have to patient and accept that this will take time. I am grateful beyond words that we have found a place where Benny has been include and where he is expected to complete the same curriculum as his peers. I just wish it could be done in a manner more flexible. Even as I type this I fear that this sounds two faced, as if I am asking that he be included yet held to a different standard than his peers, and that makes me shiver inside. That is not what I want. What I want is an educational system that does not need to rely on high stakes, exhaustive testing to hold teachers accountable to teaching well and with a high bar for all. I want a system filled with talented creative teachers who can be trusted to meet the needs of all learners in diverse and creative ways. When I see Benny navigate new cities with a compass and a map, and critique public transportation systems we have never seen, I know he has a deep intelligence that will serve him well in life. I want Benny to be feel "smart" in school and use the gifts his disability bestows upon him in school as well as in life.

David: I am always curious about to what degree do teacher education programs across the US teach inclusive education? I know in my own, due to many different political reasons, the special education department has always maintained a separate identity. Only recently have we been able to program the inclusion course for both special and general education majors *together*, as traditional programming in a large university had meant they had taken the course in separate groups. It was a terrible irony. It's also a shame that general educators have only one course in teaching students with disabilities. I'd much rather see more integrated programs, where all teachers are educated to work *together* and support all students. I think, just as we have tried to show a successful school, I'd like successful teacher education inclusive programs to share what they've done. Given what I know of how bureaucratic and political teacher education programs are, in some places this simple idea begins to appear like a Herculean task. What do you think?

Diane: I have really enjoyed this year at Hunter now that I have special
            educators and general educators in the same classroom. It makes my
            job easier as they can draw upon each other's experiences. When we
            discuss disability, often the special educators have more experiences
            working with kids with special needs. They can dispel some of the
            myths some students come into the class with. The special educators
            also often know first hand about the horrors of segregated settings,
            because they have observed within those classes. The general educa-
            tors know first hand about the curricular demands at each grade level.
            They general education students come in with a passion for their
            subjects and together they can come up with lesson and unit plans
            that meet the needs of all students. In a few years they will be asked
            to co-teach together and it is great that now I can have them work
            together to craft engaging lessons that differentiate while holding up
            to high rigorous state standards.

David: In terms of Disability Studies in Education, this has been an interest-
            ing book to develop as what we believe in and what we do is being
            done informally all over the country but not necessarily called DSE or
            as having a DSE framework. I am hoping that the literature base in
            our field will expand to incorporate more 'DSE-flavor' books that are
            written by teachers that illustrate so many of the possibilities that can
            be achieved. I have always been concerned about how educators are
            quickly professionalized into viewing teaching as a technical endeavor,
            with special education 'scientifically' grounded, and the justification of
            deficit conceptualizations of human difference. I see our book as coun-
            tering that narrative, providing alternative explanations and under-
            standings, that can be useful—especially when teachers find themselves
            mired in all of the traditional discourses of special education.

Diane: I hope this book can expand that vision. I see already within the
            course you designed and I teach, that the DSE framework is brand
            new to some students. As the semester progresses more and more of
            them reach that point where they have some sort of epiphany and sud-
            denly understand the profound shift that this perspective can affect.
            I recall our conversation when I took on the inclusion course at Hunter.
            I expressed my fear that including my personal story in the course
            might somehow weaken my role as an instructor. I was still in the
            mindset of my own upbringing, where teachers were by and large
            objective conveyors of facts and skills. You encouraged me to inte-
            grate the story and to make it part of the fabric of the class. It made
            me nervous at first to share so much of my personal story but I saw
            quickly how it enabled the ideas of the course to be digested. I was
            able to connect with my classes on a level that was new to me and very
            exciting. It was an interesting confluence that I encountered Boulder

School, where boundaries fell with abandon at the same time that I began to teach from a place of my own passion and heart. I hope this book can expand the reach beyond my classroom and the hundred or so students I teach each semester.

David: Me too. Another desire I have is to see research more user-friendly to teachers. However, a career-long experience of educational research-ers and teachers being far apart with each "side" insufficiently con-nected leaves me desirous of teachers being action researchers in the broadest sense, sharing "what works" in their context.

Diane: I would love that as well. As an adjunct I am somewhere in the middle. I was not trained to do high level research, yet I read the literature all of the time. I try to find articles that will resonate with my students, but sometimes that is difficult. I also find it hard at times even to access the latest scholarly research as the publications require large fees for access. I so enjoy the DSE publications that come out regularly as they tend to be more accessible to my students. I also love Disability Studies Quarterly because it is free and accessible to all. This project has been so meaningful to me in that our partnership has given me an academic voice and enabled me to share my story and see it grounded in the current DSE research that is your specialty. In many ways our collaboration is an example of what you are recommending in your last comment. Perhaps this will pave the way for more teachers and researchers to partner together.

David: Altogether, I hold hope for the future. We have seen many changes for the better. At the same time, I feel we have to be vigilant and pro-active in not only supporting the inclusive agenda, but seeking to replace how the business of schools should be done. We have noted for years that being included into an inadequate and dysfunctional system defeats the purpose of inclusion. It's the whole system that needs to be constantly critiqued with view to suggesting changes.

Diane: I agree completely. Almost every semester, on the first day of my course on inclusion, one of my students reports a horrendous story of inclu-sion gone sour. I listen patiently and then I ask the student how the school operates in other ways. Almost every time the student reports a school filled with chaos, decisions made for financial reasons rather than educational, an administration that is not in collaboration with its teachers. I am quiet and listen again with patience. Then I suggest that we critique the whole school and not simply the one instance of inclusion gone wrong. It seems to be when the school is healthy, and the relationships between professionals is good, then inclusion can flourish. I don't think we need extra fancy bells and whistles, or teach-ers trained in the intricacies of 100 disabilities. We need cooperative, open, flexible staff members who are willing to connect deeply and sincerely with the community, and are open to the wonderful ways our children can shape the school. Inevitably they will begin to appreciate the diversity that all our students can bring into the classroom.

David: So, in closing... here's to teacher education working toward more inclusive certification programs, schools that develop them, and the teachers, support staff, kids, and families who help make them work.

EPILOGUE

Where Are We Now?

Adam is in grade 6. He is excelling academically and commanding large roles in the school play and chorus concerts. He seeks out moments to shine and handles his responsibilities with grace. Adam does not need to spend too much time on his studies. His school work comes easily to him, and his teacher's appreciate his wit and humor. Despite beginning the school year in the hospital for complications from his epilepsy, he returned to school to secure a part in the fall play. His ease in social situations is something we all admire and strive for. Adam encouraged Benny, now in grade 8, to try out for the school play as well. They are enjoying one year in school together before Benny leaves for high school in the fall.

Benny graduates middle school as we write the last sentences of this book. He is taking an honors level curriculum because that is what everyone in this school district does. He is in the drama club and the performance chorale. Benny still has a small and loyal group of friends, many from elementary school, but he has made some new ones as well. He is a handsome young man with a mysterious air that draws others to him. Benny's sincerity and dedication to his friends, family and responsibility make him stand out to his peers and teachers.

He is struggling academically, and doing his best. The topic of disability has come into our daily discussion as for the first time he really feels the impact of his differences. While we see tremendous growth and celebrate the fact that he is taking Regents Earth Science and Algebra as an 8th grader, he is face to face with the fact that he studies for hours on end and still gets grades which are way lower than those of most of his peers. We come to the moment from different perspectives. David and I are delightfully surprised at all he can do while Benny is increasingly aware of his challenges (differences or struggles, maybe). I try to respond by pointing out the struggles we all have in different areas and the strengths he has that make him stand out. We speak about the way our school system requires a type of work that is challenging for him. Benny realizes that he has to study many more hours than most just to get by, but in the end there has not been anything he could not learn with time and effort.

We still recall the horror we felt at the time he was given multiple diagnoses and as we watched him writhe in pain in the hands of his first elementary school teachers. I know without a doubt that this move into the hands of Boulder school saved him from a dismal fate. He is a happy confident teenager because of the move. That is not to say life is easy for him, but he has learned to work very hard, and he is grateful for the supports he receives. While deep down I always knew he had a genius inside and a heart full of warmth and goodness, I wish that I had more confidence when faced with the naysayers. I lost some time when my children were young and I could have been more carefree. Instead their early childhood was weighed down by my fears for the future. I hope this story will help parents believe in their children, and stand up to a society that, to a degree, values conformity over all else.

As a teacher with nearly 30 years experience, I see that we need to teach our students how to persevere in times of difficulty. I see Benny has developed that skill and I am trying to cultivate that in others: the ability to work hard in the face of challenge.

At the end of at our most recent talk with my students at Hunter, when I questioned Clark, about why inclusion works at Boulder, I think within his answer we have an important part if the secret. He replied, "If I walked down the halls of Boulder school with a goat at my side, no one would be alarmed." The kids expect difference because it is built in to the fabric of their day on many levels. Teachers can be themselves, they can bring their passions into the classroom, their penchant for the color pink, their desire to bake, to share stories of their travels, and to be open and honest about their own idiosyncrasies.

Regrets?

What, if anything, do I regret? I pass a young mom today with her two small children, maybe one of them is 2 years old and a baby of only several months, just the ages when we heard the worst predictions for Benny and his future. Her hair is carelessly tossed in a ponytail; she walks with an easy gait. It is spring and she is showing her children the blossoms. They are in that space that seems eternal, before the pressures of school, when days roll on top of days and every step takes her children further into the world, with her at their side, coaching, cheering, and delighting. They will go home soon to cookies and apples and a good book. Then they will have baths and bed. Tomorrow they will do it all over again, almost the same except for the infinitesimal growth that deepens their beauty, brings her children closer to eventual independence.

I regret that I was never that mom who could walk about without carrying gravity in her step. In retrospect, I realize that as soon as Benny was born I sensed difference in him and I did not know how to embrace it. I tried to ignore it at first and then to change him. Once he failed to walk or talk on time we had Benny evaluated. Then the nightmare began. As speech eluded him he grew frustrated and I saw options close ahead of us. I saw children growing around me gaining skill while my son was regressing, and this was accepted as part of his disability. Parents around me looked forward to an expansion of talent and opportunity and I instead began to feel suffocated as possibilities ahead seemed to narrow and vanish with every passing minute. When I managed to feel joy out on a walk with my two small children I felt inside a sort of shame sensing that this joy was actually a consequence of the denial I was in about the depth of his delays. Partly this came from me, an internal pessimism, but much came from knowledge found in books, websites, and from prominent doctors. I wish more people had told me that anything was possible as a precious few did. I wish I had the chance to read about children who flourished despite profound language and social delays. If I had, maybe I could have enjoyed his differences earlier.

That is my only regret. I am glad for all else. Though I still yearn for the city, I am grateful that we do not live too far and we can visit often. I cherish my position at Hunter College and the opportunity it provides me to shape in some small way the city I have always loved. Though our finances have not recovered from the move I do not care, as money never motivated me much. I appreciate, too, the softer side in me I have found, that likes to garden and go for a walk in relative solitude. I am not sure I could have written this book in the noisy busy city with so much to see and do. In the absence of so much stimulation, I found another way to channel my energy.

Moving Ahead

As high school approaches I see other nervous parents, and I am not. Instead, I have that feeling I once yearned for, the feeling of joyful anticipation of the possibilities on the horizon. After cowering as I turned the corner to take him to kindergarten in the city, day after day for months, and then holding my breath out here as he made his way through the middle and elementary grades, I am finally here, in a place where I know beyond all doubt that he will continue to grow, to find new skills, to expand his talents, widen his social circle and to make his way more and more into the world. I am excited as a parent might be on sending her child to preschool for the very first day. I can't cry any longer for Benny, I can only cheer him on. I am beginning to get used to his achievements in school, his performances, and his talents that flow freely by now. I no longer live in two worlds when he performs; I no longer wallow in what might have been, at least not in the moments made for celebration.

I do think often, when alone, of where he would have been had we listened to the advice of many and moved him into a class for 6 severely disabled children in a school that was far from our neighborhood. I can't say for certain that every child in that setting would find the success that Benny has found. I can say for certain that had Benny spent the past five years with 5 other non-verbal children in a program for the autistic, he would not be reading and writing on grade level, he would not be singing in a performance chorale, horsing around with his friends on the subway, or dancing as an Ozian in *The Wizard of Oz*. He would not stay awake late at night chatting to Adam about all of the friends they have in common. He would not be able to offer Adam such good advice about how to play with who he wants to at recess or to give Adam a heads up on the teachers they have shared. He would not fall asleep each night with laughter on his lips and walk to school with a skip in his step. I know without his peers talking to him relentlessly about the most intriguing of subjects, Benny would not be conversational.

Had we not moved here I would not have learned once again that we are all unique and that it is not only okay, but wonderful to be ourselves. I shudder to think of how many children are denied the opportunity to develop fully while still holding on to what makes them unique. It saddens me to think of how many students are cut off from traditional academic programs as a result of expressive and receptive language delays, apparent cognitive impairment, and emotional behavioral "disorders" which may mask ability but do not prevent competence or even mastery of certain academic and/or social skills.

Contributing Member of Community

I see that Benny is not the only one on the receiving end. His friends would not have seen the city multiple times or learned the names of every subway line. They might never have met a child who could play two recorders at once or who could read a book upside down and backwards before forwards. They would not have learned how to hold their head up high while skipping and flapping so gracefully while walking down a busy street. He graduates from middle school a full member of his class, contributing to the dynamic in every way, beloved and loved, having shaped the culture of his class in ways no other child could have done.

I hear of many students who are included academically but never socially accepted. As Ferri (2006) says, "A particular challenge in teaching inclusive education is not simply working to get disabled students in the door, but rather finding ways to encourage general education teachers to rethink their basic perceptions about who their students are" (p. 292). Later she writes about inclusion that does not truly include, stating, "This type of inclusion calls to mind general education classrooms where the disabled are included but only nominally. They are invited into an existing structure but the structure is not changed or modified in any substantial way" (p. 295).

It is the small moments that move me most, the times Benny and I walk together down the street or wait for a bus, or watch him laugh with Adam, a robust uncontrolled laughter, the sort only brothers can share. It is then that I am conscious of the ease with which we make our way through the world, the times when I can be happy and know that my happiness is not simply and naively a product of my failure to accept. I walk now with my boys down the tree-lined streets and we watch the pink blossoms blow and count the dandelions on the lawns. I walk with a skip in my step, a freely flowing joy in my heart and pretend in the narrow slips of time between activities and responsibilities that the boys are still small, as they once were, and realize that ahead of us, individually and as a family is a great expanse, filled with possibilities.

We close this book by sharing the perspectives of Benny and Adam.

Diane: Over the 14 years of your life so far, you have overcome so many challenges so beautifully, with your dedication, and talent. What have your teachers at Boulder and SSMS done for you that has been especially helpful?

Benny: Elementary school, teachers read questions. My teachers gave me a lot of support, kept saying "you can do it, you can do it." I wish I were smarter though, I wish I were not failing so many tests. I wish I were smarter.

Diane: Over the years you have been involved in many activities—dancing, drama, track, swimming, volunteering at the library. Which activities have you enjoyed the most and why?

Benny: Drama club, because I did the spring play and it was fun. I was an Ozian and a Winkie in The Wizard of Oz.

Adam: Drama club, acting is spectacular.

Diane: What advice do you have for youngsters who have similar struggles? What keeps you going even when it is 10 PM and you still have hard homework to complete? What drives you to persevere even when you are crying with frustration?

Benny: When my parents help, I calm down, Maybe I get help from a lot of people. I want to do well, I feel happy when I pass tests.

Diane: What does inclusion mean to you?

Adam: Inclusion means you are grouping both the undisabled and the disabled together because they belong together.

Diane: How do you think your life would be different if you and Benny went to different schools?

Benny: It would be not good because we would not get to see each other in school that much.

Adam: We would not be able to do clubs together.

Benny: I wouldn't have done drama club if Adam did not do it and asked me to come to the auditions.

Adam: Benny would not have learned much if had stayed in the segregated classroom. It was too small. And the other kids did not speak. How would Benny have learned to speak that way?

Diane: You often say that Boulder school is the best elementary school in the universe. What makes you feel that way?

Adam: The principal obviously, I don't think any other principal would put on tights, or get a fauxhawk, or be dunked in a tank, or helped us that much. Or have so many fun events.

Diane: We talk often about how little we like the word "disability." What suggestions might you have for a new word that we could use instead?

Adam: Someone has a struggle or an obstacle?

Benny: Someone who is floundering?

Diane:	What are your career plans? Where do you see yourself in 20 years when you are 32?
Adam:	Actor, singer, game show host and a father and a husband and a son, a nephew, a grandson and an uncle.
Benny:	I want to drive a bus and live in NYC- maybe Brooklyn or the Bronx? I am not sure…I will figure it out. Maybe I will get married. Maybe I will have kids.
Diane:	If you could make your disability go away, would you?
Adam:	I am not sure. There are pluses and minuses to epilepsy. I don't like the restrictions but it is part of who I am. Being different is cool. And I like my mind. Maybe it makes my mind more interesting.
Benny:	I would give away my disability right away, for sure, because then I would not feel so stupid in school.
Diane:	Did you feel that way in elementary school, in Boulder? When did it start?
Benny:	Well maybe I am not stupid…maybe it was when I got a 38 on that math test last year. I didn't feel stupid in Boulder. But middle school got very hard and I don't pass that many tests.
Diane:	Well you have accomplished a lot in middle school too. You took two High School Classes this year! And you had a nice role in the school play. What are you the most proud of from middle school?
Benny:	Well I passed the math Regents and I got an award at graduation for working hard—the PTA, A- for Effort award.
Diane:	How did you feel when your teacher called you to tell you how well you did on the Algebra 1 Common Core math Regents?
Benny:	I was very excited. I couldn't stop smiling. It was phenomenal.

Reference

Ferri, B. (2006). Teaching to trouble. In S. Gabel & S. Danforth (Eds.) *Vital questions facing disability studies in education* (pp. 289–306). New York: Peter Lang.

INDEX

A

ableism, 61
acceptance, 176
acceptance, of limitations, 109, 114, 115
acceptance, social, 245
accountability, 20
ADHD (Attention Deficit Hyperactivity
    Disorder), 59, 108
adhocratic model of education, 130, 131
aides, 57
Annamma, S. A., 66
announcements, 124–25, 128–29
appropriateness, 30, 33–35
ASD Nest Program, 7
assessments, 232, 234–35
assistant teachers, 63, 64
asylums, 181
Attention Deficit Hyperactivity Disorder
    (ADHD), 59, 108
attitude, 192–93, 234
audacity, 115

Audacity of Hope, The (Obama), 115
autism spectrum disorders, 4, 7, 73
Axis Dance Company, 183, 194

B

Baglieri, S., 80
balance, 113, 114
Becoming a Great Inclusive Educator (Dan-
    forth), 234
behavior, 7, 61, 89
    and academic challenges, 108
    Benny's, 53, 56–57
    expectations of, 190
    and life circumstances, 66
    and medication, 59–60
    responses to, 65
    zero tolerance, 65
behavioral challenges, strategies for,
    189–191, 195
Behavior Disorders (BD), 8

Behavior Intervention Plans (BIPs), 7, 190,
    195–96
bigotry, 51
Biklen, D., 129, 178
BIPs (Behavior Intervention Plans), 7, 190,
    195–96
birthdays, 94, 100
Blatt, Burton, 181
Board of Cooperative Educational Services
    (BOCES), 73
Boulder School
    Benny's and Adam's perspectives on, 246
    climate at, 15–17, 21, 44–45
    distribution of students at, 55
    principal, 65
    social dynamics at, 78
    structure of, 62–63
boundaries, 157–58, 160–64, 193, 238
    See also professionalism; relationships
bridge years, 179–180
brothers, 201, 205–8, 209
Burke, J., 129
buses, 92–93

communication, 82
    conversation, 46–47, 48, 49, 75, 77, 78,
        79, 82
    between school and home, 158
    with teachers, 156, 158
community
    emphasis on, 71
    importance of, 129
community involvement, 145
compensatory skills, 232
competency, assuming, 66, 129, 196
Connor, D. J., 80
context, xiv, 94, 112–13, 130
conversation, 46–47, 48, 49, 75, 77, 78, 79,
    82
conversation starter cards, 81
cooperation, 59
cooperative learning, 226
costs, of inclusion, 83–84
cultural capital, 7
curriculum, changes in, 16
curriculum, hidden, 100
curriculum, unofficial, 147

C

Cantor, ?, 201
challenges, 108, 115, 125
change, openness to, 17
Charlton, ? , 227
child
    expectations of, 128
    as guide, 126, 131
Christmas in Purgatory (Blatt), 181
civil rights, 10, 20
class, and placements, 35
classmates, involved in therapy, 71, 75–76
classroom ecology, and successful inclusion,
    112–13
classroom management, 61, 195
    See also behavior
Common Core, implementation of, 191–92

D

dance, 139–141, 183, 194
Danforth, S., 80, 234
DEAR (drop everything and read) time,
    77–78, 82
deficit-based approach, 19, 33, 196
dehumanization, 162
delays, 66
democracy, 101
Descartes, R., 164
Deschler, Don, 180
DI (Differentiated Instruction), 80, 186–87,
    195
dialogue, 231–39
difference
    expectations of, 242
    re-thinking of conceptions of, 210–11

ways of thinking about, 49
different, vs. deficient, 204
Differentiated Instruction (DI), 80, 186–87, 195
disability
    disabled people's views of, 247
    as diversity, 19, 83, 100, 116
    expanding understanding of, 10
    and hierarchies, 96, 97
    and identity, 235–36, 247
    as liberation, 5
    social model of, 130, 146
    stereotypes of, 18–19, 227
    theorizing about, 129, 227
    understandings of, 99
    use of term, 246
    and ways of thinking about difference, 49
Disability Studies in Education (DSE), xviii, 162, 196, 237, 238
    assuming competency, 66, 129, 196
    challenge to concept of exceptionality, 179
    destabilizing thinking about fundamental issues, 22
    and issues of disability and race, 35
    link to practice, xix
    and misunderstandings of disability and difference, 210
    and perceptions of students with troubling behaviors, 66
    purposes of, 146
    roots of, 19
    strengths-based perspective, 61
    tenets of, 9–10, 35, 83, 98, 99, 211, 212, 226
    and ways of thinking about difference, 49
disabled people
    including in theorizing about disability, 129
    view of disability, 247
distribution of students, 55, 63, 64–65
    60-40 formula, 37–38
District 75, 7–8, 61
diversity
    in adults, 192

disability as, 19, 83, 100, 116
Down syndrome, 180–81, 189
drop everything and read (DEAR), 77–78, 82
drugs, 59–60, 67–68, 108, 111, 116–17
DSE (Disability Studies in Education). See Disability Studies in Education

E

education
    adhocratic model of, 130, 131
    state of, 20–21
Education of All Handicapped Children Act, 6
educators. See teachers
educators, inclusive, 176
8-1-1 class, 3
Emotional Disturbance (ED), 8
emotional growth, 16
English Language Learners (ELLs), 38
equitable model, 62
essay, Benny's, 207–8
ethics, 51
exceptionality, 179
exclusion, 148, 175, 180
    effects of, 37, 217–18, 227
    outcomes, 30
    See also restrictive placements; self-contained classrooms; special education
expectations, 107, 109, 110, 114
    of behavior, 190
    of child, 128
    of difference, 242
    of parents, 18
    for participation, 190
expense, public, 83–84
experience, 8, 63–64, 177–78
expertise, 177
extracurricular activities, 135–144, 147, 148

F

family
    importance of, 129
    inclusion in, 178
FAPE (Free and Appropriate Education),
    30, 33–35
Ferguson, P., 50
Ferri, B., 245
flexibility, 192–93, 234
Free and Appropriate Education (FAPE),
    30, 33–35
Friend, Marilyn, 62
friendships, 78, 79, 82, 87, 89–96, 98, 100
Frost, Robert, 181

G

Garland-Thomson, R., 97
Gartner, A., 6
goals, 124, 126, 169, 176, 231–32, 247
goals, social, 169, 176
Goffman, E., 96
graduations, 224, 226
    Adam's, 219–222
    Benny's, 218–19
Gramsci, A., 164
grouping, 220
group work, 187
guide, child as, 126, 131

H

Habib, Betsy, 48
Habib, D., 20
Hehir, Tom, 37
Heshuisus, L., 49
heterogeneous group work, 187
hierarchies, 96–97
high school, transition to, 179–180
hope, 115
hostility, 51

hyperactivity, 108

I

IDEA (Individuals with Disabilities Educa-
    tion Act), 30
IDEIA (Individuals with Disabilities Edu-
    cation Improvement Act), 6, 33–35,
    208–9, 213
identity, 235–36, 247
IEPs (Individualized Education Programs),
    34, 49, 50, 57–58, 116, 122, 126,
    129–130, 196
impulsivity, 108
Including Samuel (documentary), 20, 48,
    178, 196
inclusion
    after high school, 233
    as civil right, 20
    commitment to, 32
    costs of, 83–84
    desirability, 194
    as earned, 19, 29, 35
    effects of, 8, 9
    in families, 178
    limits of, 188–89
    messiness of, 114
    misconceptions about, 16, 18, 95
    models of supporting, 62
    most important ingredients for, 192–93
    need to develop philosophical practices
        of, xv
    in New York City, 63–65
    and non-disabled children, 226
    part-time, 29–30, 180–81
    re-thinking limited notions of, 234
    and school climate, 23
    search for program, 29–33
    shifting to, 21–23
    understanding, 194
inclusion, social, 245
Inclusion and School Reform (Lipsky and
    Gartner), 6

inclusion specialist, 55, 63, 64
Individualized Education Programs (IEPs),
    34, 49, 50, 57–58, 116, 122, 126,
    129–130, 196
Individuals with Disabilities Education Act
    (IDEA), 30
Individuals with Disabilities Education
    Improvement Act (IDEIA), 6, 33–35,
    208–9, 213
instinct, 4, 18, 47, 50
intelligence, 232–33
interaction, 48, 217, 227
intolerance, 51

J

Junior Announcers, 124–25

K

Kluth, P., 80
Kudlick, C. J., 22
Kunc, Norm, 235

L

labels, 9, 10, 35, 66, 220, 232
language
    and conception of disability, 5–6
    and misrepresentation of students, 66
law, 6, 30
    See also Individuals with Disabilities
    Education Improvement Act
Lawrence-Brown, D., 80
leadership roles, 100
learning, as social activity, 79
learning, cooperative, 226
Least Restrictive Environment (LRE), 6, 34
Lewis, Jerry, 18, 227
limitations, accepting, 109, 114, 115
Linton, Simi, 178

Lipsky, D. K., 6
listening, learning new ways of, 4
Long Term Absentees (LTAs), 38
Losen, D. J., 35
LRE (Least Restrictive Environment), 6, 34

M

medication, 59–60, 67–68, 108, 111,
    116 17
medicine (field), 19
middle school, transition to, 179–180
minority identities
    hierarchies within, 96–97
    See also race
misery, 27, 28
mothers
    assessment of special education practices,
        xiv
    characterization of, 18, 50
    devaluing knowledge of, 18
    including in theorizing about disability,
        129
    responsibility for children's outcomes, xiv
    See also parents
music, 153–57

N

NCLB (No Child Left Behind), 10
*The Newtonian Mechanistic Paradigm, Special
    Education, and the Contours of Alterna-
    tives* (Heshuisus), 49
New York City, inclusion in, 63–65
New York City Department of Education,
    37–38
New York State Education Department, 112
No Child Left Behind (NCLB), 10
Noddings, N., 51
normalcy, 61, 211
    concept of, 83
    emphasis on, 35

and inclusion, 19, 73, 83
and medication, 60, 67
norms, 67

O

Obama, B., 115
obsessions, 93
Orfield, G., 35
ostracization, of parents, 96

P

panels, parent, 198
panels, student, 197–98
paraprofessionals, 63, 64–65
parent panels, 198
parents, 233
    characterization of, 50
    devaluing knowledge of, 18
    estrangement from professional discourse,
        50
    expectations of, 18
    instincts of, 47, 50
    ostracization of, 96, 97–98
    power/privilege of, 35–36
    support for, 191
    See also mothers
participation, 127, 148, 162
    expectations of, 190
peer group, power of, 59
personality, emergence of, 174
Pervasive Developmental Disorder–-Not
    Otherwise Specified (PDD-NOS), 1
pity, 18
placements, 208–9
    District 75, 7–8, 61
    8-1-1 classrooms, 3
    justifying, 33
    Least Restrictive Environment, 6, 34
    and race/class, 35
    6-1-4 classrooms, 8

12-1-1 class, 3, 25
    See also exclusion; restrictive placements;
        self-contained classrooms; special
        education
placements, restrictive. See restrictive
    placements
play dates, 90–92, 93–94
poetry chairs, 121
potential, 107
power, 4, 35–36
practice, linking to theory, xix
principals, 65, 192–93, 225
privilege, 4, 35–36
professionalism, 159–160, 193
    See also boundaries; relationships
psychology, 19, 232–33
pull out model, 55
push in model, 55

R

race
    and medication, 68
    and placements, 35
    Racial Inequality in Special Education (Losen
        and Orfield), 35
regrets, 243
relationships, 71, 81–82, 158
    friendships, 78, 79, 82, 87, 89–96, 98, 100
    with principal, 151
    with teachers, 153–57, 159, 161, 193
    See also boundaries; siblings
research, 238
residential settings, 181
resources
    access to, 4
    on inclusion, 80
restrictive placements, 3, 8
    conditions in, 27–28, 30
    costs of, 83–84
    District 75, 7–8, 61
    effects of, 30, 31, 37
    and interaction, 48

preference for, 5, 61–62
as protection, 61
See also exclusion; self-contained classrooms; special education
The Road Not Taken (Frost), 181

S

sadness, 27, 28
Sapon-Shevin, M., 80
school climate, and inclusion, 23
schools, environment in, 51
school-to-prison pipeline, 30
science, 19
segregated classroom. *See* exclusion; restrictive placements; self-contained classrooms; special education
self-advocacy, 148
self-contained classrooms, 30, 175, 188–89
See also exclusion; restrictive placements; special education
sensory issues, 190
shame, 205, 209–10
Shapiro, A., 80
siblings, 201, 205–8, 209
6:1:4 classrooms, 8
60-40 formula, 37–38
Skrtic, T. M., 130
SNAP (Special Needs Athletic Programs), 217, 227
social dynamics, 71, 73–74, 77, 78
social goals, 169, 176
social inclusion, 245
social interaction, 48
socialization, 96, 144, 146, 224–25
extracurricular activities, 135–144, 148
social model of disability, 130, 146
social skills
linked to academic skills, 81, 82, 84
as reason for inclusion, 79
See also communication; relationships
special education
effects of, 210

hierarchy of stigma within, 96
impact of, 37
resistance to inclusion, 37
in teacher education, 236
See also exclusion; restrictive placements; self-contained classrooms
special education law, 6, 30, 33–35
See also Individuals with Disabilities Education Improvement Act
Special Needs Athletic Programs (SNAP), 217, 227
special needs child, use of term, 5–6
speech therapy, 75
stereotypes, 18–19, 227
stigma, 96, 205, 209–10
Strategic Instruction Model, 180
strengths-based perspective, 61, 129
student panels, 197–98
students of color, 35, 68
supports, 191–92
from siblings, 205

T

TA (teaching assistant), 55, 56
talents, discovering, 144, 147
teacher education, 16, 19, 185–198, 236–37, 239
teachers
absorption of professional discourse, 49
and accountability, 20
attrition, 20
communication with, 156, 158
effective, 176
experience of, 8, 63–64
freedom for, 192–93
hostility to inclusion, 112
professionalism, 159–160, 193
qualifications, 63
relationships with, 153–57, 159, 193
in restrictive environments, 8
Teach for America (TFA), 63–64
teaching assistant (TA), 55, 56

Teaching Fellows (TFs), 63, 64
team teaching, 22
Temporarily Able Bodied, 178
terminology, 66
theory, linking to practice, xix
therapist, acting like, 47, 49
therapy, 81
    classmates' involvement in, 71, 75–76
Tomlinson, C. A., 195
tracking, 220
trains, 92–93
transportation systems, 92–93, 94, 100
trust, 65, 116
12-1-1 class, 3, 25

U

Udvari-Solner, A., 80
Universal Design for Learning (UDL),
    79–80, 148

V

Valle, J. W., 50, 80
values, 51
Van Hove, G., 50
variety show, 141–44
visibility, 75–76
Vygotsky, L., 128

W

Willowbrook, 181

Z

zero tolerance, 65
Zone of Proximal Development, 128

Susan L. Gabel and Scot Danforth
General Editors

Historically, inclusive education developed as a reaction to the exclusion of students of minoritized identity groups marked by race, language, sexual orientation, disability, etc. Our position in this series is that inclusion can and should be more. It can be understood as embracing and planning for difference, building relationships across difference, teaching and learning that acknowledges and supports difference while also minimizing the use of identity categories as the foundation for arguments about inclusion. In other words, the silos of educational discourse based on identity categories need to be broken down, little by little, to reconceptualize inclusion as just, compassionate, and creative ways of living, teaching, and learning in a complex and diverse world. Inclusive teaching depends on deeply respectful relationships between teachers, students, and community members.

Books in the series must make clear connections between theory and practice. Both are necessary ingredients for inclusion. This series will help teacher educators prepare teachers to be knowledgeable and skillful in teaching all students, regardless of their differences.

For additional information about this series or for the submission of manuscripts, please contact:

Susan L. Gabel and Scot Danforth
susan.gabel@wayne.edu | sdanforth@mail.sdsu.edu

To order other books in this series, please contact our Customer Service Department:

(800) 770-LANG (within the U.S.)
(212) 647-7706 (outside the U.S.)
(212) 647-7707 FAX

Or browse online by series:
www.peterlang.com